The archives of the valuation of Ir

The archives of the valuation of Ireland, 1830–65

Frances McGee

FOUR COURTS PRESS

Set in 11 on 12.5 point Ehrhardt for
FOUR COURTS PRESS LTD
7 Malpas Street, Dublin 8, Ireland
e-mail: info@fourcourtspress.ie
www.fourcourtspress.ie
and in North America for
FOUR COURTS PRESS
c/o IPG, 814 N. Franklin Street, Chicago, IL 60622.

© Frances McGee and Four Courts Press 2018

A catalogue record for this title
is available from the British Library.

ISBN 978–1–84682–136–3

All rights reserved. No part of this publication may be reproduced, stored in or introduced into a retrieval system, or transmitted, in any form or by any means (electronic, mechanical, photocopying, recording or otherwise), without the prior written permission of both the copyright owner and the publisher of this book.

Printed in England by
TJ International, Padstow, Cornwall.

I do not believe any country in Europe possesses so magnificent a work as the Ordnance Survey and valuation of Ireland. I do not believe that France has such maps or such a valuation; I do not believe that England has such maps or such a valuation; I do not believe that Germany, or any country in Europe, is possessed of such a thing. I look upon it as very useful for the purposes of taxation, the franchise, letting, income-tax, surveys, confidence in the government, and the establishment of a good feeling between the landlord and the tenant, and also a clear understanding between them.[1]

– John Townshend Trench, 1869.

---

1 *Report from the select committee on general valuation, etc (Ireland) together with the proceedings of the committee, minutes of evidence, and appendix*, HC 1868–9 (362–1), question 4205 (hereinafter cited as *Report from select committee on valuation, 1869*).

Contents

LIST OF ILLUSTRATIONS		9
CITATION CONVENTIONS AND ABBREVIATIONS		11
ACKNOWLEDGMENTS		13
Introduction		15
1	Development of the system and the work of valuation	22
2	The valuation staff	47
3	The manuscript books and other documents of the valuation	60
	A. Field books	61
	B. House books	72
	C. Quarto books	83
	D. Mill books	90
	E. Townland valuation appeal books	94
	F. Townland valuation printed books	100
	G. Tenure books	102
	H. Other series	109
	I. Administrative documents and correspondence	114
4	The maps of the valuation	117
	A. Valuation maps	118
	B. Valuation town plans	131
5	The *Primary valuation*	136
6	Appeals against the *Primary valuation*	157
	A. Appeals under the 1846 act	157
	B. Appeals under the 1852 act	179

7	Keeping the archives safe		193
	A.	Management and preservation of archives in the Valuation Office	193
	B.	Archives now held in the Valuation Office, Dublin	195
	C.	Valuation archives in the Public Record Office of Northern Ireland	196
	D.	Local archives and local-studies libraries	197
8	Conclusion		198
Appendices			200
	A.	Procedures for appeals under valuation acts of 1826–52	200
	B.	Chronology of principal measures and amendments, 1826–64	204
	C.	Field work in Townland Valuation and Tenement Valuation	207
	D.	Start dates of field work, by county, 1830–57	208
	E.	Table of main book types extant, by county	210
	F.	Table of main map types extant, by county	212
	G.	Classification of buildings	214
	H.	Statutes, 1826–64	216
	I.	Research in the valuation archives	218
BIBLIOGRAPHY			225
INDEX			227

Illustrations

FIGURES

3.1	Quarto book, Dunboyne, Co. Meath, OL/7/40 (1840)	85
4.1	Diagram showing how sets of maps made in the Townland Valuation were reused in the Tenement Valuation	121
5.1	Simple letting arrangement	144
5.2	Letting arrangement with subletting	144
5.3	Letting arrangement with several levels of subletting	145
5.4	Data in *Primary valuation* and in manuscript books	149
5.5	Data on houses in *Primary valuation* and manuscript house books	152

PLATES
Between pages 128 and 129

1. Tenement Valuation original field map (drawn on Townland Valuation original field map), Co. Galway, sheet 122, townland of Crannagh, parish of Kilmacduagh, OL/11/11/958 [1842].
2. Townland Valuation original field book, townland of Crannagh, parish of Kilmacduagh, Co. Galway, OL/4/5485, p. 9 (1842).
3. Townland Valuation original house book, OL/4/5485, p. 42 (1842).
4. Tenement Valuation original house book, townland of Crannagh, parish of Kilmacduagh, Co. Galway, OL/5/1022, p. 3 (1853).
5. Tenement Valuation tenure book, townland of Crannagh, parish of Kilmacduagh, Co. Galway, OL/6/796, p. 4 (1853).
6. Valuation town plan, Ballina, Co. Mayo, OL/12/21/8 [1841].
7. Townland Valuation house book, Ballina (town), Co. Mayo, OL/4/3114, p. 36 [1841].
8. Quarto book, Ballina (town), Co. Mayo, OL/7/280, p. 33 (1842).
9. Tenement Valuation house book, Ballina (town), Co. Mayo, OL/4/3115, p. 31 (1854).
10. Townland Valuation appeal book, barony of Castlerahan, Co. Cavan, OL/13/9 (1840).
11. Townland Valuation printed book, parish of Munterconnaght, barony of Castlerahan, Co. Cavan, OL/14/3, pp 8–9 (1841).

12 *Primary Valuation, County Cavan, union of Cootehill*, 1857, parish of Munterconnaught (barony of Castlerahan), Co. Cavan, p. 59.
13 Tenement Valuation appeals (1846 Act), parish of Killabban, barony of Ballyadams, Queen's County, OL/19/24/1, p. 13 (1850).
14 Tenement Valuation appeals (1852 Act), parish of Moyrus, union of Clifden, Co. Galway, OL/20/11/3, p. 70 (1855).
15 List book, barony of Ardoyne, Co. Carlow, OL/10/1 (1843)
16 Tenement Valuation rent book, parish of Kilmeen, barony of Duhallow, Co. Cork, OL/16/32 (1851).

Citation conventions and abbreviations

The vast majority of the footnotes concern valuation documents in the National Archives, and the prefix NAI has been omitted in the footnotes that refer to those documents. It has been included in references to other documents in the National Archives.

The *Primary valuation* is now accessible online free of charge at askaboutireland.ie/griffith-valuation, and on microfilm in the National Archives, National Library and local-studies libraries. The references to the *Primary valuation* are to the original published books and give the abbreviated title *PV*, the county and barony or union and the year of publication. All of the *Primary valuation* books were published in Dublin and the place of publication has been omitted in the references.

The Parliamentary Papers are now available online free of charge (see dippam.ac.uk/eppi). The papers available on this website have been used, and the references include the year and the number of the paper in round brackets, but omit the volume numbers and manuscript pagination.

The following abbreviations have been used:

CSO Chief Secretary's Office
NAI National Archives of Ireland
NLI National Library of Ireland
OL   Reference code of archives of the Valuation Office (Oifig Luachála) in the National Archives
PV *Primary valuation* or *Griffith's valuation*

Acknowledgments

This guide to the archives of the valuation of Ireland was first suggested many years ago by the late Phil Connolly, then my colleague in the National Archives. The work was always facilitated and encouraged with great personal generosity by the former director, David Craig, for whose support I remain most grateful. I wish to thank especially those who read the draft: Sarah Ward-Perkins who contributed her own great knowledge of the subject and also Claire Foley and Ken Hannigan who made many valuable suggestions and saved me from error. William A. Smyth kindly gave me access to his thesis and shared information with me. In the National Archives I wish to thank the director, John McDonough, for permission to publish the photographs of documents. I am grateful to Tom Quinlan for his unflagging support and assistance and also Brian Donnelly, Martin Fagan, Aideen Ireland, Noreen Lynch, Hazel Menton, Niamh McDonnell, Zoë Reid and the staff of the reading room for responding cheerfully and efficiently to my requests for large quantities of documents, especially Ken Robinson and Ken Martin. Special thanks are due to Eamonn Mullally who took the photographs within the book, and Elina Sironen, who took the cover photograph.

In the National Library, Colette O'Flaherty, Elizabeth Harford and the staff of the reading rooms were most helpful as always. I am indebted to Siobhán Fitzpatrick and the staff of the Library of the Royal Irish Academy, Paul Ferguson in the Glucksman Map Library (TCD), Joanne Rothwell in Waterford Archives, Jacqui Hayes in Limerick Archives, Declan Macauley in Kilkenny County Library, the staff of the Dublin City Archives, Patricia Kernaghan and Brendan Campbell, former staff of the Public Record Office of Northern Ireland, Brian Donovan, Ríonach uí Ógáin and Sean Hennessy, as well as Sam Tranum of Four Courts Press. Thanks to Mariane Picard for the diagrams and tables. In the Valuation Office, I wish to acknowledge the commissioner, John O'Sullivan, for maintaining the interest in the past work of the office, and also Anne Durkin, Pat McCarthy and Mary Smyth for their assistance over many years. I would like to thank retired staff Bobby Roche and Pat Gallagher for sharing their deep knowledge of the documents and the mysteries of valuation.

I am grateful to Marian Lyons for her valuable guidance with the text and for her kindness and patience in the lengthy gestation of this guide. And, lastly, thanks to my family who have lived with this for a very long time.

Introduction

The valuation of Ireland was initiated by an act of parliament in 1826 and continues in operation to the present day. The work of valuation generated a large trove of archives, which has been described as 'one of the richest sources for the social and economic history of nineteenth-century Ireland'.[1] The valuation was a complex and technical process, about which there was public discussion on an almost continuous basis in the years before the first act in 1826 and long after the completion of the initial valuation in 1865. The large number of parliamentary committees, inquiries and reports that concerned themselves with the valuation and the related matter of local taxation from the late eighteenth century onwards showed that it was possible to define both what was wrong and what the desired outcome was, but there was no clear answer as to how this might be achieved. Unlike the Ordnance Survey, whose success in producing accurate maps demonstrated that their technical methods were correct, there was no general agreement about the manner in which property should be valued.

The valuation of Ireland was dominated by the figure of Richard Griffith, who was commissioner of valuation between 1829 and 1868. This was in addition to his many other roles in the Board of Works, the Boundary Survey, the Bog Survey and as geologist, builder of roads and general expert on engineering matters. It has been pointed out that his involvement in many other enterprises is one of the elements in the confusion that surrounds the valuation archives.[2] Griffith held strong views about the valuation, and expended a great deal of time and energy on defending his system, in which the valuation of land was based on an examination of soil and a fixed scale of prices for agricultural produce, and on the potential letting value of houses. This often exasperated his contemporaries, who, on the whole, preferred a more readily understandable valuation based on the rental value of individual holdings.

The name and identity of the organization took some time to establish. In the relevant acts of parliament the organization was not named and the work was defined in terms of the commissioner, under whose supervision it would be carried out. The first valuation act in 1826 required that a commissioner

---

1 W.E. Vaughan, 'Richard Griffith and the Tenement Valuation' in G.L. Herries Davies & R.C. Mollan (eds), *Richard Griffith, 1784–1878* (Dublin, 1980), p. 104.   2 Jacinta Prunty, *Maps and map-making in local history* (Dublin, 2004), p. 146.

of valuation be appointed for every county, although Griffith was the only person to hold these offices, and in 1834, this arrangement was replaced by one commissioner for the entire country. In the years between 1826 and 1852, the valuation was variously identified as the 'general', 'government', 'uniform' or 'Ordnance' valuation, and by persons outside the organization as 'Griffith's' valuation. This was at first to distinguish it from other contemporary, statute-based valuations (such as those made for tithes from the late 1820s, the poor law from 1838 and earlier grand jury valuations), and later as a recognition of the scale of the achievement. That appellation has endured, although usually in relation to the Tenement Valuation. Throughout the nineteenth century the organization was generally known as the General Valuation of Ireland. The title 'commissioner of valuation' continues in use for the head of the Valuation Office and is one of the few titles nearly 200 years old still used in the public service.

The valuation was an experiment carried out at a time of great change and against a background of growing state activity, from the census to the police and national schools. There was a convergence of ideas and technical developments that brought together a willingness to solve the long-standing problem of local taxation, with a new ability to create truly accurate maps. This involved three organisations, each working in its own sphere, but linked to the others by a common purpose: the Boundary Survey established official boundaries; the Ordnance Survey made the maps, replacing the old maps of varying origins, including the seventeenth-century plantations, with a national map based on the latest science; and the valuation put a value on every piece of property in Ireland. It can be argued that these undertakings helped to shape our common understanding of the recorded landscape. In the process, unique and important contemporary information was recorded. This was happening in a time of optimism, following decades of war in Europe. The report from the select committee that examined the matter in 1824 commented that 'all former surveys of Ireland originated in forfeitures and violent transfers of property; the present has for its object the relief that can be afforded to the proprietors and occupiers of land from unequal taxation'. It also recognized that the 'general tranquillity of Europe' meant that the army was available to carry out the mapping.[3]

The work of valuation falls into two periods. The first was the initial valuation that identified and valued every unit for the first time, recording lands, buildings and their occupiers throughout the entire country between 1830 and 1865. The archives created by the initial valuation relating to counties now in the Republic of Ireland are held by the National Archives in

---

3 *Report from the select committee on the survey and valuation of Ireland*, HC 1824 (445), p. 10 (henceforth cited as *Spring Rice Report*).

Dublin, and are the subject of this guide. In the second period, the work consisted of revision of the initial valuation so that it was kept up to date. This took place from approximately 1855,[4] continued until the mid-1990s and still applies to buildings other than domestic dwellings. The archives of the second period of the work are held by the Valuation Office in Dublin.[5] In the early 1920s, a Valuation Office was set up in Belfast and most of the archives relating to the six counties of Northern Ireland are now held by the Public Record Office of Northern Ireland,[6] with a small quantity held by the National Archives in Dublin.

The initial valuation took place first under the Townland Valuation and then under the Tenement Valuation. The Townland Valuation was carried out between 1830 and 1852 under acts 1826-36 and valued approximately three-quarters of the country. It was so called because the townland was the smallest unit of land valued. Information was collected on agricultural land and some houses, and was set out in townlands, parishes and baronies, but individual holdings were not defined. The Tenement Valuation took place between 1844 and 1865 under acts of 1846 and 1852. It valued the remaining quarter of the country and then went back over the counties previously valued in the Townland Valuation. The Tenement Valuation valued individual holdings or 'tenements'. At the end of the Tenement Valuation the entire country was valued in tenements. In theory the work of the initial valuation took place once in each location but in practice some of the work was done twice in some counties because additional information was required after the change from townland to tenement. However, the transition from townland to tenement was not a simple one, and in the period between 1844 and 1852 the old and new systems overlapped. At this time, three separate systems were in operation simultaneously: the Townland Valuation continued in some counties, a new Tenement Valuation for poor law purposes was started in others and in some counties the Townland Valuation was revised into a Tenement Valuation.[7]

The valuation archives were created for the purpose of establishing the valuation of property and identifying the persons who were liable to pay tax on that property, the lessor and the occupier. County cess was paid to the grand jury entirely by the occupier and, later, poor rates were shared between the occupier and the immediate lessor, and paid to the local board of

---

4 Some parts of the country were ready for revision before the Tenement Valuation was completed in others.   5 Valuation Office, Irish Life Centre, Abbey Street Lower, Dublin 1. The Valuation Office is due to become part of a new organization, named Tailte Éireann, which will include the Property Registration Authority (formerly the Land Registry) and Ordnance Survey Ireland. A similar body was proposed by Griffith in 1855, see OL/2/14, pp 230-2.   6 Trevor Parkhill, 'Valuation records in the Public Record Office of Northern Ireland', *Ulster Local Studies*, 16:2 (Winter 1994), p. 46.   7 Sarah Ward-Perkins, unpublished paper (1978).

guardians. All of the documents were made because the data they contain was required for the work of valuing. They were intended for internal use in the office by specialized staff and are, of necessity, technical. The data is fragmented because it was collected in separate series of documents, each of which had a specific function. The series of documents are closely related and need to be consulted in conjunction with one another. Changes were also made in the content of the work and the documents over the period. For these reasons, the valuation archives can appear difficult for the researcher to use. One of the series of documents, the *Primary valuation* or *Griffith's valuation*, is very well known. It is the most accessible and is now available online, but it is only a small proportion of the total, and of the information available.

The archives of the valuation can be read at many different levels, from a search for family names, to analysis of social and economic factors recorded uniformly over the entire country. An explanation of the original function of the documents and the information recorded should assist the researcher in understanding their content and in obtaining maximum benefit from consultation. The legal basis of the valuation lies in acts of parliament, of which there were no fewer than twelve between 1826 and 1864.[8] This large number can be explained by the fact that the work was novel and alterations were found to be necessary. Also, the official and legal environment in which the valuation was carried out was itself changing in related areas of the poor law, the development of municipal government and the parliamentary franchise.

The success of the valuation can be seen in the fact that over the course of the nineteenth century it was seen as a reference for matters beyond its immediate purpose of local taxation, and became associated with dealings in land and property. From the early years, requests for private valuations were received from landowners, but these were usually refused.[9] Griffith claimed that the valuation was preferred to assessments based on estate rentals in connection with the purchase of land, and was used in London to raise money on Irish estates.[10] The valuation was cited in the sales catalogues (known as 'rentals') of the Encumbered Estates Court and its successors.[11] That rents should be not be greater than the valuation was one of the demands of the Land League in the early 1880s.[12] Over the second half of the century it became the official reference for income tax, duty on licensed premises, identification of properties liable to stamp duties and death duties, *ex gratia* sums paid in lieu of rates on government property, determination

---

8 In 1826, 1831, 1832, 1834, 1836, 1846, 1852, 1853, 1854, 1856, 1860 and 1864.   9 OL/2/12, p. 55.   10 OL/2/10, pp 19–20.   11 *Report from select committee on valuation, 1869*, questions 713–15.   12 James S. Donnelly Jr., *The land and the people of nineteenth-century Cork* (London, 1975), pp 264 and 268. See pp 277–82 for an account of how the valuation was offered instead of the rent on some estates.

of the jurisdiction of courts relating to title, application of statutes relating to property (for example, rent restriction acts) and was used in defining what areas of the country were congested districts. In addition, it set limits of eligibility for a wide range of state services, including grants, benefits and subsidies. A similar vision of a valuation that would be linked to income for local authorities, to development of infrastructure and social services and to the franchise was outlined by Sir Denham Norreys in a letter to the grand jury of Cork in 1844.[13] It is a testimony to Griffith's achievement that the valuation became so deeply integrated into the relationship between individual citizens and the state. It is also a tribute to the system devised in the early 1830s that the documents it created were in use until 1984, when rates on agricultural land were abolished. W.E. Vaughan has described the public and visible nature of landed property, and the relationship between landlord and tenant.[14] A similar observation can be made about the valuation: its work took place in public view, its procedures followed prescribed form and its outcomes were submitted to appeal.

The valuation archives have a unique importance as a research source on nineteenth-century Ireland. The social and economic context of the period in which they were made, as well as the manner in which the valuation was organized, add to their significance. They contain a vast mass of information on individuals, including their names and addresses, details of the houses they lived in and information about the location and value of their farms and holdings. It is possible to identify the precise house in which they lived; to ascertain its quality, size and shape; to see the extent and quality of farms and the kind of farming or other activity carried on; and to expand this to the immediate surroundings and to wider areas. Many of the documents contain additional detail on family and social connections as well as general information on the area. The archives can be used for family and local history, as well as to study large-scale social and economic subjects. Examples of how valuation archives, in conjunction with other sources, allow detailed examination of small areas are seen in work on the parish of Shanrahan, Co. Tipperary and the Smyth estate in Co. Wicklow.[15]

The archives date from a period from which there are relatively few other sources. They cover the entire country, including rural and urban areas. They were collected in a standardized manner for a central authority by

---

[13] *Report from the select committee on Townland Valuation of Ireland; together with the minutes of evidence, appendix and index*, HC 1844 (513), appendix 1, p. 161 (hereinafter cited as *Report from select committee on Townland Valuation, 1844*). [14] W.E. Vaughan, *Landlords and tenants in mid-Victorian Ireland* (Oxford, 1994), pp 1–5. [15] William J. Smyth, 'The Famine in the Co. Tipperary parish of Shanrahan' in John Crowley, W.J. Smyth & Mike Murphy (eds), *Atlas of the Great Irish Famine* (Cork, 2012), pp 385–97; Matthew Stout, 'The Smyth estate in Baltyboys, Co. Wicklow' in Crowley, Smyth & Murphy (eds), *Atlas of the Great Irish Famine*, pp 354–7.

trained professional observers who visited every field and documented every house. They are comparable from one place to another. They record the basic facts about the occupiers, their circumstances and property from the period before the Famine to the changes in rural geography and urban occupation in the years immediately afterwards. The complex interrelationships of the factors involved were taken into account in the data written into the documents by the staff. The notes on the parishes and towns give first-hand accounts of the situation, and the data shows the extent of depopulation and impoverishment over the period. Given the loss of other major record series, such as the nineteenth-century census returns and many parish records, the valuation archives are a rich repository of information on families, localities and social and economic conditions. It is an irony that the least useful aspect of these documents is now the valuation of soil and land, and that the science, of which Griffith was so proud, is superseded.[16]

This guide is concerned with the archives created by the initial valuation between 1830 and 1865, which established the facts about property and occupation. It is intended to help the reader in understanding the complex data and the many changes that took place over the period and in seeing the research potential of the archives. The guide will look at the background to the valuation, the development of the practice, and the work itself before explaining in detail the major series of documents, what they contain, and how they relate to each other. While the documents and the work were standardized and were governed by legislation, instructions and circulars, the researcher will need to bear in mind that the rules were not always applied to their full extent. Some variations were introduced on foot of new instructions and, in other cases, the instructions ratified conventions that were already in use. It is difficult to be categorical about how the systems worked when there are many exceptions that need to be taken into account.

The books and maps of the initial valuation, 1830–65, are divided into separate series of documents in accordance with the manner in which they were originally created and used as a body of reference material – for example, field books or house books. The books were made by civil parish and county and are arranged by parish, barony and county within their series. The valuation maps are arranged by county, in Ordnance Survey sheet number order. The town plans are arranged by the name of the town, within the county. Each document is entered separately in the lists in the National Archives, and introductory notes explain the series and the variations in the documents. Researchers need to look at all of the documents for the place of interest because of the variations present. While the valuation archives are

---

16 John Lee, 'Richard Griffith's soil survey as a basis for farm taxation' in Herries Davies & Mollan (eds), *Richard Griffith, 1784–1878*, pp 77–101.

voluminous, some documents have not survived. There are gaps for individual parishes and in certain cases entire series are not present for a county. All of the archives for the initial period of the valuation are now held by the National Archives. Some series that have previously not been available to researchers, because of their fragile condition, will be made accessible in digital or other surrogate form.

I

Development of the system and the work of valuation

BACKGROUND

The background to the valuation of Ireland was long-standing dissatisfaction with the system of local taxation in Ireland. Counties were administered by grand juries, which had civil as well as judicial functions and were responsible for public facilities such as roads, bridges, infirmaries, asylums and county gaols, all funded from a tax on property known as county cess. Grand juries were largely composed of landowners appointed by the high sheriff of the county, and did not represent the occupiers of property, who financed their activities.[1] A small number of permanent officials served the grand jury, including a county secretary and county treasurer, both of whom were to have a role in the early part of the valuation. Counties were divided into baronies and subdivided into civil parishes, townlands and smaller areas, where officialdom was represented by high constables of baronies, and church wardens and vestry committees at parish level.

The grand jury met at sessions known as assizes in various locations in each county, determined its monetary needs for the year and made 'presentments'. The county treasurer raised the money by levying county cess on occupiers of land. He issued warrants to the high constable of each barony, who in turn apportioned or 'applotted' the amounts to be paid by individuals and appointed a collector in each townland.[2] The problems associated with this system included unregulated collection and a lack of redress for aggrieved taxpayers. Difficulties also arose from the fact that the acreages of baronies and other divisions were not established, were disregarded or were believed to be incorrect. In an extreme example in Co. Waterford, cess was traditionally paid equally by 'ploughland' but in one barony the size of a ploughland varied between 148 acres and 9,000 acres.[3] The grand juries' own records of land were not standardized. In some cases the records were kept in a document known as the 'old book', but the figures were thought to be based on surveys made, at best, in the seventeenth century, including the Down Survey and the Strafford Survey.[4] Apart from the fact that many were

1 Virginia Crossman, *Local government in nineteenth-century Ireland* (Belfast, 1994), p. 27. 2 *Spring Rice Report*, appendix A, pp 20–1. 3 *Report from select committee on county cess (Ireland); with the minutes of evidence, appendix and index*, HC 1836 (527), questions 1198–1203 (hereinafter cited as *Report from select committee on county cess, 1836*). 4 J.H. Andrews,

inaccurate in the first place, no account was taken of changes since that time. This meant that the payment of county cess was based on a principle that was known to be erroneous and was unequally distributed.

There was widespread criticism of this system and several parliamentary investigations took place in the early years of the nineteenth century. A bill introduced in 1819 was withdrawn on the undertaking of the government that it would bring in its own measure. Further pressure led to the setting up in 1824 of a select committee charged with considering the more equal apportionment of local tax and of providing for a general survey of Ireland, under the chairmanship of the Kerry landowner Thomas Spring Rice. This coincided with the expansion of the military cartography activities of the Board of Ordnance, which was already engaged in the primary triangulation of Britain under the charge of Colonel Colby, who testified to the committee.

The Spring Rice Committee published its report in June 1824. Three major bodies that still exist today – the Valuation Office, the Boundary Survey and the Ordnance Survey – have their origins in this seminal document. The report advocated a standardized solution to the problem of local taxation in Ireland, and distinguished between the survey and the valuation. It made clear recommendations on mapping: a map showing the boundaries and content (or square area) of townlands as well as the boundaries of parishes and baronies was essential; the survey should be carried out by the Board of Ordnance; and the maps should be made at the scale of six inches to the mile. With regard to the valuation, the conclusions were non-committal; although the committee had looked at cadastral surveys in other countries, it had not found an appropriate model. The report stated the expectation that a bill would be introduced in the next session of parliament, and set out three general principles for the valuation. It should: (1) have a fixed and uniform principle that would enable comparison; (2) be directed by a central authority appointed by the government; and (3) use local assistance, which would provide information and protection of private rights. Griffith was a witness at the select committee and gave his view of the valuation. In a short submission, he outlined how a valuation might be organised, but without any details of the work.[5]

After decades of discussion and delay, events now moved quickly. The two acts promised in the report were passed, setting up the Boundary Survey in 1825 and the valuation in 1826.[6] Before the maps could be made, the boundaries of the various divisions of land needed to be ascertained and the areas named, all in a standardized manner.[7] Griffith was named boundary surveyor

---

Plantation acres (Belfast, 1995), pp 366–85. 5 *Spring Rice Report*, pp 3–10, 138 (appendix F). 6 6 Geo. IV, c. 99 and 7 Geo. IV, c. 62, respectively. 7 See list of Boundary Survey archives in the National Archives.

in 1825,[8] and then appointed commissioner of valuation in August 1829.[9] Since that time, the positions of chief boundary surveyor and of commissioner of valuation, although created separately, have always been held by the same person. Meanwhile, the Ordnance Survey had started the triangulation of Ireland, followed by the field survey. The valuation field work began in June 1830 in Co. Londonderry. The work carried out by the three bodies was separate but closely linked, as the work of one was determined by the needs of the other. The Boundary Survey established authoritative boundaries that separated the baronies, parishes and townlands, either by recognising existing boundaries or by creating new ones, and named all units of land. The boundaries were handed over to the Ordnance Survey, enabling the map survey work to be carried out. The maps were drawn, corrected, engraved, printed and published. They showed the boundaries and the other basic information needed by the valuation, including land, buildings and physical features. Once the maps were available, the valuation could proceed.

Territorial divisions and organization
The recommendations of the Spring Rice Committee determined some of the data that was shown on the printed six-inch maps, and in turn this had an enduring influence on the valuation, shaping the manner in which the work was organized, and in consequence the archives. The common purpose behind the mapping and valuation was the taxation requirement of the grand juries, which traditionally used baronies, parishes and smaller divisions in the local administration. It was agreed that the Ordnance Survey maps would show these divisions and that the townland would be the smallest unit.[10] These were the boundaries printed on the maps and the work of the Townland Valuation was organized according to these divisions. The barony and parish became the references and identification points for all the documentation. However, within ten years of the start of the valuation, a new administrative structure was devised for the poor law system, and further territorial units were formed in poor law unions.[11] These were composed of unions of townlands, were not related to parishes, baronies or counties, and were overlaid on the existing territorial units. As well as being much larger than baronies, they frequently did not have boundaries in common with baronies, and many crossed county boundaries. Poor law unions were not printed on the Ordnance Survey maps because the decisions about the maps were made before they came into existence. The boundaries of poor law unions were always added manually to the valuation maps.

8 J.H. Andrews, *A paper landscape: the Ordnance Survey in nineteenth-century Ireland* (Oxford, 1975). 9 OL/2/2, p. 209. 10 *Spring Rice Report*, p. 6. Baronies are old territorial divisions of counties. They number 327, vary in size and do not generally cross county boundaries in a significant way. 11 1 & 2 Vict., c. 56. Poor law unions numbered 130 at first, but later more were added.

In the Tenement Valuation the work continued to be based on baronies even though from the late 1840s the valuation was made for the union-based poor law system. It is likely that the reuse of existing documents and maps (made in baronies and parishes) influenced this situation but new field and office maps were also all made in baronies. The *Primary valuation* was published in baronies until 1852–3 and after that in poor law unions. However, all the fair-copy maps of the Tenement Valuation were made in poor law unions and were known as 'union' maps. The 'cancelled books' (in the Valuation Office) are arranged by poor law union and electoral division.[12] This rather confused-looking situation should not impede access to the documents for the researcher, as once the name of a townland or parish is identified, the corresponding barony or poor law union can be found and the basic reference of the Ordnance Survey sheet number remains the same.

Baronies are large areas and always require several Ordnance Survey sheets. Sheets covering the margins of a barony also show parts of the adjoining baronies. Poor law unions are larger again and, similarly, sheets covering the margins of unions show more than one. The relevant divisions can be found in the *Townland index, 1901* and on logainm.ie/en.

THE DEVELOPMENT OF THE SYSTEM OF VALUATION

As the Spring Rice Committee had not made recommendations about the valuation, the system needed to be created from the beginning. Griffith favoured a method similar to that used in Scotland, and through legislation, instructions, training and constant engagement with the work, he shaped the system in the years between 1826 and 1852, and created documents that remained in reference use until the end of the twentieth century.

The Townland Valuation
The 1826 act and amendments
The first valuation act was passed in 1826. It stated that there was a need for more equal levying of local taxes and that a valuation should proceed once the Ordnance Survey maps were ready. It allowed the appointment of a commissioner and valuators, and gave the lord lieutenant power to issue instructions. It outlined how the valuation would be carried out: lands were to be valued according to a scale of prices, and houses on the basis of their letting values, with one-third deducted. The work was to be done county by county and recorded in townlands, parishes and baronies. The valuators were

12 The cancelled books are the official record and contain the most up-to-date valuation. When the valuation of a property is revised, the previous entry in the book is 'cancelled' and the new valuation is entered. These books are also known as 'revision books'. See *PRONI* (pp 196–7).

required to keep records. The result was to be a list showing for each county the townlands, parishes and baronies, with their valuations and acreages and could be appealed. This valuation list was to be made available publicly through the grand jury. The smallest unit to be valued was the townland. The new valuation would be used for county cess and no new arrangements were made for applotment or breaking down the tax on the townland into individual liability.[13] While changes were made in the years that followed, the basic structure of the valuation and the work methods were set up under this provision.

However, work did not begin immediately. In August 1828, Griffith expressed impatience with the delay, wishing to create public confidence by completing one county. He also wished to find out if additional measures were required and to start training a group of valuators who would 'form the nucleus for a more extended establishment capable of proceeding with the valuation of several counties at the same time'.[14] In the summer of 1829 Griffith was again making preparations. He wrote to Leveson Gower, the chief secretary for Ireland, informing him that the maps were nearly ready and outlining the preparation of instructions and the appointment and training of valuators.[15] He contacted the secretary of the grand jury of Co. Londonderry about nominating a committee of appeal.[16] In September he was obliged to write again to several correspondents, explaining that as he had not received the maps, the valuation would not start until the spring.[17] Work was finally started in June 1830, and in August he forwarded a copy of his instructions to the chief secretary, Sir H. Hardinge.[18] Problems arose almost immediately when the valuators working in the field discovered errors and omissions in the maps that hampered their work. This resulted in the Ordnance Survey withdrawing and revising the maps.[19] There were also problems regarding the definition of property that was to be valued. Some houses shown on the Ordnance Survey maps were no longer standing by the time the valuation started, and Griffith proposed to exclude those under £5 in value.[20]

A new act in October 1831 set a threshold of £3 under which houses need not be valued, and extended the valuation to outbuildings and other buildings.[21] In November, Griffith looked for a legal opinion in relation to exempted property.[22] A third act was passed in August 1832, defining exempt buildings as those wholly of a public nature or used for charitable purposes.[23] A fourth act, passed in August 1834, removed the limit of nine valuators per county, and required the deposit of copies of field books and maps with the county treasurer, who was to make them available for public

---

13 7 Geo. IV, c. 62.   14 OL/2/1, p. 33.   15 Ibid., pp 171–2.   16 Ibid., p. 181.   17 Ibid., pp 193–4.   18 OL/2/2, p. 19 and NAI, CSO/RP/1830/1411 (5).   19 Andrews, *A paper landscape*, pp 78–80.   20 OL/2/2, p. 25.   21 1 & 2 Will. IV, c. 51.   22 OL/2/2, p. 179. See also *Report from select committee on county cess, 1836*, questions 652–7.   23 2 & 3 Will. IV, c. 73.

inspection and copying. It sanctioned the appointment of one commissioner of valuation for the entire country, but as a salary of £500 per annum was 'an insufficient remuneration' for such a position, expenses of a guinea (£1 1s.) a day were allowed.[24]

Instructions
The valuation was not only novel, but was going to take many years to complete, by separate valuators in different parts of the country. If the valuation produced at the end was to be uniform, the work needed to be carried out by the same method throughout, and formal written instructions were used to ensure consistency. Seven sets of instructions for the field work were issued between 1830 and 1853, most in printed booklets small enough to fit in a pocket and be taken into the field for reference.[25] These were supplemented periodically by circulars giving directions on specific points.[26] The instructions set out the basis for making decisions, provided model descriptions and outlined how the work was to be organized, executed and recorded. Over the period, their content mirrors the changes brought in by new legislation and also attempts to clarify difficulties, and they became longer and more detailed. The instructions can be helpful to the researcher in relation to data recorded in the field work, although some parts are technical and the early versions were somewhat disordered, and they were not always followed exactly.

INSTRUCTIONS 1830
The first instructions were printed in Dublin in 1830. An unbound copy was forwarded to the chief secretary in Dublin Castle.[27] The *Instructions 1830* contain forty-nine paragraphs, more than half of which are concerned with the valuators and their work, and the remainder of which relate to the valuation of agricultural land and houses. The valuation was to be carried out by the baronial valuator working with two assistant valuators and recorded on maps and in field books. The land was to be valued according to the scale of prices from the act. In the field the valuators were to ascertain the quality, extent and initial value of 'quality lots' into which each townland was divided and were to value houses at the annual rent they would fetch, less one-third. Mills, distilleries and other such building were to be valued as buildings only. In valuing land, local circumstances were to be taken into account, such as

24 4 & 5 Will. IV, c. 55. 25 OL/1/2/1,1830 printed pages; OL/1/2/2, 1833, book; OL/1/2/3 1835–6, printed in *Report from select committee on county cess, 1836*, appendix; OL/1/2/4, 1839, book; OL/1/2/5, 1844, booklet of instructions to valuators; OL/1/2/6, 1844, booklet of instructions to surveyors and OL/1/2/7, 1853, book. 26 Circulars are found throughout the valuation letter books. See OL/2. 27 NAI, CSO/RP/1830/1411(5), see copy in National Archives, OL/1/2/1.

exposure to winds or distance from market. Some indoor duties were also prescribed. Examples of a map and forms were attached to the instructions.

INSTRUCTIONS 1833

Following some internal circulars, further instructions were published in 1833, which were more elaborate and detailed. The 187 paragraphs are divided between the principles and the organization of the work, how to value the land and how to value buildings. The paragraphs on land include some tables and give considerably more detail than the 1830 edition in the standardized descriptions of soils. Major additions were made in the sections on houses to reflect the changes made in the acts of 1831 and 1832 in establishing a threshold of £3 under which houses were not valued, although those over £2 10s. were to be noted, and in defining properties exempt from tax. Houses were to be measured, their quality noted using a letter code and the rent of houses in towns was to be recorded. The first house tables setting out letter codes for description and condition and number codes for materials were included. A system for calculating the additional value of houses in towns was outlined.

THE 1836 SELECT COMMITTEE ON COUNTY CESS

The Select Committee on County Cess (Ireland) reported in August 1836.[28] The valuation was not the subject of the enquiry but was a matter of great interest to the committee, both because the cost of the valuation was paid by the counties and because its objective was to create the basis on which county cess would be charged, thereby affecting their future income.[29] Griffith gave evidence and suggested changes, such as the inclusion of mills and the exclusion of houses under £5, something he had long advocated.[30]

INSTRUCTIONS 1835–6

The select committee report of 1836 includes instructions consisting of the *Instructions 1833* with two separate sets of additions. The first, dated 1835, gave directions on gardens and, significantly in respect of genealogical use of the documents, required that the name of the occupier of every house that was measured be entered and numbered in the field book. The second set of additions are undated but were issued with the select committee report in 1836. They cover matters that are also important for the information recorded: quality lots were limited to between thirty and fifty acres, the advantage of proximity to towns was to be shown on the maps by marking

---

28 *Report from select committee on county cess, 1836*.   29 The entire cost of the valuation of each county was charged to the grand jury at this period. From 1860 (23 Vict., c. 4) half of the cost of the revision of the valuation was to be paid out of the consolidated fund (i.e., by the state).
30 *Report from select committee on county cess, 1836*, question 641.

concentric lines, known as 'lines of percentage' and information was to be collected on tenure in towns, on grazing lands and on mills.[31]

THE ACT OF 1836

A major consolidating act was passed in August 1836, repealing the four earlier acts but retaining many of their provisions.[32] The changes in this act are mainly concerned with the workings of the valuation. A third and final meeting of the county-level committee of revision was convened within three years of the first meeting. New measures included raising the valuation threshold for houses to £5 and valuing machinery in mills. The arrangement whereby the valuators worked in parties of three was dropped. Some administrative matters were tidied up and new requirements included the printing of the valuation lists of each barony and the presentation by the commissioner of a progress report and statement of costs to the grand jury of the county at assizes.

INSTRUCTIONS 1839

A new book of instructions was published in September 1839.[33] They incorporate the changes made in the 1836 act, repeat many of the earlier provisions and give advice about how the valuators should organize and conduct themselves. The valuators were now to work on their own, with their work being checked in a periodic independent re-valuation by the check valuator. Houses under £5 were not to be valued but those likely to be worth more than £4 were to be noted. Almost one-third of the instructions related to the valuation of water power of mills and manufactories.[34] The last two paragraphs of the instructions, added after the others had been printed, introduced a measure that had bearing on the information recorded in the archives: as field fences were now included on the Ordnance Survey maps, the boundaries of lots were henceforth to correspond to farms. This marked the beginning of the recording of individual holdings, although no mention was made of the names of the occupiers.

When the 1836 act is taken together with the *Instructions 1839*, the development of thinking and practice over the thirteen year period since the first act can be appreciated. The situation had moved from some vague sections on the workings of the valuation in the 1826 act and a small number of requirements in the *Instructions 1830* to prescriptive rules set out in the 1836 act and the substantial *Instructions 1839*. The experience on the ground exposed weaknesses and anomalies, such as the definition of exempted property or the inclusion of mills.[35] The number of changes demonstrates

31 OL/1/2/3. 32 6 & 7 Will. IV, c. 84. 33 OL/1/2/4. 34 Ibid., §205–76. 35 *Report from select committee on county cess, 1836*, question 604.

the experimental nature of the work, and this was anticipated from the beginning.[36]

The passage of five acts in ten years is a tribute to Griffith's ability to deal with difficulties at the highest level.[37] The content of the changes bears a strong similarity to the ideas that he had promoted from the outset. He retained the principle of uniformity, of a relative valuation based on a scale of prices for land and letting value for houses. He succeeded in having houses under £5 excluded and in having mills included, in defining exempt properties, in increasing the number of valuators and changing their working practices. He also strengthened his own position by being appointed commissioner for the entire country with new financial arrangements, although he was made somewhat more accountable in that he had to provide progress and expenditure reports to the grand juries. Copies of these reports are preserved in the valuation letter books in the National Archives, and provide cursory accounts of the progress of the work.[38] Annual reports on the valuation work were not required.

Difficulties for the Townland Valuation

Even after all the meticulous work, careful examination and appeals, the result of the Townland Valuation was badly understood. The determination of the liability of individual occupiers for tax, known as the 'applotment', remained the responsibility of the grand jury and was carried out by locally appointed applotters. Although the applotment was not the concern of the valuation, great pains were taken to make the outcome of the work acceptable to users. In 1834 Griffith sought a legal opinion that confirmed that he was not empowered to break down the valuation into individual holdings, but he continued to provide advice on the matter.[39] He forwarded to a correspondent 'a specimen of an applotment table which I propose to prepare for every parish, by means of which the amounts of assessments in any townland can be ascertained with great facility'.[40] Queries on applotment appeared constantly in the valuation correspondence until the act of 1852 made the valuation in tenements universal. In the 1840s a form letter explaining the process of applotment was printed, indicating a volume of queries that merited a routine response.[41] As late as 1848, Griffith wrote to the grand jury of Wexford expressing criticism of the work of the applotters that they had appointed. He had sent John Boyan, 'one of [his] best and more experienced valuators' to call on each of the applotters and report on the work. He offered to go there himself to speak to the gentlemen and to draw up the solutions relative to the applotment.[42]

36 OL/2/1, p. 33.   37 Vaughan, 'Richard Griffith and the Tenement Valuation' in Herries Davies & Mollan (eds), *Richard Griffith, 1784–1878*, p. 104.   38 OL/2.   39 OL/2/3, p. 300.
40 Ibid., p. 345.   41 OL/2/11/1.   42 OL/2/12, pp 41–3. Copies of some of the books of

In the late 1830s, when the valuation seemed to be making progress, a complication arose when the poor law was introduced in Ireland and the workhouse system, based at first on 130 poor law unions run by boards of guardians, was set up.[43] The relief of the poor was financed by a property tax, known as the poor rate, which was based on a valuation of individual tenements. This valuation was carried out separately in each poor law union by locally appointed valuators, without central control beyond the requirements of the Poor Law Act and instructions from the poor law commissioners.[44] It had no connection to the Townland Valuation. This led to confusion and complaints. In parts of the country where the Townland Valuation had been completed there were now two systems, based on different principles, and used as the bases of taxes collected by separate bodies.

Other developments also contributed to the discussion surrounding the valuation. In the context of reform of the parliamentary franchise, an examination of the Poor Law Valuation was carried out in 1841 to see if it could be used as the basis for electoral lists.[45] In 1843 an amendment to the Municipal Corporations Act made the Poor Law Valuation the basis of the electoral franchise in the cities covered by this act.[46] A tenement valuation was not a new concept. Models of tenement valuations in France, Bavaria, Savoy and Piedmont had been discussed by the Spring Rice Committee, and in Ireland the Tithe Valuation, carried out between 1823 and 1837, was based on individual holdings.[47]

Select committee on the Townland Valuation 1844

In 1844 a select committee scrutinized the Townland Valuation in order to determine whether a single valuation could be used for county cess and poor rates, and whether the Townland Valuation's principle of the townland being the smallest unit valued could be altered.[48] The establishment of the

applotment made by the grand jury in Co. Wexford in 1849 are held in the National Archives, including books made by Pierce Ryan, who had also worked as a valuator on the Townland Valuation of Co. Wexford in the mid-1840s, and again in 1849 on the check valuation, see OL/4/7473–8. **43** 1 & 2 Vict., c. 56. **44** *Copies of instructions issued by the poor law commissioners to the valuators in Ireland*, HC 1841 (353). **45** *Reports relative to the valuations for poor rates, and to the registered elective franchise, in Ireland*, HC 1841 (292–3); *Reports relative to the valuations for poor rates, and to the registered elective franchise, in Ireland*: first series: part II, HC 1841 (305–7c); *Reports relative to the valuations for poor rates, and to the registered elective franchise, in Ireland*: second series: part I, HC 1841 (308–10); *Second appendix to reports relative to the valuations for poor rates, and to the registered elective franchise, in Ireland*, HC 1841 (326); *Third general report relative to the valuations for poor rates, and to the registered elective franchise, in Ireland*, HC 1841 (329); *Reports relative to the valuations for poor rates, and to the registered elective franchise, in Ireland, with appendices*, HC 1842 (401). **46** 6 & 7 Vict., c. 93. **47** *Spring Rice Report*, pp 5–6, and titheapplotmentbooks.nationalarchives.ie. **48** *Report from select committee on Townland Valuation, 1844*, pp iv–xiii.

committee was in itself a sign of public concern and its proceedings show exasperation with what, on the one hand, appeared to be an interminable valuation under the commissioner of valuation and, on the other hand, an unsatisfactory valuation carried out in haste by the boards of guardians. A letter from Sir Denhem Norreys MP to the grand jury of Cork expressed this frustration: 'Is it not absurd to have two distinct valuations; the one to give the value of the whole, the other, by a different process, to give the value of its parts?'[49]

The Townland Valuation was criticized for its slow progress, with only twenty counties completed and the most extensive and populous counties still to come, because tenements were not valued and because there was no provision for revision. Griffith put up a vigorous defence, but on this occasion was unable to prevail against the overwhelming logic of using tenements. He argued that he was bound by law to use the townland unit and was not required to give details of farms,[50] while at the same time he indicated a certain resignation by demonstrating how the field books and field maps could be used to convert the townland work to a valuation in tenements.[51] In his turn, he was damning in his criticism of the Poor Law Valuation. When questioned about the possibility of using the Poor Law Valuation for county cess, he replied that there were big discrepancies between the two and 'that either one or the other must be very erroneous'.[52]

The report of the select committee found that the Townland Valuation could not be used for poor rates and that the Poor Law Valuation could not be used for county cess. It recommended that there should be one valuation based on tenements valued on the principles of the Poor Law Act, that it be carried out by an independent and professional officer and that it be revised periodically. As an interim measure pending new legislation, it proposed that the Townland Valuation be discontinued and that the Poor Law Valuation be revised for county cess purposes by Griffith, with tenements as the basic unit, using instructions from the lord lieutenant.[53] While these recommendations were not implemented, the report had major consequences for the valuation and set it on the course upon which it attained its definitive form in 1852. It forced the decision that the valuation would henceforth be in tenements, but gave all responsibility in this area to the commissioner of valuation and, following a period of transition, the 1852 act saw a return to the principle of valuation based on a scale of prices.

Although its content was superseded by the work of the Tenement Valuation, the Townland Valuation nevertheless created the model for the

---

49 Ibid., appendix 1, pp 159–62. 50 Ibid., question 211. 51 Ibid., questions 176–90. Model documents used to make the demonstration are held in the National Archives, see OL/4/148, OL/4/152–3, OL/4/7466–8. 52 *Report from select committee on Townland Valuation, 1844*, question 155. 53 Ibid., pp x–xii.

later work. It established the structures (draft valuation, appeal and final valuation) and operations (valuators working in the field determining the valuation according to a set of rules, with follow-up work carried out in the office and centralized control) that were retained in the tenement work. The administration and appeals were also organized in a similar manner. In spite of the criticism and the delays, Griffith's position as a public servant and his stature as a man of science can only have been enhanced as he emerged from this battle with increased control and the acceptance of at least some of his strongly held principles.

The transitional period, 1844–52
Instructions 1844
In October 1844 two short sets of instructions appeared on the same day: the lord lieutenant's *Additional instructions for valuators* and Griffith's *Instructions for land surveyors*.[54] They were issued in the expectation that legislation would be enacted without delay, but it took two more years. The *Additional instructions for valuators* made radical changes to the basis of the valuation. Every tenement was to be entered separately in the field book, with the occupier's name, the lot number, the description of the soil, the content and the value. The difficulties of including very small holdings were anticipated, and rent and tenure were to be noted. Some existing requirements were restated concerning lots not greater than fifty acres and where possible coinciding with the boundaries of farms, with a view to a future applotment of the county cess on each tenement.

The *Instructions for land surveyors 1844* required marking all tenements over one acre on the map, numbering them to correspond to the field book and noting the name of the occupier. Tenements under five acres were to be measured by chain survey,[55] as the calculation of square area from the maps was not sufficiently accurate. In towns, the square area of gardens was to be given, and roads and streets were to be noted as 'waste ground'. Very small holdings in towns were to be grouped together on the map but distinguished in the field book. Houses were to be measured and given a quality letter as usual. The different cases where names were to be recorded were set out.[56]

The act of 1846
New legislation was expected following the select committee report but in 1845 a valuation bill failed in the House of Lords. On 28 August 1846 the 'Act to amend the law relating to the valuation of rateable property in Ireland' was passed.[57] This long and complex act was to apply to six counties

54 OL/1/2/5 and OL/1/2/6. 55 This was a survey carried out using a surveyor's chain to take measurements on the ground and calculating the figures to obtain the square area of the tenements. 56 OL/1/2/6. 57 9 & 10 Vict., c. 110.

and four cities that had not been valued by the Townland Valuation,[58] and the 1836 act was to continue in force in other counties. The act authorized a valuation in tenements that would be used for poor law purposes in the named counties and that would be restated in townlands for county cess purposes. Administrative matters were covered, including remuneration, the appointment of the commissioner and valuators, the power of the lord lieutenant to engage staff and issue instructions and the use of Ordnance Survey maps.

The first part of the 1846 act established the Tenement Valuation. It was to apply to every tenement that was a 'rateable hereditament' under the Poor Law Act and was to be based on the 'net annual value (that is to say) the rent', less costs. The names of occupiers and immediate lessors were to be noted. Other provisions included the possibility of grand juries requesting a tenement valuation, matters relating to towns rateable under other acts, the valuation in tenements of parts of poor law unions that crossed county boundaries and periodic revision. The draft valuation (the *Primary valuation*) was to be printed and circulated through the boards of guardians. A new system was set up for appeals against this draft valuation, with a second appeal to the court of quarter sessions (see appendix A for details of appeals). The second part of the act dealt with the valuation for county cess purposes. On completion of appeals and amendment, the Tenement Valuation was to be converted to the townland scale of prices, based on the table of agricultural prices in the 1836 act, and the valuation was to be issued in townlands. The existing Townland Valuation system of appeals was to continue through the committees of appeal and revision. A new valuation was to take place every fourteen years.

At the date of the new instructions in October 1844 most of the work of the Townland Valuation was complete. The valuation was in operation in ten counties.[59] In eight further counties the work was finished and the period between preliminary and final committee of revision meetings was under way.[60] Six more counties were expected to be ready in late 1844 or early 1845, and Clare and Kilkenny were well advanced. Work had barely started in Waterford, Tipperary and Dublin, and no work had been done in counties Limerick, Cork and Kerry.[61] There is no record of a decision regarding which counties should be finished under the Townland Valuation and which

---

58 Cos. Dublin, Cork, Kerry, Limerick, Tipperary and Waterford and cities of Cork, Kilkenny, Limerick and Waterford. 59 *Returns of the date of the commencement of the Townland Valuation in each county in Ireland, and of the final meeting of the committee of revision*, HC 1851 (268): Cos. Antrim, Armagh, Donegal, Down, Fermanagh, Londonderry, Louth, Meath, Monaghan and Tyrone. 60 Ibid.: Carlow, Cavan, Kildare, Longford, Leitrim, Roscommon, Sligo and Westmeath. 61 *Report from select committee on Townland Valuation, 1844*, questions 6–10; Andrews, *A paper landscape*, appendix G, p. 1. Six-inch maps: maps of Dublin and Limerick were published in 1844, Cork in 1845 and Kerry in 1846.

should be valued in tenements. In the six almost-ready counties and in Clare and Kilkenny, the Townland Valuation work was continued to completion. Counties where little or no work had been done were brought under the tenement provisions. The work there was started on the authority of the *Instructions 1844* and by the time the 1846 act passed, good progress had been made in those counties.

The change from townland to tenement work is illustrated in some of the documents. The valuation in tenements was authorized in late October 1844. Work on a house book in the parish of Ballyboghill, Co. Dublin started under the Townland Valuation in November 1844, noting only houses valued over £5. In early December the valuator went back over the townlands already completed and entered all the other houses using the Tenement Valuation instructions.[62] In Terryglass and a number of other parishes in Co. Tipperary there are field books from both valuations. The first is a standard Townland Valuation book containing the townlands in quality lots, made in April and May 1844. Terryglass was valued again in April 1846 by the same valuator, in a field book of the Tenement Valuation, with tenements numbered, occupiers named and the qualities of land in each tenement differentiated.[63]

The 1846 act attempted to reconcile the different strands of theory and practice and is the most challenging text of all of the valuation acts. In addition to making an important alteration in the content of the valuing work, it changed the relative importance of the organs of local government, although for the moment the old and new systems operated in parallel. The grand jury, the high constable of the barony, the churchwarden and select vestry of the parish as well as the grand jury-appointed committees continued to have a role. However, under this act new responsibilities were given to the boards of guardians of the poor law unions in a process controlled by central government that presaged the expansion of their activities into other local functions as the century progressed.[64]

One of the difficulties with the Townland Valuation was the long time-lag between the beginning of the field work and the issue of the valuation for appeals, the holding of appeals and then a further period of up to three years before the valuation was finalized. In the years 1844–52 this resulted in an overlap between the old system and the new, with the Townland Valuation still completing its work in eight counties,[65] and the Tenement Valuation starting work in counties that came under the 1846 act. Moreover, in some counties, the two valuations appeared to be carried on simultaneously at this

62 OL/4/5270. Similar books were made in neighbouring Dublin parishes of Clonmethan, Ballymadun and Garristown. 63 OL/4/4471 (1844) and OL/4/6961 (1846). 64 Crossman, *Local government*. 65 Cos. Mayo, Galway, King's, Queen's, Wexford, Wicklow, Clare and Kilkenny.

time. In Co. Kilkenny, the Townland Valuation field work was started in July 1843 and completed in 1847, the preliminary committee of revision meeting was held in May 1848 and the final meeting in May 1851. In the meantime, the entire work of the Tenement Valuation had been carried out: the field work began in June 1847, the *Primary valuation* was published in 1849–50 and the last tenement appeals were held in December 1850, five months before the final ratification of the Townland Valuation. It was not surprising that this resulted in criticism and impatience. The 1846 act was replaced within a short time by a further act in 1852. Although there was a lot of parallel activity in the transitional period, it created a large quantity of unique and interesting archives.

The Tenement Valuation from 1852
The act of 1852
In February 1852, Griffith wrote to Somerville, the chief secretary for Ireland, in relation to the completion of the townland work: 'I cannot go another year with the present act, without incurring an *enormous additional expense*, as well as universal opposition.'[66] A new valuation act passed into law on 30 June 1852.[67] The Tenement Valuation made under the 1846 act was to be used for both poor rates and county cess, subject to amendment under the new act. A new tenement valuation was to be made of counties not yet valued in tenements, and this was also to be used for both purposes. The valuation in townlands was to be discontinued. The earlier acts were repealed but were to remain in force until valuations already made were altered. Valuations made under the earlier acts were to be amended to the new scale of prices set out in this act. Tenements were to be valued separately based on an estimate of the net annual value with reference to the new scale of prices, and buildings were to be valued on an estimate of 'net annual value', that is, the rent with expenses deducted. Buildings of a public nature continued to be valued but remained exempt from tax. The valuation was extended to include other property, such as mines, railways and fisheries, and improvements became eligible for relief for seven years. Revision of altered property was authorized. Arrangements similar to those already in place for circulation of the *Primary valuation* were outlined. Some existing provisions were restated, salary rates were set, and the commissioner's powers in relation to the hiring of staff were widened. Appeals were simplified and were now made directly to the commissioner (see appendix A). This act tidied up previous provisions and established the tenement as the basis of all valuation, creating the model that survives to the present day. Griffith had finally lost the battle about tenements, but he prevailed in using the scale of prices and had strengthened

---

66 OL/2/13, opposite p. 288.   67 15 & 16 Vict., c. 63.

his position of centralized control of a single valuation. There were further valuation acts later in the century but they covered only minor or administrative matters.[68]

Instructions 1853

New instructions were issued in 1853 consisting of 345 separate paragraphs with sample forms and tables, in a dense little volume. A copy of the geological map of Ireland published by Griffith in 1853, one of his favourite projects, was folded into the front cover. Many of the paragraphs had appeared in previous versions, but this became the definitive version for the tenement work. The *Instructions 1853* begin and end with paragraphs relating to the manner in which the valuators and surveyors are to go about their business, keep records and generally behave, including the habitual exhortation to maintain discretion. They are divided into three principal areas – land, buildings and water power – with smaller sections covering records, definitions and duties. They deal with an astonishing range of matters, from identifying the components of soil to valuing a railway by examining 'receipts for a year or two, taken at each station along the line' to seventy-two separate paragraphs about houses. They are interspersed with tables or ready reckoners for every eventuality, from the rotation of tillage crops to the formula for calculating the profit on butter to the allowance to be made for transporting seaweed on a hilly road.[69]

The detailed and comprehensive nature of the instructions shows how specific it was found necessary to be, in order to maintain uniformity over a large-scale project that took place over a long period. W.E. Vaughan, in his examination of how the main tables in the instructions could have been applied, suggests that their complexity and gaps means that they were used as 'a valuator's equivalent of a bench-mark; they fixed the top of a scale for measuring the relative value of land'.[70] The centralized control of the work, the importance of uniformity and the strong personal involvement of the commissioner are illustrated in a matter that arose in 1855, when Griffith was asked to exempt the residence of the Sisters of Mercy in Enniscorthy, Co. Wexford. He refused because it was complicated with 'many and very nice distinctions', and 'I always find if I relax in the least degree that I cannot recover lost ground.'[71]

---

68 Further amending acts relating to valuation were passed in 1854 (17 Vict., c. 8), 1856 (19 & 20 Vict., c. 63), 1860 (23 Vict., c. 4), 1864 (27 & 28 Vict., c. 70) and 1874 (37 & 38 Vict., c. 70). The 1860 act made payment of half of the cost of revising the valuation the responsibility of the central government and brought the valuation under Treasury control. 69 OL/1/2/7, §318 (discretion), §65 and others (soil), §169 (railway), §172–243 (houses), §98 (tillage crops), §106 (profit on butter), §139 (transporting seaweed). 70 Vaughan, 'Richard Griffith and the Tenement Valuation' in Herries Davies & Mollan (eds), *Richard Griffith, 1784–1878*, p. 113. 71 OL/2/14, p. 296.

HOW THE WORK WAS DONE

In the initial valuation, the work always took place in four stages: (1) field work in which the data was collected, (2) office work in which the field data was used to prepare a preliminary valuation for appeals, (3) appeal hearings and follow-up work, and (4) production of a final valuation that was applied to taxation. The content of the work and its organization and execution were determined by the acts and instructions and by practice adapted from experience. The distinguishing features of the valuation were to be its uniformity, its relativity and the fact that it was carried out by a centralized and national body. This required collecting and processing the data in a standardized manner, using the evidence in the documents as the basis of decisions and retaining the records as proof. The archives bear testimony to the methodical and meticulous work carried out to this end. In common with other enterprises funded from public monies, the strictest economy was to be observed in every element of the work. The broad outline of the work is given below and the main series of documents created by each stage are set out. Further details will be found in the chapters on the series of archives.

Over the period between the acts of 1826 and 1852, a number of changes were made that determined what records were made and what information they contained. Some changes were piecemeal, such as the requirement to collect additional information at various dates, and some were radical, as in the adoption of the tenement as the only unit valued in 1852. The work was organized by place, the changes were not introduced everywhere at the same time and, in the period 1844–52, several different kinds of work were carried on in parallel at the same time. The objective of the valuation also changed over this time, and the initial valuation became the baseline to be used for ongoing revision.[72] See appendix C for the dates of the work in each county.

Work under the Townland Valuation
Field work valuing land and houses

A valuator was assigned to a barony and worked through each parish, townland by townland, recording the information on land and houses specified in the instructions. He was equipped with notebooks and copies of the printed Ordnance Survey maps that covered the barony and was assisted by a labourer. After a general look around, and having examined the soil by digging, he subdivided the townland by type of soil into 'quality lots'. He marked these in outline on his field map (see p. 123) and numbered the lots to correspond to the entries in his field book (see pp 61–72), where he wrote

---

[72] There are several descriptions of the work given to parliamentary committees: see *Report from select committee on county cess, 1836*, questions 595–9; *Report from select committee on Townland Valuation, 1844*, questions 19–49.

a description of soil and also noted the price per acre (known as the 'field price') that he considered each lot was worth.[73] Before 1836, the field work was carried out by three valuators working together, who made separate field books; after 1836 each valuator worked alone and made one field book and one house book per parish. A separate check valuation was made to ensure consistency.

The field valuator also did some desk work. He made a copy of the map, which he used to calculate the square area, or content, of each quality lot, using one of two methods.[74] He wrote up information that was later used for reference, including a scale of prices, a list of the main landowners, a general account of the parish and notes on townlands, describing the land and local circumstances. The field price assumed that the lot was 'in an ordinary situation' and the price adjusted for local circumstances was written in another column. Matters affecting specific areas rather than the wider locality, such as steep land, were noted immediately. More general circumstances, including the advantages of good climate or access to lime, and the disadvantages of elevation or distance from markets, were taken into account later. In the early years, this work was done by the valuator while still in the county, but from the mid-1830s it was done in the office in Dublin. The valuator's familiarity with the area was seen as essential, and he was required to complete his notes to the fullest extent before forwarding the documents to the office or moving to another district.[75]

House books were used to record houses. A system based on measurement and observation was first outlined in *Instructions 1833*.[76] Houses likely to be near the threshold of £3 and £5 were recorded, but as most houses in rural areas did not meet this requirement, the numbers noted were small. In rural areas, qualifying houses were entered in the house book and marked on the field map. After 1836, houses in urban areas were usually recorded in separate house books and marked on the town plans. Most houses in rural areas were omitted but most houses in towns were included because they were more valuable.

The main series of documents created were:

- Townland Valuation original field books and check field books (OL/4)
- Townland Valuation original house books and check house books (OL/5)
- Townland Valuation original field maps (OL/11)
- Valuation town plans (OL/12)

---

73 OL/1/2/2, §25–9. 74 Ibid., §34: areas were to be computed 'either by triangles or by parallel lines drawn through the map, at the distance of 20 perches from each other'. 75 Ibid., §38–60, OL/1/2/4, §30–65. 76 OL/1/2/2, §143–81.

Office work in preparation of the draft valuation for appeal
When the field work in each parish was completed, the documents were forwarded to the office in Dublin, where the next stage was carried out by a separate team of clerks and draftsmen. The office work included copying the field books, recalculating the field price by the scale of the act and making allowances for circumstances, completing calculations, renumbering documents and collating the data to make a draft valuation. The total acreage in each townland was double-checked and made to match the figure provided by the Ordnance Survey, using registry books (see pp 109–10). The data on houses was calculated and collated. Quarto books (see pp 83–90) were used to record the additional value of houses in towns. Mill books (see pp 90–4) were also made in the office. Calculations were usually done twice in different books as a check on accuracy, using calculation books (field) (see p. 64). A summary of the data on each county was entered in the list book (see pp 110–11). The original field books and calculation books (field) have a printed worksheet at the back that lists the office operations, noting the name of the clerk and the date. A typical example shows that fourteen office staff carried out nineteen separate operations over a period of five months in 1839.[77] When the office work was finished in each barony, a draft valuation list for appeals was printed for circulation through the grand jury. Copies of these lists are attached to the Townland Valuation appeal books.

The main series of documents created were:

- Townland Valuation copy field books (OL/4)
- Townland Valuation office maps (OL/11)
- Townland Valuation calculation books (field) (OL/4)
- Townland Valuation registry books (OL/8)
- Quarto books (OL/7)
- Townland Valuation mill books (OL/9)
- List books (OL/10)

Appeals against the Townland Valuation
A complex multi-level system of appeals was set up under the 1826 and 1836 acts and remained in operation until 1852 (see pp 94–9 and appendix A).

The documents created were:

- Townland Valuation appeal books (OL/13)

[77] OL/4/504.

Documents of record of the Townland Valuation
On completion of the appeals, record copies of the documents stating the valuation were made, including printed books (see pp 100–2). Copies were given to the grand juries and used in the levying of tax.

The main documents created were:

- Townland Valuation fair-copy field books (OL/4)
- Townland Valuation fair-copy maps (OL/11)
- *Townland Valuation* printed books (OL/14)

Work under the Tenement Valuation
The Tenement Valuation took place in three phases. In the first phase, from 1844, the tenement work was started in counties that had not been valued by the Townland Valuation. In the second phase, from 1848, it was extended to some counties that had previously been valued by the Townland Valuation. Under section 15 of the 1846 act, where part of a poor law union was valued in tenements because it was located in one of the six named counties but other parts of the union were in an adjoining county, the poor law commissioners could request the valuation in tenements of the parts in the adjoining county. Under sections 11 and 73, town authorities and grand juries of counties could apply for valuation in tenements.[78] In the third and final phase, the 1852 act was applied to all other counties, also valued by the Townland Valuation. The first and second phases can be seen as the transitional period between the two valuations, when different methods of work were tried and the townland work also continued at the same time. The experience of this period resulted in the 1852 act, which swept away the complications of parallel work and henceforth applied one system to the entire country.

Under the Tenement Valuation, the same four stages of field work, office work, appeal and final valuation were carried out. The Tenement Valuation had to deal with a vastly increased workload at all stages. Where the Townland Valuation field work had recorded townlands divided by quality of soil and a limited number of houses, the valuation in tenements needed information on all houses, the extent and location of every tenement and the names of the occupiers of each holding. In consequence, the office work also expanded. This change was initiated at a time when the population was at its highest. In May 1845, Griffith wrote to the chief secretary, Sir Thomas Fremantle, that the new system 'will have the effect of changing the entire system of the valuation and of increasing the detail at least twenty fold'.[79]

78 9 & 10 Vict., c. 110.   79 OL/2/10, p. 236.

Tenement Valuation in counties valued for the first time
The valuation in tenements began in 1844, authorized by instructions of the lord lieutenant and by the 1846 act. It was applied in the first instance to named counties (Cork, Dublin, Kerry, Limerick, Tipperary and Waterford) and cities (Cork, Kilkenny, Limerick and Waterford) where the Townland Valuation work had not been carried out and that were now valued for the first time.

FIELD WORK VALUING LAND AND HOUSES
The field work was carried out as previously by parish, but now by a surveyor and valuator working together. The surveyor carried out the preliminary work by 'perambulating' the tenements. He established the boundaries and noted the occupiers' names and other information, using field maps, field books, and a new book, known as a tenure book or perambulation book (see pp 102–9). He also collected information on buildings in the house book. The valuator followed, valuing the land and recording his data using the field book and a second map, and also noting his decision on the value of the houses and other related matters. Houses in towns were noted in the house books and on the town plans. Preliminary books (see p. 67) were made in some cases and the square area of holdings under five acres was measured by survey and recorded in survey books (see pp 67–8).

The main series of documents created were:

- Tenement Valuation original field books (OL/4)
- Tenement Valuation surveyor's and valuator's house books (OL/5)
- Tenement Valuation tenure books (OL/6)
- Tenement Valuation surveyor's and valuator's field maps (OL/11)
- Valuation town plans (OL/12)
- Tenement Valuation preliminary books (OL/4)
- Tenement Valuation survey books (OL/4)
- Tenement Valuation check field books (OL/4)
- Tenement Valuation check house books (OL/5)

OFFICE WORK
The office work under the Tenement Valuation was onerous and the volume of work increased considerably. There were not only far more tenements than quality lots, but the square area of each different subdivision by quality of land in each tenement and the total were also required. The calculated figures were reconciled with the Ordnance Survey figures in the registry books, but no registry books for counties valued in this phase have survived. Rent books (see pp 111–12), consisting of abstracts of rent, were made in baronies and in some cases in parishes. Comparison books (see p. 68) were

made in some cases. At the end of the office work, the preliminary valuation was printed in books as the *Primary valuation*, in preparation for appeals (see pp 136–56).

The main series of documents created were:

- Tenement Valuation office maps (OL/11)
- Tenement Valuation calculation books (field) (OL/4)
- Tenement Valuation copy field books (OL/4)
- Tenement Valuation copy house books (OL/5)
- Tenement Valuation comparison books (OL/4)
- Tenement Valuation rent books (OL/16)
- Mill books (OL/9)
- List books (OL/10)
- *Primary valuation* (OL/18, available at askaboutireland.ie/griffith-valuation)

APPEALS AGAINST THE *PRIMARY VALUATION*

Appeals against the *Primary valuation* were heard by sub-commissioners of valuation (see pp 157–79). Documents were prepared for the appeals and some check field work was also done at this time. Further survey work and office work of amendment was carried out following the appeals.

The main series of documents created were:

- Tenement Valuation appeal books (1846 act) (OL/19)
- Revision book of revising surveyor (OL/19)

Extension of the Tenement Valuation to counties previously valued

The second phase of the Tenement Valuation saw it extended to other counties under the 1846 act. From 1848, the grand juries of Co. Kilkenny, Co. Carlow, Queen's County and the city of Drogheda requested a valuation in tenements under section 73.[80] From 1850, under section 15, the poor law commissioners requested that the parts of some poor law unions be valued in tenements.[81] Using this provision, parts of Cos. Clare, Kildare, Meath, Wexford, Wicklow and King's County were valued in tenements in advance of the other parts of those counties.

Once the Tenement Valuation was extended to counties beyond those originally named in the act, a new situation obtained. In these counties part

---

80 OL/2/12, p. 8, Kilkenny, 9 Mar. 1848; OL/2/12, p. 107, Queen's County, 27 July 1848; OL/2/12 following p. 478, Carlow, 31 July 1850; OL/2/12, p. 369, city of Drogheda, 1 Mar. 1850 assent of lord lieutenant.   81 OL/2/12, p. 451; OL/2/13, pp 91, 209, 220, 221, 223. Unions of Celbridge, Limerick, Roscrea, Parsonstown, Mountmellick, New Ross and Rathdown.

of the work had already been done by the Townland Valuation and some of the data could be reused. In order to make the valuation in tenements, additional data was required on the extent and location of every tenement, and all houses were valued, which led to a new round of field work in the counties concerned. It was then necessary to put the new information together with the old records on land quality in order to establish the quality of the land in each tenement.

In some parts of these counties the valuation was at first carried out by re-plotting the existing data in tenements in a manner that was intended to minimize the work involved. This method was outlined by Griffith at the 1844 select committee,[82] and in June 1848 he described a 'trial of the system' that was to be applied in two baronies in Co. Kilkenny.[83] The results of this experiment can be seen in some printed *Primary valuation* volumes, where a note at the end of the parish states 'arranged in tenements'.[84] The system was quietly discontinued. The work methods in this phase were similar to those used under the 1852 act, described below, and documents of the same description were created.

Tenement Valuation from 1852
The third phase of the valuation in tenements took place following the 1852 act and applied to the remainder of the country. The work followed the same stages of field work, office work, appeal and final valuation. All counties covered by this provision had already been valued under the Townland Valuation. The existing documents continued to be used – always to some extent and in many cases widely – but this varied from one county to another. The lists in the National Archives give details for each county.

FIELD WORK VALUING LAND AND HOUSES
New field books were not made by the Tenement Valuation but some check field books were made and varied use was made of the existing maps and books. The field work was carried out by a surveyor and a valuator working parish by parish and now consisted of plotting the same land in tenements. The surveyor established the boundaries of the tenements, and recorded the houses, the names of occupiers and other information, using field maps, field books, house books and tenure books. Tenement boundaries were marked on maps – either existing Townland Valuation field maps or new maps. New

82 *Report from select committee on Townland Valuation, 1844*, questions 176–84. 83 OL/2/12, p. 91. In Co. Kilkenny, only the barony of Ida was valued using this method. 84 *Primary valuation*, Co. Carlow and Queen's County (all baronies); Co. Clare, baronies of Bunratty Lower and Tulla Lower (part); Co. Kildare, barony of Salt North; Co. Kilkenny, barony of Ida; King's County, baronies of Ballybritt, Clonlisk and Philipstown Upper; Co. Wicklow, barony of Rathdown.

house books were made to cover the additional houses now included, and some of the Townland Valuation house books were revised. The valuator followed the surveyor, checking the valuation of the land and valuing the buildings. Houses in towns were recorded and noted on town plans, although most had already been covered by the Townland Valuation. Further enquiries were made in Dublin and Belfast using query sheets (see pp 112–13). In theory, after the 1852 act houses were no longer measured and the rent was used as the basis of valuation, but this varied from one place to another.

The main series of documents created were:

- Tenement Valuation original field maps, drawn on Townland Valuation original or copy field maps, or drawn on new maps (OL/11)
- Valuation town plans (OL/12)
- Tenement Valuation original house books (OL/5)
- Tenement Valuation tenure books (OL/6)
- Tenement Valuation check house books (OL/5)
- Tenement Valuation query sheets (OL/17)

OFFICE WORK

The office work was the same as under the 1846 act. The existing Townland Valuation office maps were, almost without exception, reused in this work. The office calculations were carried out as before but in the greatly increased numbers required by the work in tenements. The *Primary valuation* was produced at the end of this work with the same content as under the 1846 act.

The main series of documents created were:

- Tenement Valuation office maps, drawn on Townland Valuation office maps or on new maps (OL/11)
- Tenement Valuation calculation books (field) (OL/4)
- Tenement Valuation copy house books (OL/5)
- Quarto books (OL/7)
- Tenement Valuation registry books (OL/8)
- *Primary valuation* (OL/18, available online)

APPEALS

Under the 1852 act, the appeals were investigated by a revising valuator and a decision was issued by the commissioner (see pp 179–92). Some further field work was carried out where tenements were appealed.

The main series of documents created was:

- Tenement Valuation appeal books (1852 act) (OL/20)

FINAL VALUATION UNDER 1846 AND 1852 TENEMENT VALUATION ACTS
The final valuation was made in manuscript in documents known as 'cancelled books' that are still retained in the Valuation Office and that were updated continuously since the outcome of the *Primary valuation* appeals was decided. The cancelled books covering the counties of Northern Ireland are held in the Public Record Office of Northern Ireland in Belfast, and the digitized books can be found on the website, nidirect.gov.uk/proni.

2

The valuation staff

The valuation was an entirely new enterprise and within the limits of the legislation Griffith had freedom to create the organization as he envisioned it. Valuation of property was not an exact science, and in the early 1830s the profession of valuator was recognized but without formal qualifications, although surveys and valuations of estates were common.[1] Griffith always recognized that the calibre of the staff was critical, and in the early years he was able to recruit, train, manage and dismiss as he saw fit and to control pay. The valuators and other staff who worked in the field were the linchpin of the entire system, as all the other work was built on their competence and trustworthiness. Griffith was demanding, and expected everyone in the organization to be committed to high standards.

The first task was to mould a disparate group of men into a corps of valuators who would share the objective and be capable of the technical work. Griffith identified the first valuators by obtaining, from landowners in Cos. Londonderry and Tyrone, the names of men who had carried out such work. The 1826 act permitted the employment of nine valuators per county, and these were taken on and trained directly by him in the field for two months before they began work.[2] Assistance was provided by an office clerk and three labourers.[3] This core group was used to train further valuators. The limit was removed in 1834, and the numbers grew substantially as the work expanded. Other staff were employed to do clerical, calculating and drawing work, at first in temporary offices in Derry, Coleraine and Belfast, and from 1832 in an office in Dublin.[4] In the early stages, some staff moved from the Boundary Survey and Ordnance Survey and some were known to the commissioner from his work on other enterprises.[5] By 1845 approximately 150 staff in all grades were employed, and by 1853 this had grown to 300.[6] In 1869, when the initial valuation was finished and the work consisted entirely of revision, the staff still numbered 100.[7] The organization

---

1 J.H. Andrews, *Plantation acres* (Belfast, 1995), pp 253–7. The background to the related professions is outlined in this chapter, pp 224–57. 2 *Report from select committee on valuation, 1869*, question 1335. 3 OL/2/2, p. 209. 4 *Report from select committee on valuation, 1869*, question 1340. 5 For example, John Kelly worked with Griffith from 1812; Henry Buck worked on the Bog Survey and the Boundary Survey; and Edward Gaffney worked on the Boundary Survey; *Report from select committee on valuation, 1869*, question 2618. 6 *Report from select committee on valuation, 1869*, question 1902, and OL/2/13 p. 412. 7 *Report from select committee on valuation, 1869*, appendix 1, return of staff in Apr. 1869, p. 224. These 100 staff were: 1

47

comprised an accounts department, office-based clerks and draftsmen, and valuators and surveyors who worked mostly in the field – all supervised by superintendents. The ratio of field staff to office staff was roughly one to two and fluctuations in numbers were related to the amount of data generated in the field work. A constant stream of unsolicited applications for jobs was received, most of which were turned down. The commissioner took a direct interest in the competence of the valuators, and new recruits were expected to work in the field for one month without pay, after which he satisfied himself personally as to their fitness for appointment.[8]

The salary of the commissioner and the maximum pay of valuators and some other staff were set out in the acts.[9] The rates were reinterpreted by the commissioner, who explained: 'I made the salaries very low, and the people employed under me were constantly complaining and writing to the *Civil Service Gazette* about the miserable pittances I gave them.'[10] Broadly, the commissioner was paid £500 a year, valuators were paid between £4 and £6 a week, and surveyors and clerks were paid between £1 and £3 per week. Travelling and lodging expenses were paid for work outside the office. Labourers received between 6s. and 9s. a week.[11] These rates do not seem to have increased over the years. Many of the valuators petitioned individually for increases; they were usually refused.[12] The expansion in the mid-1840s arose from the additional work in the Tenement Valuation, and surveyors were employed to record detail that did not call for the specific skills of the valuators. At least one surveyor worked with each valuator, and each surveyor was assisted by two labourers or chainmen. The labourers were engaged locally and were not counted in the numbers employed. The surveyor's role was described by Griffith as arduous and requiring 'tact in ascertaining the boundaries of the several holdings which some of the tenants from ignorance of the true object of the survey point out erroneously. Hence only a practical man well acquainted with the people and who is a well-known land surveyor is eligible.'[13]

Although it was an official enterprise, the valuation did not become a government department until 1860.[14] Many staff worked over decades without security as they were employed for the work at hand and were let go, or 'discontinued', when it was completed. Notices about the discontinuation of service were issued as work on counties was completed. For example, in February 1856 a circular warned that, as work in several counties was about to conclude, and as the Tenement Valuation of the northern counties could not begin until the maps were ready, a number of staff were to be discon-

commissioner; 13 chief officers; 29 revisors or valuators and 57 office assistants. 8 OL/2/5, p. 5. 9 Acts in years 1826, 1834, 1836, 1846 and 1852. 10 *Report from select committee on valuation, 1869*, question 1422. 11 See OL/2/4, p. 69 for pay of labourers. 12 See example at OL/2/7, p. 40. 13 OL/2/10, p. 185. 14 23 Vict., c. 4.

tinued.[15] An additional month's salary was paid in this case.[16] In mid-July 1856, a further reduction of staff was announced for the end of the month, with pay until the end of August for those discontinued.[17] The documents make little reference to the fate of the majority of the men who were discontinued, but many letters seeking re-employment were received. Some were taken on again for various periods as the work dictated.[18] Some found employment in private firms,[19] and some emigrated.[20] A special effort was made to accommodate the six sub-commissioners of appeal when these posts were abolished due to the change in the appeal system in 1852. They were offered positions as revising valuators, but at a one-third reduction in salary, which was later further reduced.[21] Five of the six accepted, and one returned to his original profession of engineer.[22] Of the five, three remained in the service until their retirement in 1861–2.[23]

The staff had no entitlement to pensions and, in the mid-1850s, several factors brought dissatisfaction on this matter to a head. Pensions had been introduced for government officials in 1855, and in early 1856 the reductions in staffing were imminent, but the valuation was not yet part of the civil service. A number of staff had served for long periods, including time in other official enterprises, and some were likely to have been approaching retirement age. The case of John Kelly, who retired in 1853 without a pension after 40 years of service, seems to have been well known.[24] In 1856, John Boyan, one of the longest-serving valuators and a man greatly trusted by Griffith, wrote a letter of petition on behalf of staff. The letter has not

---

15 OL/2/14, p. 336. 16 Ibid., pp 359, 365. 17 Ibid., p. 379. 18 *Return of staff employed, 1867*, HC 1867 (484), p. 6; *Report from select committee on valuation, 1869*, question 2114 and appendix 2, *Return of persons dismissed or discontinued, 1850–69*, pp 229–30. 19 *Report from select committee on valuation, 1869*, question 2526. 20 OL/2/12, pp 383–5. 21 9 & 10 Vict., c. 110, sec. 77: their pay was £1 10s. a day and expenses. Under 15 & 16 Vict., c. 63, sec. 37, the pay was to be £1 per day plus 10s. hotel expenses and actual travelling expenses. In a circular of Dec. 1852, the expenses were further reduced to 7s. 6d. for hotel plus actual travelling expenses, see OL/2/13, p. 410. 22 OL/2/13, p. 402. 23 *Return of officers and salaries, 1867*, HC 1867 (484), p. 6. 24 Several references to the case were made at the 1869 select committee. John Kelly had worked with Griffith continually since 1812 and was put in overall charge of the administration and office work from the early 1830s. It was generally believed that he deserved much of the credit for the instructions of 1833, 1836 and 1839, and he had also worked on the geological map. Griffith said that he had 'great confidence in particularly Mr John Kelly, who was with me many years before; I very soon made him superintendent of valuation' and that he was 'a very able man'. Kelly was replaced as superintendent by J.B. Greene, who was Griffith's choice to succeed himself as commissioner. Kelly left the valuation in 1853 without a pension. It was alleged that his departure was related to a disagreement with Griffith about charging private work to the official service. The matter was raised by several committee members and mentioned by witnesses sixteen years after this event, and Henry Duffy, who was a divisional superintendent at the time, told the enquiry 'I think he was very badly treated. A man who had been in the public service for so long, and had been so valuable an officer, ought to have had a pension.' *Report from select committee on valuation, 1869*, questions 2522, 1339, 1343, 2554, 1904.

survived, but Griffith's response was sympathetic, if not very helpful, and he recommended that the staff send a memorial to the Treasury on the subject.[25] In 1860, the valuation came under Treasury control, and conditions for staff improved as civil service rules on recruitment and pensions were applied.[26] The commissioner's powers in relation to recruitment were limited to proposing the names of suitable candidates for the Civil Service Commission competitive examinations. Following a Treasury examination, the posts were re-graded and many staff received increases.[27]

Management of the staff was not an easy task. Griffith's style could be described as robust, an approach he justified by writing that: 'In a large establishment rules must be attended to or system will be lost.'[28] Fluctuations in the workforce, their dispersal around the country on field work and the complex technical work added to the difficulty. As well as guidance on the content of the work, the instructions and circulars set down the basic rules, such as the hours of work, and put forward advice on conduct. They give an insight into what must have been real problems, and reprimands and references to disagreements are also found throughout the correspondence. Failure to apply the rules was countered with strong discipline. Incompetence, mistakes, inappropriate behaviour or conflict with those outside the valuation were dealt with through a range of sanctions, from admonitory letters, to the threat of dismissal,[29] to summary removal. The most senior members of staff were not exempt from reprimand; in May 1853, such a letter was sent to Edward Gaffney who, until the previous year, had been sub-commissioner of appeal.[30] All documents created in the work underwent minute examination, and failings were unlikely to escape detection.

Reasons for dismissal included poor work and bad behaviour. David Williamson was let go because he was unable to 'discriminate between the respective values of arable and pasture lands'.[31] A similar departure was in store in March 1845 for Thomas O'Brien, a house valuator, because of his 'habits of intemperance'.[32] The same close supervision applied to the office staff, and many such cases are noted in the correspondence, including that of a clerk who was dismissed with one day's notice because he had made sixty errors in the parish he had calculated.[33] Griffith lamented the shortage of good staff: 'There is no class of person so difficult to find, and not one out of twenty who profess to know the business can value either houses or lands with due regard to their relative values.'[34]

The field staff inevitably had contact with landowners and the public, with potential for conflict and for damaging the reputation of the valuation.

25 OL/2/14, p. 330. 26 23 Vict., c. 4. 27 *Report from select committee on valuation, 1869*, questions 110 and 1906. 28 OL/2/14, p. 1. 29 OL/2/11, p. 17. 30 OL/2/14, p. 155. 31 OL/2/11, p. 26. 32 OL/2/10, p. 216. 33 OL/2/11, p. 22. 34 OL/2/7, p. 58.

The general policy was to mollify the complainants, as the support of landowners and other important persons was seen as necessary in obtaining public acceptance. In 1841, Griffith wrote in soothing terms to the bishop-elect of Killala regarding an apology from the valuator Thomas Cox to the parish priest of Ballycastle, Co. Mayo. It is not clear what was at issue, and Cox's apology was not immediately forthcoming.[35] Griffith advised another valuator, Thomas Keogh, following his appearance at Thurles petty sessions in 1845, not to take official action against a person who had obstructed his work, but to inform the magistrate of the situation:

> It is my wish that no notice should be taken of trifling obstructions or of any observation. You are to proceed with your duty steadily and when addressing any person you should be very civil and conciliatory in your language and deportment.[36]

In some cases the official response acknowledged that the staff had a difficult job to do. When a General Annesley complained in 1848 that Edward Gaffney had been carrying no identification while performing his duties, Griffith wrote to the latter in terms that are critical of the general: 'I am quite aware that General Annesley is a very peculiar person and exacts unusual deference being paid to him. We should always dismiss the hostility of such persons by unusual civility.' He asked Gaffney to meet the general, whose full title he included in order to avoid further offence.[37] In May 1850 Charles Cobbe of Newbridge House in Donabate, Co. Dublin protested about 'two persons who were walking through my demesne, the one with a rod and the other with a spade, making holes in my lawn'. Griffith regretted the misunderstanding and advised meeting the valuator, John Boyan: 'You will find him a very sensible man and a good judge of the relative value of land.'[38] Where staff were accused unfairly, Griffith defended them. He dealt coldly with a complaint from the chairman of the petty sessions in Ballineen, Co. Cork, who was also a member of the grand jury. The latter wrongly conflated a dispute between a valuator and the poor law guardians (who were seeking to have him dismissed) with a case heard before the court in May 1848 in which two chainmen, or labourers, were charged with forging signatures on a 'Repeal and physical force petition'. The matters were not connected, but the surveyor was instructed to dismiss the chainmen instantly for aiding 'a political movement of the most injurious character' and faced the same fate if he was involved.[39]

The high professional standing of the staff can be seen in the requests

---

35 OL/2/9, pp 23-4. 36 OL/2/11, p. 27. 37 Ibid., p. 85. The general's title was Lieut. General the Honble A. Annesley. 38 OL/2/12, p. 408. 39 Ibid., p. 57.

received from landowners and official bodies for the services of a valuator. Private work by the staff was forbidden, and even when approached officially, Griffith usually refused and sometimes in very lofty terms, although he did not extend this prohibition to himself. He wrote to John Parnell in Avondale in 1845 that it would be 'impossible for me to employ the public valuators on private business',[40] but exceptions can be found.[41] However, Griffith's response showed his pride in the reputation of the staff and the service. He was prepared to relax the rule for the common good and in 1844 he allowed David Williamson to act as judge in a ploughing match, although he said that it was contrary to practice.[42] On occasion he was helpful, as when he recommended a recently discontinued surveyor to the poor law commissioners.[43] In 1845, he assisted the commissioners of education in nominating a man to teach land surveying at the new agricultural school in Glasnevin.[44] In 1846 several staff were proposed for secondment to relief works during the Famine,[45] and some were transferred for the duration.[46] When the new commissioner, J.B. Greene, was questioned about dissatisfaction in the office, he replied that there was not 'more than would be likely to arise in any large office where there are a couple of hundred people, and every man wants to be higher than he is'.[47]

Over the period of the initial valuation, the development of professional competence in the staff and of management confidence in the operation of the system can be seen throughout the documents. The original tentative arrangement of three valuators working together was quickly replaced by valuators working alone. Specialization was developed in areas such as town valuation (Robert McMicken and James Montgomery), or check valuation (Robert Purdon and John Boyan). A comparison made in 1869 between the staff of the early years, some of whom had minimal literacy skills but were first-class valuators, with the highly qualified persons who were employed at that time, showed how far the situation had changed.[48] The original staff came from a wide variety of backgrounds – they were land managers, agriculturalists, surveyors, valuators and civil engineers[49] – and were shaped in accordance with Griffith's vision. This could also be said of the surveyors, many of whom carried out very responsible work, although they were paid far less than the valuators.

---

40 OL/2/10, p. 168. 41 OL/2/12, p. 55. 42 OL/2/10, p. 48. 43 OL/2/12, p. 404. 44 OL/2/10, p. 186. 45 OL/2/4, p. 108. 46 OL/2/13, p. 110. 47 *Report from select committee on valuation, 1869*, question 105. 48 Ibid., questions 2255–7, description by James Lynam. 49 Ibid., appendix 3, pp 233–4.

RESEARCHING INDIVIDUAL MEMBERS OF STAFF

The valuation archives contain a good deal of information about individual members of staff and some, at least, of their careers can be followed. The three main sources for this are the valuation documents themselves, the valuation letter books and parliamentary papers. There are no administrative documents for the period of the initial valuation apart from the letter books, and personnel documents, as they would now be understood, do not exist.

Names of the staff who carried out the work appear throughout the valuation books. The rules required signing and dating field books, but other stages of the work were also noted. Original field books and calculation books had printed worksheets attached where office staff signed and dated each task completed. Other work, such as copying or calculation, was also signed and dated. The names of up to twenty different staff members might be found in an original field book. The lists of the archives in the National Archives feature the names of valuators and surveyors who carried out the field work but not the names of office staff. The valuation letter books contain numerous references to individual staff members, and it should be possible to find names in the indexes, although these are not comprehensive. Matters concerning staff in the letter books include requests for positions and pay increases, appointments or refusals, instructions about the work, reprimands and expenses. The correspondence includes references for staff seeking employment elsewhere, and these can provide useful information about previous employment.[50] Parliamentary papers contain lists of staff in the mid-1830s and again during the period 1860–9. These were provided to select committees (in 1836 and 1869) and in returns made to parliament from around 1867. These documents contain information on dates, grades, duration of service and the overall staff structure of the valuation. The lists referring to the contemporary situation are likely to be accurate, and there is a good deal of information about staff employed in the late 1860s. The lists made in the 1860s covering earlier periods seem to be selective, as some obvious names are omitted, and are useful but limited. There is a long gap (1835–60) in the parliamentary papers, but it may be feasible to fill this to some extent from the valuation documents and the letter books.

Using these documents, it is possible to follow the careers of individual valuators and some surveyors. The sequence of parishes on which they worked can be found in the lists for each county from the National Archives, most usefully the lists of house books, field books and tenure books, and the precise dates of presence in a parish can be seen in the books. Some informa-

---

50 OL/2/3, pp 312–17, references for staff who worked in the early years on the valuation but who had previously worked privately for Griffith on projects such as road-building.

tion can also be traced in relation to clerical staff. George Hitchcock worked for his entire career in the office. He was first engaged as a temporary assistant in 1839, and he retired in October 1870 with a pension of £233.[51] His signature can be seen in his work on documents in the 1840s,[52] and by 1860 he had risen to the grade of divisional superintendent.[53] It would be possible, but laborious, to look through books for the names of staff believed to have worked in the office. However, almost nothing can be established about the labourers who worked with the field teams. They were recruited locally, their names do not appear in the books except randomly,[54] and, apart from the two labourers charged with forgery mentioned above,[55] they are referred to in the correspondence only in relation to rates of pay.

Robert Warwick, a civil engineer originally from Dublin,[56] was one of the first persons employed in 1830, and he worked on the earliest field book held in the National Archives (parish of Kildollagh, Co. Londonderry), dated June 1830.[57] He was described as a 'baronial valuator' and was paid £1 per week.[58] He later worked in Cos. Fermanagh, Armagh, Cavan, Meath, Kildare, Kilkenny, Tipperary and Limerick, as well as King's County. He scarcely appears in the correspondence except in relation to instructions, but in December 1849 Griffith reproached him for the poor quality of his valuation in the barony of Iffa and Offa West in Co. Tipperary in 1846–7.[59] Warwick's field books for this barony are in the National Archives and show that the work was in every case redone by other valuators in 1851–2. At the time of the letter, Warwick was working in Co. Limerick, where he signed books up to March 1850 but parishes there valued by him were also re-valued in 1850–1.[60] He died before 1869.[61]

---

51 *Return of the names of all officers either dismissed or removed from the general valuation service of Ireland from 1 January 1869 to 1 January 1871, together with a statement of their length of service; whether they were discontinued at any time; and, if so, for how long; salary when removed; and superannuation allowance, if any*, HC 1871 (191). 52 OL/4/5489. 53 *Returns of the names of divisional superintendents in the General Valuation Office, Dublin, in charge of counties during the years 1860 and 1865 respectively; and, of the names and salaries of all officers and assistants in the General Valuation Office employed in superintending or performing any work unconnected with the making or revision of the Tenement Valuation of Ireland, in each year, from 1 May 1860 to 30 April 1870; etc.*, HC 1871 (36), no. 1, p. 2. 54 OL/4/5427, notes on first page: the spadesman Pat Horan is mentioned incidentally by Thomas Cox in relation to difficulties in gaining access to Merlin Park, Oranmore, Co. Galway, the property of Charles Blake. See also OL/6/261/1, a receipt for payment from a local labourer named Isaac Lord in Killinane, Co. Kerry in Sept. 1852. 55 OL/2/12, p. 57: the two labourers were James Lane and Matthew White. 56 *Report from select committee on valuation, 1869*, appendix 3, p. 233. 57 OL/4/1070. 58 *Report from select committee on county cess, 1836*, appendix 3 (B), p. 5. 59 OL/2/12, p. 303. Griffith used the check valuation by James Lynam as comparison with Warwick's work. The following year, he discredited Lynam, who believed he used John Boyan's work to discredit his own work in Co. Kerry. Lynam mentioned this case in his evidence to the 1869 select committee, see *Report from select committee on valuation, 1869*, question 2299. 60 OL/4/4317. See National Archives list for Co. Limerick. 61 *Report from select committee on valuation, 1869*, appendix 3, p. 233.

Robert Innes, from Newtown Limavady in Co. Londonderry,[62] joined the valuation in 1833.[63] From then until 1853 he worked in Cos. Tyrone, Armagh, Louth, Monaghan, Longford, Kildare, Carlow, Wexford, Galway and Kerry, as well as King's County and Queen's County – in several counties as check valuator. There is some correspondence with Innes over this period, including an attempt to have his son Robert taken on.[64] In August 1849, while he was working near Dunmanway in Co. Cork, Griffith wrote to him on learning that he had resumed his 'destructive habit of drinking which is alike ruinous to your public as well as your moral character', a matter that had apparently previously arisen while Innes was working in Queen's County in 1843. Griffith was concerned that the local landowner in Cork, Lord Lansdowne (then a cabinet minister), might hear that he employed 'a person of dissolute habits and unsteady conduct as a valuator', but gave him another chance on account of his family: 'I do not wish at *once to throw you on the world* but I give you this *final* notice.'[65] The letter appears to have had effect, and in October 1853 Innes was working in King's County. In 1856, Griffith wrote another letter warning him about the quality of his work, and sent him to Donegal.[66] There is no trace of him after this, and he seems to have left before the first paid retirements in 1860. George Innes, likely to be another son, was employed from 1854, and by the late 1860s was listed as a middle-ranking second-class officer, earning £220 a year.[67]

Thomas Cox was employed as a valuator from 1836 and retired in July 1863 after twenty-seven years of service. His retiring allowance was £157.[68] He was originally from Frenchpark, Co. Roscommon and his professional background was 'surveyor and valuator'.[69] During his career he worked in Cos. Armagh, Down, Donegal, Cavan, Mayo, Wicklow, Galway, Waterford, Limerick and Tipperary. He valued land and houses and also carried out some check valuations. He frequently wrote long, perceptive descriptions of the parishes he valued, displaying awareness of the socio-economic situation and empathy with the occupiers. Like many other members of staff, he received a number of reprimands over the years, but he appears to have been held in esteem by the commissioner as he was one of a small number of staff proposed for supervising Famine relief works in 1846,[70] and he was made a revising valuator for the new system of appeals under the 1852 act.

John Boyan was from Kilmean, Co. Westmeath and was described as an 'agriculturalist and valuator'.[71] He was employed from 1834 and retired in

---

62 Ibid., p. 234. 63 OL/2/3, p. 42. 64 OL/2/12, p. 386, 27 Mar. 1850. His son received a reference from Griffith when his temporary post of surveyor ended in 1843, see OL/2/9, p. 200. 65 OL/2/11, p. 117. 66 OL/2/16, p. 14. 67 *Return of staff employed, 1867*, HC 1867 (484), p. 4. 68 *Return of staff who have retired or died, 1867*, HC 1867 (484), p. 6. 69 *Report from select committee on valuation, 1869*, appendix 3, p. 233. 70 OL/2/4, p. 108. 71 *Report from*

May 1860 after twenty-six years of service, with a retiring allowance of £135. In the early years he worked in Cos. Tyrone and Down and he later worked as a check valuator in most counties. He is the only member of staff for whom there is any physical description. Boyan's former colleague James Lynam described him rather unkindly as a 'moderately old man' (in the late 1840s) who weighed more than nineteen stone and was in consequence incapable of examining the land correctly.[72] Griffith, however, held him in the highest regard throughout his career.[73] A man named Michael Boyan, who may have been his brother, was an engineer in the Office of Woods and appears in the letter books in occasional correspondence with Griffith (wearing one of his other hats).

Robert Purdon, who came from Huntington, Co. Westmeath, was employed in January 1835. He was described as a 'surveyor and valuator'. He worked in Co. Antrim in 1835 and after that in most counties as check valuator. He gave lengthy evidence to the Select Committee on the Townland Valuation in 1844, where he described his training in the field under Griffith. He was also a witness at the hearings of the Devon Commission in 1845.[74] He was appointed sub-commissioner of appeals under the 1846 Tenement Valuation Act, but he died unexpectedly in April 1846. Augustus Purdon, who worked in the office, may have been his brother.

Some staff that left the valuation achieved distinction in other areas, and information about them can be found in other sources. Patrick Ganly worked in the Boundary Survey and Ordnance Survey and was employed by the valuation from 1833 as a draftsman at 4s. 6d. a week.[75] From June 1837 until the mid-1840s he was engaged, unofficially, on geological field work on Griffith's behalf,[76] and he made a big contribution to the geological map. He retired in May 1860, with a retiring allowance of £55, and went on to become a renowned geologist.[77] John Montgomery, who started as a draftsman in

---

select committee on valuation, 1869, appendix 3, p. 233. 72 Ibid., question 2291. Lynam left the service following disagreement about the valuation of parishes in the barony of Magunihy, Co. Kerry. His field books are in the National Archives and the work was redone in all parishes. Lynam claimed Boyan had played a part in the matter, but the latter valued only one of the fourteen parishes. Boyan's age is not known. If a direct contemporary of Griffith (b. 1784), in the late 1840s he would have in his late 50s, and at the time of his retirement nearly 80. It seems likely that he was somewhat younger, but Griffith himself did not retire until the age of 85. 73 Ibid., question 2287: 'From his great experience, I am in the habit of leaning to Mr Boyan.' 74 Royal commission on the state of the law and practice in respect to the occupation of land in Ireland, 1843–5. 75 *Report of select committee on county cess, 1836*, appendix 3 (B), p. 7; *Return of staff who have retired or died, 1867*, HC 1867 (484), p. 6. 76 Ganly letters, RIA Library, 12 E 26–8; Jean Archer, 'Richard Griffith and the first published geological maps of Ireland' in Herries Davies & Mollan (eds), *Richard Griffith, 1784–1878*, pp 143–71. 77 *Dictionary of Irish biography*. Patrick Ganly was discontinued in Feb. 1851. He declared his intention of going to America and received a glowing reference from Griffith, see OL/2/13, p. 110. In 1853, he was re-employed but with a warning that he was to follow the rules ('You have already suffered from

1831[78] and was then made valuator, retired in 1860 and obtained a 'high place' in Liverpool as a revising valuator.[79] James Lynam had also worked in the Ordnance Survey and Boundary Survey and was one of the favoured valuators until an acrimonious falling-out with J.B. Greene led to his departure in 1851. He then had a successful career as a civil engineer in private practice. He gave strong testimony against the valuation at the 1869 select committee, where he described how he provided expert advice to persons contesting the valuation and how improvements were made to the valuation as a result of these interventions.[80] In the early 1870s, he discovered a rare error in the Ordnance Survey work on the water levels of Lough Erne.[81]

In a number of cases, several members of the same family appear to have worked in the valuation but, although the likelihood is high, it is not possible to be certain of the relationship unless there is other evidence. The Innes family is described above. The fact that William E. Jones was the son of the valuator William Jones is attested to incidentally by a letter, but it is not known if Francis P. Jones, who was employed from about 1854, was another son.[82] Stephen Coffey worked as a draftsman for a time before 1865 and is likely to have been a brother of Martin, who was a valuator for nearly thirty years.[83] Staff names from the early days included Bell, Deering, Freeman, Hampton and Montgomery, and the same family names appear in the lists printed in the late 1860s. Griffith himself referred to 'my cousin Mr Henry Buck', who had worked with him in the Bog Survey, the Boundary Survey and the valuation.[84]

No account of the work by a valuator is found in the valuation archives, but it is not difficult to imagine that it was a challenging life. Travelling the length and breadth of the country, walking the ground, through wild terrain and mountains, in all weather, as well as completing the field documents in the regulation manner, was a not a task for the faint of heart. Six staff members were acknowledged to have died in service,[85] one died by his own hand,[86] and the health of others is likely to have suffered.[87] The correspondence contains incidental information on travel and lodgings, mostly in

---

an inclination to act on your own opinion'), see OL/2/14, p. 1. 78 *Report of select committee on county cess, 1836*, appendix 3 (B), p. 7. 79 *Report from select committee on valuation, 1869*, question 2509. 80 Ibid., questions 2226–300. 81 Andrews, *A paper landscape*, pp 110–11. 82 OL/6/1447/1. William E. Jones is listed in 1869 as an officer of the third class with 15 years' service and a salary of £150; see *Report from select committee on valuation, 1869*, appendix 3, p. 232. 83 Ibid., question 2618, refers to staff from the Boundary Survey who joined the valuation in 1841, including the Coffeys. 84 OL/2/3, p. 321. 85 *Return of staff who have retired or died, 1867*, HC 1867 (484), p. 6. 86 *Report from select committee on valuation, 1869*, question 1415. 87 In the case of John Kelly, the deterioration of his health was an issue in his departure. See *Report from select committee on valuation, 1869*, question 1904. Ganly's geological letters make many references to the colds and chills caught while working in wet weather.

contested expenses claims, where the hire of horse-drawn cars figures prominently. In correspondence where he was also reprimanded for having taken a first-class train, Robert Innes mentioned having to transport his horse from Dundalk to Ferbane in King's County.[88] Griffith himself famously claimed that he always travelled by night in order to save the day.[89] Little information can be gleaned from the documents about the itinerant life of the staff. The diaries of work, or 'time bills', found in some of the field books, state the work done each day, and some list books also contain a calendar of work.[90] The weather was obviously a preoccupation, and periods when outdoor work was prevented or hindered by bad weather are accounted for in these lists.[91] An 1839 field book contains Hall's weather almanac for March 1839.[92] In Patrick Ganly's geological correspondence, wet weather features as an impediment to progress.

Incidental information indicates that many of the staff were interested in the world around them, and in furthering themselves through learning. Patrick Ganly studied in his spare time in Trinity College and obtained a degree.[93] While on the geological field work, he taught himself French.[94] John Kelly sketched a golden-crested wren in the back of his appeal book,[95] and Edward Gaffney wrote out a poem in French in another.[96] A field book from Co. Sligo contains a notice about evening classes in Dublin.[97]

Although lodging expenses were paid, field staff were expected to find something less than a hotel. In June 1858, the surveyor William Scott wrote to Robert Bell that he would take up his quarters at Desertmartin, Co. Londonderry, as he was unable to get a house in Maghera.[98] An example of a minor practical difficulty can be seen in the claim that in 1836 there was only one stationer's shop in Co. Donegal (in Ballyshannon).[99] The valuation took place over the period of the Famine and its aftermath, and the staff are likely to have witnessed scenes such as those described in 1847 by John Locke, a surveyor in private practice, of the poor dying in the streets of Kenmare.[1] Despite the professional tone of the field documents, many record the strong reaction of the staff who every day faced poverty and poor conditions. It is likely that their work was not very different, but possibly less

---

88 OL/2/14, p. 14.   89 *Report from select committee on valuation, 1869*, question 1324. Griffith claimed that he travelled from the north to the south of the country forty times a year.   90 OL/10/1 and OL/10/9.   91 See examples in Townland Valuation field books in Cos. Longford (OL/4/6242) and Monaghan (OL/4/6583).   92 OL/4/6221.   93 James Maguire and James Quinn (eds), *Dictionary of Irish biography*, 9 vols (Cambridge, 2009).   94 Ganly letters, RIA Library, 12 E 26, 8 Aug. 1837: Ganly wrote to John Kelly that he was learning French grammar and should be able to read with the aid of a dictionary. He asked the latter to obtain a Bible in French from the Bible Society in Sackville Street and to forward it to him.   95 OL/19/24/9, back endpaper: 'golden crested wren, got November'.   96 OL/20/21/5, back page.   97 OL/5/4295, back page.   98 OL/20/7/8/1.   99 *Report from select committee on county cess, 1836*, question 709.   1 NLI, MS 3566, 24 June 1847.

comfortable, than the description of the survey of the Martin estate in Co. Galway carried out in 1853 by Thomas Colville Scott.[2] The practical difficulties of transport and suitable lodgings must have been similar to the experiences of John O'Donovan, who, working for the Ordnance Survey in Co. Galway in 1839, described walking to Portumna and getting 'wet not only to the skin but to the very centre of the heart', and then having to sleep in a damp bed. He also wrote a long account of the hazardous and expensive journey to the Aran Islands.[3] In January 1858 William Jones, working at the time in Co. Donegal, wrote: 'I have just come in right tired, wet and chilly after spending a miserable day in the rain.'[4]

CONCLUSION

This was a remarkable group of staff, whose competence, stoicism and dedication allowed the novel enterprise to come to a successful conclusion. The management style was robust, and the tone of many of the letters to staff would now be considered unacceptable, but the fact that many staff served for long years – or, in some cases, their entire working lives – must demonstrate a level of satisfaction on both sides. Despite the difficulties, the professional pride in the work is clear from the documents, as is the reliance on staff in the field. The archives contain good information about individuals, but it requires assembly from a range of documents. The printed lists in the parliamentary papers are a good starting point, despite the gap between the mid-1830s and 1860. Searching through the lists of valuation archives in the National Archive for individual names is also likely to be fruitful.

2 Thomas Colville Scott, *Connemara after the Famine*, ed. Tim Robinson (Dublin, 1995).
3 Michael Herity (ed.), *Ordnance Survey letters: Galway* (Dublin, 2009), pp 171, 499–501.
4 OL/20/7/3/2.

3

The manuscript books and other documents of the valuation

The work of the valuation generated a vast amount of data. From the beginning this was actively managed so that it would be available for further work and would be preserved as evidence. Books were used as a compact and secure method of keeping the data in an accessible format. The 1826 act required that a new book be started for every parish,[1] but the complexity of the work meant that several books were actually needed, with specific data in each. This created series of 'field books' or 'house books' where each book was unique and identifiable for the parish concerned. This system was also used in the office work. The data relating to any one parish across the series of books was used to make the valuation of that place, much as related databases would be used today. Each type of book was printed in columns, which, along with the detailed instructions given to field staff, helped to ensure that the work was standardized, uniform and complete. The book format also assisted in managing the documents, breaking them down by subject (for example, field or house), place (county, barony and parish) and type (original or copy). It was then possible to control the books by putting them in order by county, barony and parish and to retrieve the data as required.

The term 'field book' is somewhat ambiguous as it was commonly applied to all books that were used in the outdoor work in the field, including work on houses, and to distinguish these from books created in the office. Once stored in the office, the books became known by their subject matter and continue to be known by those names. For example, field books deal with agricultural land in fields and house books deal with buildings. Some 'books' were originally completed as loose pages and bound at a later date. The National Archives now holds approximately 15,000 books covering the work of the initial valuation, 1830–65. Many copies were made of the books, and in most cases it is possible to distinguish between the original books and the copies. Most original books were dated and signed by the valuator, but individual practice varied widely. The words 'this book copied' written on a

---

1 7 Geo. IV, c. 62, sec. 9. The books vary slightly in size but are mostly near the metric size of A5.

book usually means that it is the original book, from which a copy was made.[2] Books designed for one purpose were sometimes used for another and, for example, field books were on occasion used for house data.[3]

In the Townland Valuation the main series of books are field books, house books and quarto books. In the Tenement Valuation, the same series were continued and a new series of tenure books was added. There are also other series, including mill books, rent books, list books and appeal books.

A. FIELD BOOKS

The field books are the notebooks where information on agricultural land was collected during the field work. The field books, with the field maps, are the fundamental documents of the valuation. In general, the field books cover rural areas, and urban areas are covered by house books. The field books were made between 1830 and 1852, with some later revisions. As the work took place county by county, the date in each county varies. There is only one original field book for each parish, as the information on land was recorded only once. The National Archives holds more than 7,000 field books relating to every county, including parts of Northern Ireland. From the outset, the field books were considered to be documents of the first importance. They were sent to the office in Dublin when the work in the field was complete, they were always well looked-after and they were in continuous use for reference in the Valuation Office until 1984, when rates on agricultural land were abolished. From the earliest date, the correspondence and annotations on the books show that the commissioner took the time to look at them carefully.

The field books of the initial valuation under both the Townland Valuation and the Tenement Valuation were made over a period of twenty-two years, and the information was recorded in the same manner throughout. They were labelled by parish, barony and county, with the townland name written at the top of every page. The pages were printed in columns in a format that remained practically unchanged throughout: lot numbers, sub-denominations and observations (the description), quantity of land in acres, roods and perches (ARP),[4] value per statute acre,[5] amount of land in money

2 The copying and calculation were carried out by office clerks who were paid by the line or by the number of calculations. See OL/5/0674, marked 'copy'; note at beginning: 'copied and calculated by J. Clarke 26/3/50; numbering of holdings copied from rough book'; note at end gives number of lines copied (723) and number of items calculated (1,502). 3 OL/5/1307, Dunshaughlin, Co. Meath. 4 Acres, roods and perches are imperial square measures: 1 acre contains 4 roods and 1 rood contains 40 perches. The metric equivalent of 1 acre is 0.404685 hectares. 5 The acts required that the areas be recorded in statute acres, although Irish or plantation acres were widely used by occupiers and owners; 1 Irish acre = 1.619 775 775 5 statute

(meaning the valuation in pounds, shillings and pence) and the amount of houses in money with one-third deducted. A column for local circumstances was added in 1834.[6]

The field books of the Townland Valuation

In the Townland Valuation, the units valued were the 'quality lots' into which each townland was divided. In 1836 the lots were limited to areas of between thirty and fifty acres,[7] and from 1839 they were to coincide with the boundaries of farms.[8] The result of the work was to be a summary valuation in townlands and the apportionment of occupiers' liability for tax was to be made at local level. The land was to be valued 'at the rent for which a fair landlord would let it to a respectable tenant, such valuation being made with reference to the average price of agricultural produce for the preceding five years'.[9]

Before 1836 the field work in each parish was carried out by a team of three valuators, with each creating a separate book. The books were printed to allow for noting the several opinions.[10] After 1836 the valuator worked alone and made one field book for each parish. Houses near the valuation threshold were also valued as a separate valuation price for buildings was required. The field books comprise several different types of related books, including original field books, check field books, calculation books (field) and fair copies. There are also small numbers of other books. In some counties combinations were made by binding books together, most commonly the original field book with the original house book. The books of the Townland Valuation were all made in civil parishes, except check books, which can cover several parishes or a barony.

Townland Valuation original field books

The original field book was filled out by the valuator as he worked in the field, noting immediately the lot number, the description of the soil and the field price of every quality lot in the townland. Other columns were completed later. The calculations of the figures were carried out in some of the field books. Work on houses was done separately, and those over the valuation threshold were added into the field book at the end of the entry for each townland, or a note was made that there was none. Most field books

---

acres. **6** The format of the pages is first given in the *Instructions 1839*, OL/1/2/4, p. 99, but the column for local circumstances is omitted. See letter from Griffith stating that this column has been added to books, 30 Sept. 1834, OL/2/4, p. 26. **7** OL/1/2/3, additional instructions §10. **8** OL/1/2/4, §311. **9** OL/1/2/2, §21, reworded in *Instructions 1839* (OL/1/2/4), §25: the valuator was to value the land as if 'employed by a liberal landlord, to value land for letting to respectable tenants, at the then average price for agricultural produce' and this valuation will be corrected in the office work to the scale of prices for agricultural produce in the act. **10** See examples in Donegal and Fermanagh.

have a general note on the parish, notes on individual townlands, lists of landlords and a scale of prices. The field book was frequently first written in pencil and 'inked' later when indoors (see plate 2).[11]

Although it was not a requirement to record occupiers, in a number of counties names are noted. From 1839 quality lots were to coincide with the boundaries of farms.[12] In counties where work took place from around that time, some names of occupiers are noted, as well as names of middlemen and agents.[13] The manner of recording was not standardized, and the names can be found in a number of places in the field books: in the text of the descriptions of the lots, in the margins, in separate summary lists or in the notes on the townlands that also include information on tenure and rents. In some books, the names are difficult to find and few are noted, and in others, only large landholders are recorded, with a note stating that the land is let to under-tenants, but without naming them. However, the early date and the details associated with the names (size, quality and location of farms or houses) make this useful and interesting information. The names of occupiers of houses in small towns and villages are also recorded in the field books. This is explained under *house books*.

Townland Valuation check field books

The check books contain re-valuations of sample areas of parishes or baronies made by a different valuator as a verification of quality. He used the original field map and a new book. This system was introduced formally in 1836, but examples of check books made before that date can be found.[14] The check books were either kept as separate books or the pages were bound into the original field book of the parish. Where the check valuation superseded the original work, the pages in the original field book are usually crossed through.[15] Occasionally the original valuation was preferred.[16] Where significant discrepancies were found, further examination was ordered. The check field books record the lot number, the description and the check valuator's field price, but no names are noted. The results of the check valuation were carried into the final version of the valuation in the fair-copy field books, and the name of the check valuator is given along with that of the valuator who did the original work.

---

11 See example in OL/4/4468, Kilbarron, Co. Tipperary. 12 OL/1/2/4, §311. 13 See National Archives lists for Cos. Carlow, Galway, Kildare, Kilkenny, Longford, Louth, Mayo, Meath, Roscommon, Sligo, Westmeath, Wexford and Wicklow, as well as King's County and Queen's County. 14 OL/1/2/3, additional instructions §21; OL/4/3852 (1835), Co. Antrim; OL/4/4542 (1835), Co. Tyrone. 15 OL/4/6240, p. 3 (Templemichael, Co. Longford) and other examples where copies of the check valuation are bound into the original field book. 16 OL/4/6246, p. 32, Moydow, Co. Longford, 'field valuation adopted'.

Townland valuation calculation books (field)

The calculation books were made by copying from the original field book the lot number, the content and the field price but omitting the description of the land. Calculations were usually carried out in duplicate, once in these books and once in the original or a copy. Multiple calculations were needed, including the square area of each lot multiplied by the rate per acre, with percentages added or subtracted for local circumstances. The acreages and valuations of lots in each townland were totalled, and the figures for the townlands were added to give the parish total. The house calculations were done separately, and the price and names of occupiers were copied into the calculation books and the original field books, but the names of the occupiers of land were not copied. Where a small town or village is included in the rural parish, a separate list of occupiers is normally attached to the calculation book.[17]

Townland Valuation fair-copy field books

The fair-copy field books are the final manuscript document in the Townland Valuation. They were created as the document of record and are not merely copies, as their name implies. They were compiled from the field books, house books, quarto books, check books and calculation books. The fair copies were usually made in advance of the county-level appeals, and many contain notes of amendments made to townlands or parishes at the appeal meetings.[18] Some books are signed as correct by the committees of appeal and some are certified copies.[19]

The fair-copy field books are in parishes in the usual format, with the column for local circumstances omitted. They contain standardized descriptions of the quality lots of land, and the valuation prices of the lots and houses. The names of occupiers of houses valued are noted and the houses are numbered to correspond to the Townland Valuation fair-copy map. The house numbers are not related to the lot numbers, as was later the practice in the tenement work. Where there are no houses valued, a statement is made at the end of each townland. Lists of occupiers of houses in towns and villages were also copied into these books. The fair-copy books were written in a good hand by a copyist in the office. They are easily legible but do not contain all the background information of the field and house books, and omit many of the houses noted in the original house books that the office calculations put below the limit. They contain the detailed information on

---

17 OL/4/2317, Aughinish, Co. Donegal.   18 For an example of certified correct, see OL/4/1024, Gallen, King's County; for an example of alterations noted, see OL/4/3600, Liskinfere, Co. Wexford.   19 See field books for Co. Longford, where many additional copies are certified.

which the summaries published in the *Townland Valuation* printed books were based. These books were made under the Townland Valuation only.

From 1834 certified copies of the field books and maps were lodged for public inspection with the county treasurer.[20] Some of these documents were later transferred to the Public Record Office of Ireland in the 1890s, and were destroyed in 1922.[21] Copy field books for Co. Meath are the only ones now held in the National Archives.[22]

The field books of the Tenement Valuation
As described above, the tenement work was carried out in three phases. New field books were made only in the first phase, which took place between 1844 and 1852 in counties being valued for the first time. In the second phase (from 1848) and third phase (from 1852), new field books were not made, as the counties concerned were previously valued in field books by the Townland Valuation. The old format of field book continued in use in the tenement work and combinations of books were bound together by parish. A new type of book was made by the Tenement Valuation: the tenure or perambulation book. The field work created original field books, check field books and calculation books (field), and also preliminary books, survey books and comparison books. The work took place by parish as before, with a surveyor and valuator working together.

Field books in counties valued for the first time
New field books were made in the first phase of tenement work and information on land was collected *ab initio*.[23]

TENEMENT VALUATION ORIGINAL FIELD BOOKS
Although the valuation for poor law purposes under the 1846 act was based on the letting value, the recording of data on agricultural land continued as previously. A new field book was started for every parish. Tenements were numbered to correspond to the field map and the names of occupiers were noted on each tenement in the field book. Some of the information previously collected was now omitted, including the scales of prices and, in the majority of books, the valuator's description of the parish, but notes on rent and tenure are frequent.

Each quality of land in a tenement was described separately, with the square area and the rate per acre. Various notations were used for the different qualities of land, including numbers or lower-case or italicized letters, until the *Instructions 1853* prescribed index figures added to the

---

20 4 & 5 Will. IV c. 55, sec. 8. 21 2006/35/1–32, for index entries relating to documents destroyed. 22 See 2006/35/22, pp 119–21. 23 Cos. Cork, Dublin, Kerry, Limerick, Tipperary and Waterford, and the cities of Cork, Kilkenny, Limerick and Waterford.

tenement number, for example, lot 5 with three subdivisions is noted 5^1, 5^2 and 5^3.[24] Separated parcels of land belonging to the same tenement were given capital letters, as in 5A and 5B. Where there was more than one building on a tenement, these were noted with lower-case italicized letters. This showed the relationship between the different parts of the land and with the buildings, but was not always applied consistently. The figures were calculated in these books and the valuation price was written in. The presence of a house in the tenement was noted, in some cases with a perfunctory reference and in others its valuation was entered. In other cases the waste (area not valued) of the house is recorded. Many of the entries are renumbered more than once because the sequence was altered, changes were made in boundaries or the new notation was applied from 1853.

TENEMENT VALUATION CHECK FIELD BOOKS
The check field books contain data on sample townlands. Names are not usually included in the check books. Check field books can cover a parish or several parishes in a barony. The check valuation can be in separate books or bound into the field book.

TENEMENT VALUATION COPY FIELD BOOKS
Copies of the field books were made so that duplicate calculations could be carried out. These books include names and many are full copies. Large numbers of copies were made in this phase of the work and in many cases there are several books for a parish. In some cases the copy field books were revised.

TENEMENT VALUATION CALCULATION BOOKS (FIELD)
The calculation books were made by copying the minimum data from the original field books. The number of calculations carried out in the tenement work increased greatly because figures were needed for a much higher number of units and their subdivisions (see office work in *How the work was done*, p. 42). Calculation books do not usually contain names.

Counties previously valued by the Townland Valuation
In the second and third phases of the Tenement Valuation new field books were not made but check field books were created as a verification of the earlier work.[25] The existing Townland Valuation field books were used for reference and remained unaltered. However, it was now necessary to establish the extent and location of the tenements. This was described in 1869:

24 OL/1/2/7, §27.   25 OL/4 Tenement Valuation check books for Co. Kilkenny.

the valuator kept no field book describing the soil of the other [previously valued] counties, because it was already described in the Townland Valuation. He merely went over the lands and changed the prices and settled the valuation in this book or a similar one.[26]

In the second phase of the Tenement Valuation counties that were already valued in townlands requested a valuation in tenements.[27] In some counties the existing data was re-plotted in tenements. See *How the work was done: extension of the Tenement Valuation to counties previously valued* (pp 43–4). In the third phase the Tenement Valuation was to cover the entire country under the 1852 act.

TENEMENT VALUATION PRELIMINARY BOOKS
Preliminary books are informal notebooks where information was recorded at an early stage in the work, probably when the staff had a first look around. With the exception of one notebook in Co. Donegal, they were all made in the tenement work. Some record quite detailed information on names and acreage, and some are more summary. These books are listed with the field books (OL/4).

TENEMENT VALUATION SURVEY BOOKS
Survey books contain the measurements of small tenements in counties valued under the 1846 act. Surveys were needed to measure the square area of tenements under five acres. The method used up to that time of computing square area, which was accurate within acceptable limits for large areas such as quality lots, could not be applied to very small holdings. Surveys were carried out using a surveyor's chain to measure the holdings and the figures obtained were calculated. It is likely that many more survey books were made than the small number now extant. Surveys are also on occasion found noted in field books and tenure books.

The survey books contain the names of the occupiers, the lot numbers, the measurements, the survey diagram and a calculation of the square area of the holding.[28] Some books are copies used in the office for the calculations, and the results were written back into the original book. The data in these books varies a good deal. Some have only minimal information, but many

---

[26] *Report from select committee on valuation, 1869*, question 2218, evidence of Henry Duffy, office divisional superintendent. [27] This concerned all of Cos. Carlow and Kilkenny, Queen's County, the city of Drogheda and parts of Cos. Clare, Kildare, Meath, Wexford, Wicklow and King's County. [28] The measurements are usually links of chains. A standard surveyor's chain measured 66 feet and contained 100 links. Each link represents 7.92 inches, or just over 20 centimetres.

contain small sketch plans of the holding, including a house if there was one. Many of the holdings are very small indeed, well under one acre. In the townland of Rush, in Lusk, Co. Dublin, 800 individual lots measuring less than five acres were surveyed.[29] A number of survey books for parishes in Co. Dublin contain sketches of plots and outlines of houses, some with measurements.[30]

TENEMENT VALUATION COMPARISON BOOKS

A very small number of comparison books remain. These books list the figures arrived at by different valuators in tables for comparison. They contain some comments but no names.

An enormous scientific effort went into the creation of the field books, but they are now used for purposes other than that for which they were originally made.[31] The books can appear dense and technical but they vary greatly and contain material that is useful to the family or local historian, as well as a wide range of information on social and economic circumstances. Although the number of names in rural areas is small, the presence of names at this period is valuable and may repay the work of investigation.

The columns in the field books are usually filled in carefully and comprehensively. In the Townland Valuation books, in addition to the standard data, other information is present in the notes on the townlands, in the general description and in the incidental comments written by the valuators in many books. The notes on the townlands usually include the names of the lessors and in some cases information on rent and tenure. The general note outlined the local circumstances that needed to be taken into account in valuing the parish, covering matters such as roads and access to markets, availability of manure, elevation and exposure, but they can contain other information, including notes on farming and crops, conditions of tenure and rent. They provide detail and context that cannot be deduced from the body of the text and were made at a time when this information in respect of the parish may not be recorded elsewhere. The descriptions vary but are of interest as firsthand descriptions by professional observers. The content of the notes ranges from short lists of lessors of townlands to lengthy descriptions, such as the one written by the valuator Edward Gaffney in May 1844 on the parish of

29 OL/4/7421. Rush townland contained 1,160 acres. See *Census of Ireland, 1871: alphabetical index to the townlands and towns of Ireland* (Dublin, 1877) (hereinafter cited as *Townland Index, 1871*). 30 OL/4/7425, OL/4/7429, OL/4/7432, OL/4/7430, OL/4/7434, OL/4/7436, OL/4/7440 and OL/4/7444. 31 John Lee, 'Richard Griffith's Land Valuation as a basis for farm taxation' in Herries Davies & Mollan, *Richard Griffith, 1784–1878*, pp 77–101.

Tisaran, King's County, where he gives his observations on rent, farming, crops and the prosperity of the parish.[32]

The valuator Thomas Cox valued the Aran Islands in August 1844 under the Townland Valuation, and his note in the field book for Inishmore island shows his sympathy for the inhabitants. He comments on livestock and farming practice, the high rents and the £200 paid by the islands in county cess, despite the fact that they 'still have never got a single perch of road made by the county'. He includes the following description:

> Land fit to be cultivated is so scarce and population so fast increasing that they are barely able to produce sufficient potatoes for consumption in the island. The people seldom either buy or sell potatoes. No oats or other grain would be sown here, only for the straw which they require to thatch their houses. The land they have for potatoes is so shallow and lying on a rock that a stranger can scarcely imagine it possible how potatoes can be produced on such soil. Still where there is any depth of earth, the weed and manure being so plenty, that enormously large potatoes are produced on it in a good year.[33]

The Townland Valuation field books can also provide background to later data. The parish of Killulagh, Co. Westmeath was valued in 1839 and the valuator's note lists the names of the lessors and the letting arrangements, the farming practice and the rents paid in each townland. In the townland of Ballygillin, the immediate lessor was William Synnott but the townland was under the court of chancery.[34] The land was taken by Mr Briens, who relet it at a high price: 'The land lies well, has good roads and water but no turf bog. There is an abundance of manuring but no mud.[35] All well divided and fenced.' The townland of Dryderstown was let as a grass farm to Mr Reynolds at 40s. per Irish acre: 'There is plenty of manuring, gravel and mud, with good roads and water. All his work. Mr Reynolds holds this farm during the minority of Mr Fetherston, with a clause not to till any of the fields.' Ballygillen was in seven lots with no houses and Dryderstown contained eleven lots and no houses.[36] The printed Townland Valuation of 1843 gives only the total price for lands and buildings of the townland, without details.[37] By the time of the *Primary valuation* in 1854, the two

---

32 OL/4/6653. 33 OL/4/5384, inside front cover. Inishmore, Co. Galway. 34 The owner was bankrupt and administration of the estate was taken over by the court. 35 The term 'mud' described a type of clay that was used for making bricks and was considered an asset as it provided a locally available building material. 36 OL/4/7115, notes in original field book; OL/4/1721, fair-copy field book; OL/4/1720, certified copy of fair-copy field book. 37 OL/14/1/45, p. 16.

names originally listed in Ballygillin were no longer present, and the entire 230 acres of Dryderstown townland was in the possession of Richard Fetherson, with no tenants.[38] The Townland Valuation notes of fifteen years earlier explain the background to this situation.

The descriptions of the parishes outline the situation at the time. In the parish of Kiltoghert, Co. Leitrim, the valuator wrote in 1837: 'I consider this parish in a medium situation as compared to the county, having Carrick-on-Shannon market in one end of it and Drumshambo another good market for produce in the other end and pretty well off for roads.'[39] Notes on the parish of Tibohine, Co. Roscommon describe the rural economy in 1838:

> This parish is solely agricultural, having no manufactures except for home consumption, such as friezes, flannels and a small portion of coarse linen for housekeepers' use. Cattle, butter, sheep and pigs are the principal commodities for exportation. Oats are also carried on cars to Sligo. The farms are very small, from three and five to ten Irish acres. It is unusual to find a small holder of land to have a horse and one half of the inhabitants have not even an ass. I have met many holders of land renting five acres having neither horse nor ass, but having two milch cows, pigs, sheep and calves. In general it is by the profits of the latter that money is obtained.[40]

Examples of related notes made by the valuators can also be found, including notebooks for some parishes in Co. Donegal that give the numbers and type of livestock, observations on the rent, on the agricultural practices including the increase in tillage and comments on the difficulty in finding a relationship between the value and the rents.[41] Also in Donegal, the book for Inishmacsaint contains a copy of the valuation of the Pettigo Estate in the parish of Templecarn that had been made for the owner, Mrs Leslie, by James Frain in 1833.[42]

Some Townland Valuation field books, especially those made in the 1830s, contain diaries of work, or 'time bills' as they are usually headed. These summarize the work carried out each day, and frequently record inclement weather that affected the outdoor work. The list made by the valuator John Hampton in the parish of Templemichael, Co. Longford noted the very bad weather in the days preceding the 'night of the big wind'. On the actual night, 6 January 1839, he wrote 'Sunday, dreadful tempest at night'.[43]

The Tenement Valuation field books have the advantage of recording the

38 *PV, Co. Westmeath, union of Castletowndelvin* (1854), pp 37–8.   39 OL/4/6037, inside front cover.   40 OL/4/6720, introductory page.   41 OL/4/2284–8.   42 OL/4/5261.   43 OL/4/6229.

data on all property and the names of all occupiers, affording the researcher a complete view of a townland or a larger area. However, while incidental comments are made in some books, the majority do not contain general notes. An exception to this can be seen in a comparison book for the barony of Kinsale, Co. Cork about 1851, which also exemplifies the difficult environment in which the valuators worked:

> the Poor Law Valuation of Kinsale was made by an old farmer named David Herve, living near Timoleague, and revised by a man named Tresilian who afterwards ran away to America, having sold all his stock and left heavy arrears of rent unpaid while Boyne of Bandon thought he had security in a large haggard of corn not being stirred, which on examination proved to have been all threshed out and straw re-built up in form of stacks before he parted with his stock. So that there remained neither stock not produce. Herve was a drunkard and would do anything for whoever would treat him well. Tresilian was a rogue who for a trifle would revise any man's valuation in such a way as would satisfy him.[44]

Conclusion

The Townland Valuation field books contain few names, but they are an important source of other information. They contain detailed data on agricultural land, its ownership and use and are a main source for identifying the quality of land in any given area. Although partly made before the period when specific information on individual farms and occupiers was collected, they provide the background to this later knowledge, in some counties up to twenty years earlier. The books were made in a uniform system throughout the country, allowing one area to be compared with another. The descriptions of the land are technical, but the price per acre and the valuation are given. Reference can be made to the instructions.

The Tenement Valuation field books were made for six counties only and contain the details that connect individual occupiers to houses, buildings and farms. The circumstances of the occupiers can be deduced from the acreage and quality of the farm and a great deal of information about the house in which they lived can be found in the associated house book. Later alterations made to these documents show changes in relation to both individual families and wider communities. The Townland Valuation books, and to a lesser extent the Tenement Valuation books, have useful contemporary notes made by the valuators on parishes, on townlands and on holdings, including details

---

44 OL/4/7461, inside front cover.

of rent and tenure relating to individuals. Where links are made between the field books and documents from the other series, it may be possible for the researcher to come to conclusions about the property or circumstances of the occupiers that are not explicitly stated in any of them.

B. HOUSE BOOKS

House books were used to record the information needed for the valuation of houses and buildings. The National Archives holds approximately 4,000 house books relating to counties of the Republic of Ireland and three house books for parishes in Co. Fermanagh. The house books were made between 1833 and 1861 as part of the valuation field work and the dates in individual counties vary. From the beginning, specially printed pages were used to record the data on houses. These were either bound together with the field book of the parish or made into separate books. Like other documents created by the field work, the house books were sent to the office in Dublin on completion of each parish. Griffith claimed that he always looked at the house books that covered the large houses of gentlemen in order to deal with problems that might result in an appeal.[45]

The 1831 act created a threshold of £3 under which houses were not valued and allowed exemption from local taxes for some buildings,[46] and this was further clarified in 1832.[47] In 1836 the threshold for the valuation of buildings was raised to £5.[48] From 1844 all houses were measured and valued,[49] and from 1852 some houses were measured and some were valued using tables.[50] Instructions issued in 1833 established the model for the valuation of houses, outlining the matters that were to be taken into consideration, how they were to be measured, providing tables and acknowledging that houses in towns were more valuable than those in rural areas.[51] These provisions were repeated in instructions in 1835–6 and 1839. Minor amendments were made in the *Instructions 1853*.[52]

The house books were made in civil parishes for rural areas and in towns for urban areas. The books are printed in columns showing the number of the property, the name of the occupier, the description, the quality letter, the measurements, the number of 'measures', the rate per measure, the amount and the total amount in money. An important feature of all house books was the rule that the name of the occupier of every house measured was to be recorded,[53] with the result that names were noted in relation to houses long

---

45 *Report from select committee on county cess, 1836*, question 610. **46** 1 & 2 Will. IV, c. 51. **47** 2 & 3 Will. IV, c. 73. **48** 6 & 7 Will. IV, c. 84. **49** OL/1/2/5. **50** 15 & 16 Vict., c. 63, sec. 11; OL/1/2/7, §172–93. **51** OL/1/2/2, §143–85. **52** OL/1/2/7, pp 100–15. **53** OL/1/2/3, §186.

before this was the practice for agricultural land. This rule first appeared in *Instructions 1835–6*, but names are noted in house books in Cos. Donegal and Fermanagh from 1833 and 1835, respectively. In both valuations, house books are commonly found bound with other books, and the researcher needs to search them out carefully. It is noted in the lists in the National Archives where a house book is combined with another book.

The house books of the Townland Valuation

In the Townland Valuation the house books were made around the same time as the field books. Apart from a small number of books for Cos. Donegal and Fermanagh that date from before 1836, all other house books in the National Archives were made after the threshold of £5 was introduced in 1836. The same basic data was recorded for all houses but the format of the book changed slightly over time. Before 1836 the columns were ruled for the separate opinions of the three valuators.[54] After 1836 two formats of house book were made, one for rural parishes and one for towns. Many of the books contain a general description of the parish and the circumstances that might influence the valuation. Several different kinds of house book were made, including original house books, check house books and copy house books.

The house books have survived to a considerable extent, including those for large towns and cities, except Dublin. The arrangement of the house books varies from one county to another. In most counties the house books for rural parishes are bound together with the original field book, while in other counties they are in separate books. In some counties both arrangements were used. The books for medium and large towns are usually separate under the name of the town. In the Townland Valuation the vast majority of houses in rural areas were omitted because they were under the threshold, but most houses in towns and villages were recorded, as they were above this limit.[55]

Townland Valuation original house books for rural parishes
The standard-format house book described above was used for houses in rural parishes. Houses likely to be near the threshold were entered in the book and marked on the field map. Summary terms described the property and the various parts were distinguished, as in 'house', 'stable' or 'byre'. The term 'office' was used for undifferentiated outbuildings. The building was examined visually, the external walls were measured and the length, breadth and height were given in feet and inches. A 'measure' consisted of ten square feet and the number of measures was calculated by multiplying the measure-

---

54 See example in OL/5/817, Muff, Co. Donegal (1834). 55 OL/1/2/2 (1833), §154: houses estimated at £2 10s. to be recorded; OL/1/2/4 (1839), §138: houses that would rent for £4 a year to be recorded.

ments together and dividing by ten. The many possible variations on this were outlined in the instructions. From 1833 the instructions included lists of codes, known as 'tables', that corresponded to standardized descriptions. Codes describing the building were entered in the house book. The rate per measure was determined by the quality letter and when multiplied by the number of measures gave the figure known as 'value by tables'.[56] The number code denoted the materials used in the building (e.g. '1' is a slated dwelling house built with stone or brick and lime mortar) and the letter code or 'quality letter' indicated the condition (e.g. 'B-' is medium, deteriorated by age and not in perfect repair). See appendix G for the house tables. The valuator noted the rent that he believed the house would fetch as well as any peculiar local circumstances. In many rural parishes the house book consists of a small number of pages because so few houses were valued.

The calculations in the office showed which houses were above the threshold; those below were eliminated and the remaining houses were renumbered. A greater number of houses will therefore be found in the original house books than in books transcribed after the office work. The houses valued were added to the original field books at the end of the townland or it was noted if there were none. In the final documents of the Townland Valuation, the houses valued were listed at the end of each townland in the fair-copy field books and were shown on the fair-copy map. In the Townland Valuation the numbering of buildings was not related to the lot numbers.

Most Townland Valuation original house books are attached to the original field book and are listed with the field books. Some were separate books, in which case they are listed with the house books. In some counties books are in both arrangements. It is noted in the lists in the National Archives when different types of books are combined (see plate 3).

Townland Valuation house books for towns

After 1836, medium and large towns were usually valued in a separate house book under the name of the town, not the parish. The name of a town can be different from any of the civil parishes with which it is connected. A town can be part of a parish, or can be in more than one parish, and a large town or city might comprise several entire parishes. The names can be checked in the *Townland index, 1901* or logainm.ie/en.

Houses in towns were considered more valuable than houses in the country and extra information was collected in order to calculate the additional value. Columns for the valuator's estimate, the yearly rent, the lease rent, the value of the garden and observations were added to the rural

---

56 OL/1/2/2, §123–67.

house book.[57] A lease was considered an advantage for the owner as maintenance and repairs were the responsibility of the tenant and the valuation was lower in consequence. Gardens were valued as if producing agricultural crops under good conditions. The observations column noted factors that affected the valuation, such as the nature and suitability of business premises, including shops (see plate 7).

From 1833 a system was developed for calculating a percentage increase in the value of town houses over rural houses and once the calculations were completed, the valuation was copied back into the house books.[58] This is described in *quarto books*. Most houses in towns were above the threshold, and those certain to remain below even after the addition of the percentage increase were noted as exempt. Rules for the numbering of houses in towns were set out in the *Instructions 1839*.[59] The market square or centre of the town was taken as the starting point and the houses were numbered systematically, working towards the outskirts. The valuator noted the corresponding numbers on the town plans. This did not take account of any numbering already on the houses.

Small towns and villages that were not valued in separate house books are likely to be found in the field book of the rural parish. A list of the occupiers and their valuation, without the details of the houses, was usually attached to both the original field book and the calculation book (field) and was also copied into the fair-copy field book of the parish. For example, the village of Prosperous, Co. Kildare was valued in 1841 and the occupiers are listed in the field book of its parish, Killybegs, although not in the house book. A copy of the list is inserted into the calculation book (field) for the parish and another is included in the fair-copy field book. The check house book for the parish, made in 1842, does not include these houses.[60] Some Townland Valuation house books were revised during the Tenement Valuation work. This provides most valuable information for the researcher as it updates the data in relation to names and buildings.

Townland Valuation check house books
In all counties except Clare and Sligo, check house books are extant from a second round of work on houses that took place within a year or two of the original work. These books are somewhat more than their name suggests, and unlike the check field books where small samples were re-valued as a check on the original work, new books were made covering all or most houses.

57 See books for Co. Donegal and Co. Fermanagh. Model pages printed in OL/1/2/4, pp 108–11. 58 OL/1/2/2, §168–87; OL/1/2/3, §168–83; OL/1/2/4, §163–205; and OL/1/2/7, §208–43. 59 OL/1/2/4, §165–8. 60 OL/4/5672, pages inserted between pp 11–12 (original field book with house book); OL/4/4137, townland Curryhill (calculation); OL/4/719, pp 8–9 (fair copy); OL/5/3859 (check).

These books are not extant for every parish, but notes on the surviving books suggest that they were made in most parishes. This work was carried out in most counties by a small team of valuators who worked through the entire county. The prices from the two books were compared by writing the price given by each valuator in the other's book. The check house books can provide revised information on the occupiers of houses and on buildings. Many of the Townland Valuation check house books are attached to the calculation books (field), while some are separate books.

Townland Valuation copy house books
Copy house books are found in some counties and the content can vary from summary information to full transcripts of the original house books. They were used to carry out the calculations on houses. Copy house books frequently contain names.

The house books of the Tenement Valuation
House books were made in all three phases of the Tenement Valuation because all of the houses omitted in the Townland Valuation now needed to be valued. The difference in the scale of the work on houses in the two valuations can be seen in the townland of Cullenwaine, King's County, where five houses were valued in 1845 in the Townland Valuation and an additional twenty-three houses were valued in December 1850 in the Tenement Valuation.[61]

Tenement Valuation house books in counties valued for the first time
In phase one, new house books were made in the six counties valued for the first time. The same formats of book continued in use for rural parishes and for towns. Some house books are attached to the field books and some are separate books. The work was again done by barony and parish and was carried out by a surveyor and a valuator. The surveyor recorded the measurements, the names of the occupiers and related information in a house book and the valuator ascribed a value to the house.[62] In practice, in rural parishes two house books were made – the surveyor and valuator each made their own book at different dates. Although not extant for every parish, notes in the existing books show that a second book existed at the time. The calculated prices were entered from one book into the other and either one of the prices or an average was taken as the valuation. Two house books are present for Cappagh in Co. Limerick: one made by a valuator in 1849 and the other by

---

61 OL/5/1353, pp 10–11 (1845) and pp 2–6 (1850). In the Tenement Valuation part of the book, the houses originally measured by the Townland Valuation were not re-measured. 62 See OL/5/1790, Aghanameadle, Co. Tipperary. Note on copy: 'Houses measured by Philip Ryan, surveyor, and lettered by Abraham Woffington, valuator.'

the surveyor in 1850. These books were further revised in 1851, as were many of the other house books.[63] Nothing in the instructions required a second house book, but this followed the pattern established in the Townland Valuation of a check house book that covered virtually all houses and where two prices were compared. Houses in rural areas were noted on the field maps, in many cases using temporary numbers that were later altered to letter references during the office work.

Houses in towns were recorded in town house books and noted on the town plan. Unlike rural parishes, only one original house book was made in towns. Related books were made, including copy house books, revised house books and a small number of check house books. Tenure books were also completed, and while they contain only summary information on houses, they are useful where the house book is not extant. The data was usually made to agree between all the books.

Tenement Valuation house books in counties previously valued under the Townland Valuation

New house books were also made in the second and third phases of the Tenement Valuation, in counties where house books had already been made in the Townland Valuation for houses over the £5 threshold. The work both made new books for houses omitted in the first round, and revised existing entries in the Townland Valuation books, updating names and other information. The new house books survive in varying degrees of completeness.[64] Houses in rural areas were noted on the field maps and those in urban areas on the town plans (see plate 4).

The same format of house book for rural parishes continued in use, with a column for observations added after 1852. The valuator's estimate was no longer recorded. The *Instructions 1853* included ready reckoners to assist in the work, and examples of these documents can be found pasted into books used in the field work.[65] Under the 1852 act, the valuation of houses was based on the rent and in some counties valued after that date, for example Galway, many houses were not measured. Where there was more than one building in a lot, the houses and outbuildings were given a further lower-case italicized letter, for example '5A*b*', usually with a single letter for several buildings. This system was not always consistently applied.

The format of the town house book was changed at this time and it gained columns for the Townland Valuation, Poor Law Valuation and Tenement Valuation prices, the immediate lessor and the probable annual cost of repairs

---

63 OL/5/1195 (valuator's book) and OL/5/1193 (surveyor's book). 64 In some counties, few of these books are extant, but they existed at the time of the tenement work, and Townland Valuation house books contain references to them. See OL/5/4766. 65 OL/1/2/7, pp 104–15. Example in OL/4/698 inside front cover, Mohill, Co. Leitrim.

and insurance, as these were matters that affected the calculation of poor rates (plate 9). In towns previously valued there is usually only one house book made in the tenement work. The town of Tullow, Co. Carlow was valued in 1851 by a surveyor and a few months later the same book was reworked by the valuator in blue ink.[66]

The most important change for the researcher is the fact that all houses were now included. The quality of the data is improved by the fact that the house connected with the land, as the numbering now linked all of the constituent parts.

The house books contain a great deal of detail that does not appear in the final version of the valuations. In the Townland Valuation this includes the names of occupiers of houses that were recorded but found below the threshold and were not copied into the fair-copy field book. In both valuations the valuators' general descriptions, the observations on premises, tenure or rent and the incidental references contain information on additional names, the condition and use of buildings, living conditions, tenure, rents, family relationships and general economic conditions.

The Townland Valuation house book for Thomastown, Co. Kilkenny was made in November 1845 and almost every property is described in detail.[67] The book for Durrow in Queen's County was made in 1843 and, in addition to descriptions of houses, leases and rent, the valuator noted the decline in business of a brewer as being due to the spread of temperance in the county and commented on an inn that was 'a most unprofitable concern' but was maintained by the lessor in the interest of having a respectable inn in the town.[68] Several books refer to the temperance movement as a factor in the loss of business, including the closure of a public house in Ballina, Co. Mayo following the visit of Father Mathew to the town.[69] The book for Graigue, Queen's County in 1843 attributes the failure of a large distillery partly to the 'teetotal business'. The same book lists the professions of occupiers including a turf woman, a seamstress, a land surveyor and a fruit dealer.[70]

The house books contain a record of the built environment in rural and urban areas over the period 1833–61. Every house and outbuilding in the country was described, measured and valued separately and to a uniform standard. The sizes and shapes of houses and other buildings can be worked out, and reference to the tables in the instructions would allow the researcher to form a fair idea of the condition and materials of any house, if not its

---

66 OL/5/2383. 67 OL/5/2919. 68 OL/5/2945. 69 OL/5/3114, p. 61. 70 OL/5/2949, pp 67, 42, 41 and 37, respectively.

design. An enormous range of buildings can be found, from cabins in laneways to the lighthouse on the Skellig with its dwellings and outbuildings,[71] from the Georgian splendour of Castletown House in Celbridge,[72] Co. Kildare and the duke of Leinster's Carton House in Maynooth,[73] to the station houses and engine house of the Midland and Great Western Railway and the Royal Canal Company in Posseckstown, Co. Meath.[74] A search through the books would reveal most kinds of structures. A house book from the parish of Aghern, Co. Cork in 1846 describes the buildings on a large farm and indicates the kind of work carried on there: 'stable, piggery, barn, potato house, cow house, cow shed, car house, gig house, fowl house, hen house, cart house, privy, turf house, barn and stable, dairy, coach house, old castle used as boiling house, belfry and gateway, green house, gate lodge, church', as well as a dog kennel that was not valued.[75] Premises described in the town of Boyle, Co. Roscommon in 1840 include the office of the agent of Lord Leitrim, the post office, a stationer and newspaper office, a chandler's shop and a shop in 'an old house in good repair inside. Roofs covered with light flags. Mrs Siggins is daughter to Mrs Perdue. She holds by lease from her mother at £20 a year, having the shop which is pretty well fitted up.'[76] In Ballina, Co. Mayo the state of a building in 1841 reflected the recent past: 'This was used as a cholera hospital and in consequence could not be since let as a dwelling. Is now let to the hunting club for the huntsman and the offices as kennels.'[77]

Interiors were not examined unless there were doubts and the number of rooms or their condition were not recorded. Sketch plans of buildings with multiple parts were made. Many of these are found for large premises, such as Borris House in Borris, Co. Carlow in 1843,[78] or St McCartan's Seminary in Donagh, Co. Monaghan in 1859.[79] Sketch plans also include smaller-scale buildings, as in Raphoe, Co. Donegal,[80] and show the relationship of buildings in streets, as in Kells[81] and Athboy, Co. Meath.[82]

Industrial and commercial activity can be seen throughout the house books. In rural areas mills are the main industrial buildings, but in towns many different enterprises can be found. In Muff, Co. Donegal, in 1834 two new flax mills in the townland of Craig and another in Drumskellan were noted.[83] In Carrick-on-Suir, Co. Tipperary, in 1846 the valuator lists timber yards, stores for corn, coal, iron and salt, and a slaughter yard (corrected as a bacon yard).[84] The house books also contain considerable information on

71 OL/5/1127. 72 OL/5/3925, pp 2–3. Castletown House was valued at £159, and the total for buildings on the estate was £376. 73 OL/5/3932, pp 14–15. Carton House was valued at £86 for the 'central part of house' (without wings) and the total value was £511. 74 OL/5/1304. 75 OL/5/659. 76 OL/5/3222. 77 OL/5/3114, p. 61. 78 OL/5/3, p. 5. 79 OL/5/1313. 80 OL/5/837. 81 OL/5/3156–7. 82 OL/5/3152. 83 OL/5/817, pp 55, 46. 84 OL/5/3277.

shops, the detail of which is almost entirely omitted from the *Primary valuation*. In Main Street, Carrick-on-Suir, there were linen and woollen drapers, haberdashers, chandlers, pawnbrokers, medical halls, grocers, a butter crane, a stationer, a watchmaker, two hotels and the premises of Mrs Jellico, described as a 'grocery and Italian warehouse'.[85] Descriptions of items for sale can be found, as in the notes on the shop of George Meares in Main Street, Moyvore, Co. Westmeath from 1853 that in addition to being a post office was also a 'bakery, grocery, tea, spirit, linen, woollen, calico, hardware, oils, colours, rod-and-bar iron, metalware, boards and nails warehouse and general country shop'.[86] A book for Trim, Co. Meath contains excellent descriptions of the businesses in the town in 1854.[87] The book for Ennistimon, Co. Clare (1845) lists in Church Street a cart maker, several shoemakers, three dyers and Mr Curran, who 'carries on the salt manufactory', in Parliament Street a butcher, a grocer, a physician and an apothecary and in New Town, 'Mr Barry is a nailor.'[88] Public houses are found throughout the house books.

In addition to the specific information on buildings, the house books contain general descriptions of parishes and notes on the local circumstances that had a bearing on the valuation. The work took place during difficult times and the poor state of buildings and towns was frequently remarked upon. The village of Killadysert, Co. Clare was described in 1845:

> Killadysert is a poor town. There are four bad fairs there in the year. There are two buying corn there at present. A bad quay. Poor shops. The houses of this town should not be rated higher than one fourth over country houses in a medium situation.[89]

The village of Muff, Co. Donegal was described in 1834 as 'a place of no trade and only two fairs in the year'.[90] The thriving activity in the town of Maynooth in 1850 was explained as due to works on the railway and the building at the Royal College of St Patrick: 'For the last four years it has been crowded with tradesmen and labourers and their superintendents. Several of the middle landlords have in consequence taken advantage of the demand for lodgings.'[91]

Notes were made on a whole variety of subjects in both rural and town books. They include the suitability of the location, proximity to 'small, mean houses', the size of the premises in relation to its function, the convenience of the access and many more factors, and these comments provide a rich source of information. Poor living conditions are frequently described.

85 OL/5/3276. 86 OL/5/3444, lot 15 Main Street. 87 OL/5/3170. 88 OL/5/2410.
89 OL/5/2418. 90 OL/5/817, p. 51. 91 OL/5/2857, inside front cover.

In some cases additional information was recorded. In 1837 in Dunshaughlin, Co. Meath the valuator noted 'school house formerly under Kildare Street Society not supported by the parish minister. The Kildare Society provides books.'[92] The houses built by Lord Listowel for his tradesmen in Ballyhooly, Co. Cork were described: 'They are comfortable, clean and airy houses and must contribute much to the health of their inmates, which is indeed the case of all those nice houses built by that nobleman for his people.'[93] The poor condition of the building in Westgate, Carrick-on-Suir, Co. Tipperary in 1846, now a trimming shop, was noted: 'A very old house, it was formerly an old castle, a shop front has been put to it some years ago which has given way and is now being braced with iron cramps to keep it from falling into the street.'[94] Other businesses in the town are listed including the lying-in hospital, 'supported by charitable subscription of the ladies of the town'.[95]

In 1853, a book notes that a house in Spring Valley, Laracor, Co. Meath 'has been unoccupied for some time and is much deteriorated. Mr Shannon intends to put it in repair and come to reside there.'[96] In 1851 in Valencia, Co. Kerry, Pat Donohue is listed as the occupier of a house in Ballyhearny West, and a note on the school building states: 'Pat Donohue is the teacher of this school.'[97] In Muff, Co. Donegal, a large house occupied by John Hart in Ardmore in 1834 had a water closet, a shower bath, servants' quarters and extensive farm buildings.[98] A note in the book for Abbeyleix, Queen's County in 1850 recorded: 'Mrs Mary Festin is wife to Wm Festin who is confined for life in the lunatic asylum in Maryborough (he having shot a man in a mad fit).'[99] In Clonmel, Co. Tipperary, the valuator noted the sad tale of the brewer who drowned himself in one of the vats in 1846.[1]

Where there are house books for parishes and towns under both valuations, the changes that took place in the interval between the two rounds of work can be seen. The period between the two valuations varies from more than twenty years in Co. Donegal to approximately five years in Co. Kilkenny. In most counties the Great Famine occurred between the two valuations. The loss to towns, many of which were already showing signs of decline, is described by William J. Smyth and is vividly illustrated by the

---

92 OL/5/1307, p. 99. This note refers to the Kildare Place Society, established in 1811, which provided non-denominational education. The national school system was established in 1831. 93 OL/5/2448, p. 90. 94 OL/5/3277, p. 42. 95 OL/5/3278, p. 37. 96 OL/5/1303 [1853] and *Primary valuation, Co. Meath, union of Trim* (1854), p. 42. The *Primary valuation* lists Patrick Shannon as the occupier of a house valued at £13. 97 OL/5/1134 (1851), pp 1–2. In the *Primary valuation*, Patrick O'Donohoe is listed as an occupier in the lot adjoining the school in this townland, but there is no indication that he is the teacher, see *PV, Co. Kerry, barony of Magunihy* (1853), p. 133. 98 OL/5/817 (1834), p. 52. 99 OL/5/2935, lot 36. 1 OL/5/3296, p. 46. I am grateful to my former colleague Ken Hannigan for this reference.

accounts of the valuators.² The town of Maryborough in Queen's County was valued in 1842 and again in 1851. Both books contain a general description by the valuator, as well as observations on individual entries that would allow close comparison.³ The books for Mountmellick were made at an interval of eight years, and the valuator wrote in the Tenement Valuation book in December 1850:

> This was the best business town in the Queen's County and in this part of Leinster formerly and it has suffered greater than smaller places of less importance from the general depressed state of the times. The houses are generally letting now at one half the rents of 1842 and 1843. There is one brewery (formerly there were four and a distillery). There is a good deal of business still done in the wool combing and woollen manufacture trades but everyone complains of the stagnation of business now as compared with what it was a few years ago and as a proof of this there are 40 or 50 houses vacant in this town.⁴

A similar decline can be seen in the Tenement Valuation description of Killala, Co. Mayo in May 1855:

> It was a first rate market town before the depression of the times but since it has gone completely to the bad, there is not more than one half of the population in the surrounding country which was in the year 1844. There are eight large corn stores in the town and three within one quarter of a mile of the town, all of which are now unoccupied except three. As also some of the best houses in town. And I think there can be no better proof of a slack business than a number of dilapidated houses, which is the case in Killala.⁵

Even in counties where the valuation work was started after the Famine, the books record the continued worsening of the situation. In 1849 the village of Castlelyons, Co. Cork was described as 'a very reduced village, very little business doing'. The revision three years later noted: 'Since the measurement, the houses have been a good deal deteriorated, many dilapidated. Poor rates are low, still the place is poor.'⁶

Where the house books are not extant, alternative sources of information on buildings are available in other series, and although these do not contain

---

2 William J. Smyth, 'The roles of cities and towns during the Great Famine' in Crowley, Smyth & Murphy (eds), *Atlas of the Great Irish Famine*, pp 240–54.   3 OL/5/2952–4.
4 OL/5/2954, front endpaper, Tenement Valuation house book; OL/5/2957 and OL/5/2959, Townland Valuation house books.   5 OL/5/3138, front endpaper.   6 OL/5/2460.

the detail of the house books, they can provide names, places and valuations. In counties valued in the Townland Valuation, the final version is in the fair-copy field books and the data on towns is in the quarto books. In the Tenement Valuation, data on towns will also be found in the quarto books for the six counties valued for the first time after 1844, and the presence of houses in rural areas and in some towns is noted in the tenure books. In Dublin and Belfast, the query sheets provide information that pre-dates the *Primary valuation*.

Conclusion

The house books are a major source of information on nineteenth-century Ireland. They are not difficult to read and the data is useful and interesting. Their early date makes them a most valuable source, in some cases a generation before the *Primary valuation*. The Townland Valuation house books for rural areas cover a limited number of houses, but the documents for towns and villages include the majority of houses and link occupiers to specific properties from the early 1830s. They contain the names and addresses of occupiers at a period when little other information of this kind is available and the precise location of the houses can be established though the town plans and the valuation maps.

The Tenement Valuation house data was used in making the printed *Primary valuation*, but in abstracted form and without the detail. The difference between the manuscript house books and the *Primary valuation* is described in chapter 5. The valuators' descriptions, notes and incidental comments cover a wide range of matters and contain much informative material. Revised books contain updated entries. In many counties, house books from both valuations are extant, permitting comparison over a period of great change. The house books also record considerable detail on buildings, including materials and condition. These books were made at periods when the data can be compared with the information on houses in the published census reports of 1841 and 1851. The fact that the house books both cover the entire country in a uniform fashion and link occupiers to specific buildings, locations and communities, makes them unique.

C. QUARTO BOOKS

The quarto books are manuscript notebooks relating to the valuation of houses in towns. The National Archives holds all of the quarto books for towns in the Republic of Ireland and one book for Belfast. These books were made between 1838 and 1853 in conjunction with the other valuation work in each county, under both the Townland Valuation and the Tenement

Valuation. Some quarto books are present for most counties, except Leitrim and Sligo, and there is only one book in Monaghan. There are books for the cities of Cork, Galway and Waterford but none for Dublin and Limerick. Several small towns may be grouped together in a single quarto book while large towns may take several books. The quarto books were made once for each town. In general the quarto books have a distinctive appearance. They are approximately square, which may explain the term 'quarto' and many have marbled paper covers.[7]

A system for calculating the additional value arising from the location of a house in a town was first outlined in the *Instructions 1833* and refined in later instructions.[8] This requirement was the same under the Townland Valuation and the Tenement Valuation, and the format of the books remained the same throughout. Some books made after 1846 have columns added in manuscript for the square area and the value of the garden. The valuation was first calculated from the data in the town house book by the standard method used for rural houses. This gave a gross price before any deductions were made and was known as 'valuation by tables' or 'tabular value'. The extra information in the town house books (on gardens, rent, and the type of lease) was used to calculate a local percentage, or multiplier, by which the valuation by tables would need to be increased in order to produce a result similar to the rent. The quarto book was made by first copying the name of the occupier, the description of the property and the valuation by tables from the house book. It is clear from the comments that the valuator visited the town in person and checked the information. He made further corrections and notes in the quarto book, usually in a different colour of ink. The multiplier was written in the quarto book and used to multiply the valuation by tables, which, when one-third was deducted, gave the valuation price. This final figure was copied from the quarto book back into the house book (see plate 8).

The quarto books are pre-printed in columns across two pages giving the lot number, name of occupier and description of the tenement, the relative value by tables (that is, as calculated), the rent by year or by lease and observations. Five more columns give the estimated value (based on the valuator's opinion of the rent the house would fetch), the relative value multiplied by (that is, the multiplier by which the figure calculated by tables is to be multiplied to allow for the situation in the town) and the calculated figure. The value finally settled and the value less one-third are in the last columns. The

---

7 The general meaning of 'quarto' in the book or printing trade was a book made from sheets of paper that were folded twice to produce four leaves or eight pages. This does not refer to a particular size of book, as paper was not made in standardized sheet sizes at the time. 8 OL/1/2/2, §168–87; OL/1/2/3, §168–83; OL/1/2/4, §163–205; and OL/1/2/7, §208–43.

No.	Name of occupier and description of tenement	Relative value by tables	Rent by the year	Rent by lease	Observations	Estimated value	Relative values multiplied by	Relative value with percentage	Value finally settled	Value deducting one-third
12	Thomas Sweeney, house office and yard	£2 9s. 7d.	Pays no rent	-	A public house, bad yard, good situation	+ situation	2.0	£4 19s. 2d. 6s. 0d. £5 5s. 2d.	£5 5s.	£3 10s.
1	Mary Durham, house office and yard	£2 17s.	-	£4 4s.	An old thatch house, lease just expired	-	2.0	£5 14s	£5 14s.	£3 16s.

3.1 Quarto book, Dunboyne, Co. Meath, OL/7/40 (1840).

books are written in black ink in a good hand and laid out with empty space between entries to allow for calculations and amendments.

The quarto book for Dunboyne, Co. Meath (fig. 3.1) shows that the premises of Thomas Sweeney had a relative value by tables of £2 9s. 7d. The multiplier given is 2 (the increase required as compared with the same house in the country), making £4 19s. 2d., to which is added 6s. for a good situation, the total rounded down to £5 5s. which, less one-third, gives a final value of £3 10s. In the same street, Mary Durham pays £4 4s. for an 'old thatch house. Lease just expired', calculated at £2 17s. 0d. When multiplied by two this makes £5 14s., which, less one-third, becomes £3 16s. 0d.[9]

Guidelines for the percentage increases according to the size of the town were included in *Instructions 1833*, and by 1839 were more precisely defined but with the warning that the valuator should use his own judgment because 'some towns, having a large population, are poor when compared with others, in which, owing to commercial industry, the population though small are wealthy'.[10] Villages and small market towns with populations between 700 and 1,300, such as Buncrana, had 25 per cent added. In moderate-sized market towns the prices were to be doubled for the best situations in the main street near the marketplace, and to be increased between 25 per cent and 50 per cent for other situations. Large market towns, with populations of 8,000–20,000 such as Tralee, had the prices for the best locations increased by up two and a half times.[11] In Birr, King's County, the multiplier for the houses in Main Street was mostly high at three or four, and the quality lettering indicated slated houses made of stone or brick, while Connaught Street, with its thatched houses, had a multiplier of two.[12] The population of Birr in 1841 was 6,336, with 1,033 inhabited houses.[13] Athenry, Co. Galway, with 1,236 inhabitants and 242 houses,[14] had a multiplier of 1.5.[15]

To allow for varying rents in different parts of a town, 'classes of situations' were made – two or three classes for small towns, and as many as eight or ten for large ones. The house book for Navan, Co. Meath, made in 1838, illustrates the manner in which the streets were classified and the close relationship between the house books and the quarto books. The house book valuator, James Harton, noted that:

> Prime situations in Market Square almost equal but from Mr Metges to Mrs Nichols rather the best. From Frances Madden's in Watergate Street up is equal to Diamond or Market Square. And

[9] OL/7/40 lot 12 and lot 1. [10] OL/1/2/4, §61. [11] OL/1/2/2, §171–2 and OL/1/2/4, §201. [12] OL/7/44 (1844). [13] *Addenda to the census of Ireland for the year 1841 showing the number of house, families and persons in the several townlands and towns of Ireland* (Dublin, 1844), King's County, p. 4 (hereinafter cited as *Addenda to the census of Ireland 1841*). [14] Ibid., *Co. Galway*, p. 3. [15] OL/5/2730 (1844).

from the courthouse in Ludlow Street. And from the school house gate in Trimgate.

He found that Trimgate Street was the best street for business, with parts of Ludlow Street and Watergate Street equal in situation.[16] The quarto book work in Navan was carried out two years later by Robert McMicken. He followed Harton's classification and decided a local percentage of up to 3.75 in the best streets. He placed the rest of Watergate Street, Bridge Street, Ludlow Street and Academy Street as equal to each other, with a multiplier of around 2.5. The third category added between 1.25 and 2.[17] The multiplier could vary within the same street, as the calculations of difference were made on each house: an example can be seen in Swords, Co. Dublin, where most houses in Dublin Street had a multiplier of between 2.5 and 4, but one was multiplied by 1.75, explained as being 'in a remote situation'.[18]

The valuation staff numbered houses in streets, as outlined in the *Instructions 1839*, in the quarto books, house books and on the town plans.[19] From 1836 houses likely to be worth more than £4 were measured and copied into the quarto books, although it was likely that some would be omitted once the calculations were complete, even with the addition of the local percentage.[20] If the calculations put some houses below the threshold, they were marked 'exempt' and the remaining houses were renumbered.[21] Houses that were not measured in the house books were also entered in the quarto book, grouped under one number and described as 'exempt not measured'. In theory, houses in the quarto books also appear on the town plans, but the numbers are key to identification. The town plans were usually numbered to correspond to the house books. If the same numbering appears in the quarto book and the house book, the buildings can usually be found without difficulty on the town plan. Where they do not correspond it is usually possible to establish a link between premises in the quarto books and the town plans by using the house book as an intermediate identification and finding names, descriptions of public or adjacent buildings, or the size or shape of the building related to the measurements in the house book. (See chapter 4, section on town plans for details.) The numbers in the quarto books and house books do not relate to the present-day numbering of the houses.

The work for the quarto book was carried out as a separate operation, often up to two years after the other valuation field work. This frequently resulted in the noting of new or revised information. An example of the changes in names of occupiers can be seen in the book for the town of Birr.[22] When the work in the quarto books was complete, the figures in the house

16 OL/5/4214. 17 OL/7/42 (quarto book, 1840) and OL/5/4214 (house book, 1838). 18 OL/7/31, p. 1. 19 OL/1/2/4, §165–8. 20 Ibid., §138. 21 An example can be seen in Birr, OL/7/44. 22 Ibid.

books were usually further corrected. There is a good deal of common data between the two books, but it is frequently not identical. The town of Kells, Co. Meath is an example. The original house book work was done by James Harton in 1838 and the quarto book work was carried out in 1839–40 by Robert McMicken, who also further annotated Harton's house book. In Back Street, the house book lists Hugh Ginty, Margaret Aughay and James Garvey.[23] The same occupiers appear in the quarto book, with the observations slightly expanded on the notes in the house book.[24] In Cannon Street, a house is described in the quarto book as 'a present from the Marquess [of Headfort] to an old servant for his own life rent free'.[25] This information was obtained from the house book,[26] and when McMicken found in the course of his enquiries two years later that there was a new occupier and that the premises was now a grocer's shop, he corrected both books but not identically. It is necessary to consult both books in order to establish the details of this.

Furthermore, some of the information in the quarto book is unique. In Watergate Street, Navan, the house book noted that the premises of Thomas Horan were in good repair.[27] McMicken described this in the quarto book as 'an old house but now in very good repair and has been made into one tenement with no. 3 which contains a most excellent shop well fitted up for the draper business'.[28] In the town of Swords, Co. Dublin, the house book listed the occupier of 48 Church Road as 'Trustees of the borough fund' with the description 'old dispensary, coal store'.[29] The quarto book valuator commented: 'This was some time ago a dispensary. Coal is given for half price at this store to the poor of the town.' The building was later included in the list of exemptions because of its charitable status.[30]

The quarto book for Mullingar, Co. Westmeath was made in 1840, also by McMicken. In this case the same numbering appears in both house book and quarto book. The quarto book contains specific information on properties. For example, Margaret Carberry kept a 'public house and shop, medium finish, lease rent £20 Irish, built part of the dwelling house and one of the offices. Lease taken in 1828 for 3 lives or 61 years.' The premises occupied by Mary Moore in Main Street was 'not occupied since the big storm, all in a state of dilapidation. In a very bad state, must be rebuilt.' Another is a 'bakery, dwelling repaired, shop not well fitted up, return old'.[31] This detail is not recorded in the house book.[32] The percentage increases in Mullingar varied between 3.5 to 4 in the Main Street, in Bridge Street around 2.5 and in Ballinderry Road about 1.5. Mullingar had a population of 4,569, with 752 inhabited houses in 1841.[33]

23 OL/5/4213, p. 80. 24 OL/7/41, p. 21. 25 Ibid., p. 35. 26 OL/5/4213, p. 126.
27 OL/4214, lots 2 and 3, Watergate Street. 28 OL/7/42, p. 2. 29 OL/5/2725, lot 48.
30 OL/7/31, pp 27, 30. 31 OL/7/314, pp 10, 12. 32 OL/5/3453. 33 *Addenda to the*

Many quarto books contain general observations on the town. In the book covering several towns in Co. Donegal, McMicken described Raphoe:

> The principal part for business is in the northwest side of the Diamond where there are some good shops. The people complain much for the want of business since the bishop left the place, one would suppose that they lived upon him altogether from what they say, but I am inclined to think they must still do their share of country business.

The multiplier in Ballybofey in the best area for business was mostly 1.5, and other areas were lower, although some of the houses scored highly in the classification, showing that many factors affected the prosperity of towns. McMicken described the town: 'On the whole it is a good little town but still wants a respectable hotel, strangers and commercial people have to put up at the hotel in Stranorlar.'[34]

In the tenement work, the requirement to increase the value of houses in towns remained, and quarto books were made in counties valued for the first time under the 1846 act. The books for Cork, Dublin, Tipperary and Waterford are in most cases similar to the books made in the townland work. Most show the multiplier or local percentage by which the additions were calculated and contain notes on individual premises and on the towns as a whole. In Co. Limerick, the information in most of the quarto books is minimal, with few notes. In some books a general percentage increase was applied to the town, and several of the books contain notes on the increase.[35] Other Limerick books used the multiplier as normal.[36] The quarto books for Co. Kerry are similar and contain few notes and no calculations.

Conclusion

The quarto books are a rich source of information about cities, towns and villages from the late 1830s. They provide an overview of towns as a whole, as well as detailed information on individual occupiers and buildings, and notes on the economic and social life of the area and commercial activity in the town. While some have only brief entries, the majority contain some comments and information that are not recorded elsewhere. The updating of the quarto books within a relatively short period of the house book also provides new information on names or premises dated between the house book and the *Primary valuation*. Researchers should always consult both quarto book and house book, as the information may not be identical. In

census of Ireland, 1841, Co. Westmeath, p. 11. **34** OL/7/197. Towns of Raphoe, Ballybofey, Stranorlar, Castlefin, Lifford, Manorcunningham and St Johnston. The last two towns were not calculated in this book. **35** OL/7/266, Herbertstown. **36** OL/7/262, Kilmallock.

cases where the house book has not survived, the quarto book may be the only source of this data on a town.

The quarto books are also an important source because the work was carried out by a small group of valuators who developed specialized expertise in the valuation of towns all over the country.[37] Their decisions on the multiplier for a town were based largely on the data about rent, but also took account of economic activity and the general situation. Their analysis of how the town functioned as a social and economic unit determined the price that the occupiers of property would pay, and many of the books contain notes of overall assessment that give a dispassionate but informed view.

D. MILL BOOKS

The mill books are volumes containing information on mills. The National Archives holds twenty-two books and some documents relating to mills, made between 1839 and 1851 under both the Townland Valuation and the Tenement Valuation.[38] It is likely that the mill books were created for reference, to facilitate comparison and as an aid to maintaining uniformity of valuation. Mills were not valued under the original 1826 act, but mill buildings were included from 1831 and their water power was valued from 1836.[39] In the instructions a large amount of space is devoted to mills, and they are the only type of building abstracted into a special series of books. Mills were important buildings in nineteenth-century Ireland, and are among the structures identified on the printed Ordnance Survey six-inch maps.

The books are by county, with the data arranged in parishes and townlands. They are printed across two pages, in columns for: number, parish and townland, proprietor, kind of mill, details of the water wheel and the fall of water, pairs of stones in corn or flour mills and information relative to different kinds of mills. A quality letter is given to the machinery and its measurements are specified. Many of the books include the figure for

37 Many of the quarto books used as examples above were made by the valuator Robert McMicken, who had worked in Navan and Kells in Co. Meath in 1839–4. He later worked extensively on towns, and in 1867 he was listed as an officer of the first class with an annual salary of £365. See *Returns of the expenditure of the general survey and valuation of Ireland for each year from 1860 to 1866, both inclusive; and for each county, distinguishing the primary valuation from the annual revision; of the numbers and names of officers employed in the service, with their salaries at present and their salaries at entering the service*, p. 4 (hereinafter cited as *Return of officers and salaries, 1867*, HC 1867 (484)). 38 There are mill books for Cos. Armagh, Cavan, Clare, Cork, Down, Galway, Kerry, Kilkenny, Leitrim, Limerick, Longford, Louth, Mayo, Sligo, Tipperary, Waterford, Westmeath, Wexford and Wicklow, as well as King's County and Queen's County, and notebooks relating to Cos. Dublin and Mayo. 39 1 & 2 Will. IV, c. 15 sec. 2 (1831) and 6 & 7 Will. IV, c. 84 sec. 12 (buildings) and sec. 13 (water power) (1836). See OL/2/2 for correspondence relating to inclusion of mills.

the value of the water power and observations on the workings or the state of business. The completeness of the books varies.

The mill books cover a sample of mills in each county. They were written in the office in a clear hand, using data abstracted from the original house books.[40] Information on the mill buildings was not transcribed but is available in the house books, where mills are interspersed through other houses and buildings. Mill buildings were subject to the same rules as other buildings, including the threshold of valuation of £3 until 1836 and £5 after that date. Technical details of the machinery and the operation were given in the original house books but were not always transcribed in their entirety into the mill books. Many cross-references were made from mill books to 'field' books, meaning the house books, and vice versa. Other series of documents, such as field books, tenure books and the printed *Primary valuation*, contain summary references to mills.

Most mills can be traced through the different series of documents. In Ballycloghduff, Drumraney, Co. Westmeath the mill book lists the corn mill of William Buckley. The Townland Valuation house book of 1840 gives the measurements and description of the building and both the original field book and the fair-copy field book have summary entries. Brief references also appear in the Tenement Valuation house book and tenure book in 1853 and in the *Primary valuation*.[41] There are examples where a mill is not returned in one or other of the books. The mill book for Co. Galway includes mills in Ballynamantan, Lavally and Ballylee in the parish of Kiltartan. They are listed in the Townland Valuation house book pages in 1843 but, as they are all valued under £5, they are not included in the summaries in the Townland Valuation original or fair-copy field books. All three appear in the Tenement Valuation house and tenure books of 1853 and in the printed *Primary valuation*, some with new occupiers.[42]

The most common mills listed were those that produced corn and flour. There were also mills for barley, oats, Indian corn, wheat, grist and malt, the latter sometimes associated with a distillery. Some are described by the process, such as shelling or threshing. Mills working in the cloth trade carried out spinning, carding and beetling. Cotton mills are described in Armagh, Kerry and Wexford and bleach mills are common. There were also paper and oil mills, and a single rope walk powered by a water mill at Castletrasna, Carrigaline, Co. Cork.[43] Tuck mills, where wool was felted,

---

40 OL/4/5486, mills on pp 36–8 and OL/9/6, p. 4. 41 OL/9/20, p. 4 (mill book); OL/4/7136, p. 61 (Townland Valuation house book description) and p. 36 (Townland Valuation field book summary); OL/4/1741, p. 44 (Townland Valuation fair copy); OL/5/2143, p. 44 (Tenement Valuation house book); and OL/6/1592, p. 110 (tenure book). 42 OL/9/6, p. 4; OL/4/5486, pp 36–8 (house book description); OL/5/1023, pp 11, 20, 15 (Tenement Valuation house book) and OL/6/797, pp 39, 56, 47 (tenure book). 43 OL/9/4, p. 9.

were among the most common types, and are found throughout the books, often in the same premises as corn mills. Other examples of multi-purpose mills include the flour, malt, saw and threshing mill ('all for private use') on the demesne of Lord de Vesci in Abbeyleix.[44] The transcriptions from the house books in William Hogg's books provide many examples beyond the ones cited here.[45]

The instructions required valuators to note the number of days worked in the year at a mill and the length of the working day, along with measurements of the water wheels, the number of float boards and the velocity of the water, the number and type of millstones and other machinery, as these affected commercial operation.[46] Most mills were used for grain produced in the immediate locality and there are many notes such as 'grinds only for the country'.[47] The valuators frequently commented on the lack of capital without which millers could work only for local producers.[48] However, the mill books include some substantial businesses such as that of John Smith in Adare, Co. Limerick which 'grinds sometimes for the country at 1½d. per stone but is chiefly employed in grinding corn for retail in Smith's own shop'.[49]

The mill books also contain information on produce, prices, economic conditions and related occupations. In the tuck mill of Michael Feenaghty, in Leitrimmore, Leitrim, Co. Galway 'there are done annually about 250 pieces of cloth, averaging about 15 bundles each piece for which Feenaghty gets one penny a bundle'.[50] The output of a mill operated by F.C. French and Miss Gascoigne in Kilfinane, Co. Limerick is noted: 'The carding mill cards one stone of wool per hour at the charge of one penny per pound. Expense of working 20s. per week. Works 10 hours per day for four months in the year.'[51] A note in the book for Co. Kilkenny made in 1846 reflects the circumstances of the time: 'Now used for grinding Indian corn.'[52] The information on prices includes, for example, 'charges 2s. 6d. per barrel for dressing and grinding wheat'.[53] Information on the wider community can be seen in Queen's County:

> This mill works 7 stone of wool per day at 2s. 6d. per stone, 24 skynes to the stone of 16 lb each skyne 1680 yards in length all here for flannels and friezes. Coarse yarn spun by hand machinery. The

---

[44] OL/9/16, p. 6. [45] W.E. Hogg, *The millers and the mills of Ireland of about 1850* (Dublin, 2000), p. 343. This volume and W.E. Hogg, *The old mills of Ireland*, 4 vols (Dublin, 2015), contain a vast amount of information on mills, including those not covered by the mill books in the National Archives. [46] OL/1/2/4, §226–46. [47] OL/9/11, p. 12. [48] OL/5/1303 ffernock, Laracor, Co. Meath. [49] OL/9/11, p. 20. [50] OL/9/6, p. 24. [51] OL/9/11, p. 18. [52] OL/9/8, p. 4. [53] OL/9/21, p. 21.

constant work of this arises from a connexion of weavers in Ballinakill and neighbourhood.[54]

There are many references to the state of business in the country such as 'not worth keeping in repair for a carding mill all the business gone to the bad'.[55] The situation and convenience of markets were taken into account and deductions or additions were made accordingly.[56] The distillery of George Birch in Birchgrove, Corbally, Co. Tipperary used a water wheel for pumping water and the 'rest of the machinery is worked by steam'.[57] In 1852, new technology was affecting traditional milling in other parts of the country; Joseph Wright of Banktown, Beaulieu, Co. Louth commented in the house book that 'the steam mills erected in Drogheda have left the country mills without anything to do'.[58] In counties for which there is no mill book, these buildings can be found in the house books, including information on measurements and production. The water mill and windmills in Skerries, Co. Dublin, now restored, are described in detail in the house book of 1845.[59]

Mills are shown in print on the Ordnance Survey maps and are numbered as buildings on the valuation maps. Although the mill books do not relate directly to the valuation maps, a mill can be found using the house book and field book to locate it on the corresponding map. Many of the buildings were large and solid and are still standing today, with some listed in the National Inventory of Architectural Heritage.[60] This gives further information about their origins and current condition, for example, the corn and tuck mill of Bridget Mullins at Garrynamann Lower, Kells, Co. Kilkenny, was valued in 1844 at £5 18s. 1d.,[61] and is now an interpretative centre and still known as Mullins Corn Mill.

Conclusion

The mill books provide researchers with a summary and a sample of mills in a county and draw attention to these prominent and common industrial concerns, but the books cover only a selection of the total. The number of mills in Ireland in the early nineteenth century is estimated at between 3,700[62] and nearly 4,200.[63] A comparison of the *Primary valuation* with the mill book for Co. Longford shows twice as many mills returned in the former.[64] For complete coverage and all the information available, the researcher needs to consult the house books and other manuscript books, as

54 OL/9/16, p. 8. 55 OL/9/21, p. 10. 56 OL/9/5, p. 14. 57 OL/9/18, pp 14–15. 58 OL/6/1025, p. 18. 59 OL/5/848, Townparks. 60 See buildingsofireland/niah.ie. 61 OL/9/8, p. 10. 62 Hogg, *Millers and mills of Ireland 1850*, appendix: 'The windmill, a wider view and summary'. 63 Mills shown on the OS maps were surveyed by W.E. Hogg. See *Grist to the Mill (Newsletter of the Mills & Millers of Ireland)*, 14 (2008). 64 Hogg, *Millers and mills of Ireland 1850*, p. 343.

well as the lists published by William Hogg. It is possible that detailed comparison may reveal some information in the mill books that is not available in the house books. The books also demonstrate the care taken in making the valuation, ensuring uniformity throughout the country.

E. TOWNLAND VALUATION APPEAL BOOKS

The Townland Valuation appeal books are the record of appeals against the Townland Valuation. The books in the National Archives cover all counties valued under the Townland Valuation Acts, except Londonderry, Tyrone and Wicklow. There is one volume per county and in some counties there are copies. The books were made between 1837 and 1850, under the 1836 act.

The principle of appeal was established in the first valuation act of 1826 where the procedure is set out in a level of detail that might indicate the difficulties anticipated.[65] There were two rounds of appeal, the first heard at barony level by a committee of appeal and the second heard at county level by a committee of revision. Both committees were appointed by the grand jury. The 1836 act created a third round by dividing the committee of revision hearings into a preliminary meeting and a final meeting to be held within three years. Following the field work and office work, the draft valuation list of each barony was printed in a large notice showing the number of acres and the total value of land and houses in each parish and townland, and stating the place and date of the appeal meeting (plate 10). The notices were posted in public and the select vestries of parishes decided if appeals should be made.[66] Only two letters of appeal are known,[67] but these must have existed in every case. The appeals were forwarded to Dublin, where papers were prepared for the hearings. Copies of the field books and maps were sent to the county treasurer for inspection by the public.[68] At first the new valuation was applied to local taxes only when the entire county was complete, but this was altered by the 1836 act to allow use as each barony was completed.

The organization and hosting of the hearings was the duty of the grand juries, but the process was initiated and led in large measure by the commissioner.[69] In general, the grand juries responded promptly, appointing committees and providing venues for the hearings, as well as other useful

---

65 7 Geo. IV, c. 62: the act consists of 37 sections on 17 pages, almost half of which concern the appeals. **66** 7 Geo. IV, c. 62, sec. 11 sets out the rules for publicizing the lists by posting them in defined public places in each parish, and for receiving appeals from the select vestries of parishes. **67** OL/13/23/5a–b. **68** OL/2/5, p. 234. Griffith wrote to the grand jury of Antrim on 9 Mar. 1836: 'Copies of the printed lists from the *Dublin Gazette* will be forwarded tomorrow, and the fair copies of the valuation maps and fair copies of the field books will be forwarded to the Treasurer's office to your care in a few days.' **69** See OL/2.

information.[70] Many were impatient to have the valuation completed as it was in their interest to have a new basis for county cess and to eliminate complaints, such as the petition to the lord lieutenant in 1839 claiming that in Fermanagh '127 townlands nearly one half of the barony of Clankelly pay no cess'.[71] In August 1843 occupiers in the barony of Tinnahinch in Queen's County requested the new valuation because they were 'much aggrieved by the unequal and oppressive manner in which the grand jury cess has been applotted under the old system of applotments according to the books in the office of the county treasurer'.[72] In counties where the appeals had progressed to the final stages, the completion was sometimes impeded by the adjournment of committee meetings because members failed to attend. This was the subject of several letters to grand juries.[73] In March 1836 Griffith wrote to the grand jury of Tyrone asking that they appoint only persons able to attend, as many of those appointed were likely not to be available 'from age or from living at a considerable distance from the place of meeting or from being absent from the county'.[74] The meeting in the barony of Shelmaliere West, Co. Wexford was adjourned from February to May 1847 for similar reasons.[75] A few days before the rescheduled date, Griffith wrote a stern reminder to the grand jury, and the meeting was held.[76]

The baronial appeals were heard by the committee of appeal in the sessions house of the barony. The appellants were expected to attend in person and explain their case. Appeals were disallowed in cases of 'no appearance',[77] and some applicants withdrew their appeals.[78] Evidence could be taken under oath. A similar procedure obtained for the county-level preliminary meeting of the committee of revision, held when all the baronial appeals were finished, and for the final meeting. The latter meetings were usually held in the county courthouse. The first county where appeals were completed was Londonderry, in 1836. The last hearings were held in May 1851 in Kilkenny.[79] During this period, both the context and the valuation itself changed: the 1836 act replaced earlier acts, the poor law was enacted with its own valuation, and the Tenement Valuation was started.

One of the main problems with the Townland Valuation was the very long period required for its completion. In addition to the time needed for the field and office work before the draft valuation lists for each barony could be

---

70 See OL/13/23: In King's County the appeal committees were appointed at the summer assizes of 1842, but the first hearing was in June 1844. The secretary of the grand jury also forwarded a list of the collectors of county cess. 71 OL/2/7, p. 76. 72 OL/2/9, pp 219, 222. In this barony it took two more years for the valuation to be agreed in Nov. 1845. See OL/13/38, barony of Tinnahinch. 73 See also OL/13/38, p. 21: The meeting in barony of Maryborough East, Queen's County was adjourned twice because of insufficient attendance. 74 OL/2/5, p. 231. See similar in Longford, OL 2/7, p. 211. 75 OL/13/44, barony of Shelmaliere West. 76 OL/2/11, p. 72. 77 OL/13/26, p. 7. 78 OL/13/39, barony of Ballintober North. 79 *Returns of date of commencement and final meeting Townland Valuation*, HC 1851 (268), p. 2.

produced, the appeals process itself was protracted. In many counties it took over a year to carry out the baronial hearings. They were usually grouped, with four or five baronies heard on successive days and then a break of up to several months before the next group.[80] The total length of time taken from the start of the field work to the meeting of the final committee of revision varied greatly. In Donegal it took eleven years,[81] but in Co. Carlow all the work was completed in three and half years.[82] After the first few counties the field work was completed more quickly, but the periods between the stages were defined in the statute. Disquiet at the length of time taken can be seen in the requirement included in the 1836 act for the commissioner to present progress reports,[83] and between 1844 and 1851, the House of Commons requested returns on the Townland Valuation on nine occasions.[84]

The appeal books usually contain documents recording the meetings at all three levels. The most detailed are those covering the baronial appeals, which include the list of appeals, the large printed draft valuation list folded to fit in the book, an abstract of the barony and the declaration made by the committee after the meeting. The documents were annotated during the hearings. The draft list (plate 10) shows the townlands and parishes in the barony, with the acreage, the value of the land and houses and the total. Exemptions are listed at the end of each parish and the information on the meeting of the barony-level committee of appeal is printed at the foot of the document. A copy of this notice was posted in the prescribed places in advance of the meeting. The manuscript corrections made to this document record alterations made at the meeting. In some cases, reference information was included, such as tables of averaged prices of valuation in the county[85] and other valuations by experienced staff, the check valuation and even the much-maligned Poor Law Valuation.[86] Some books contain other related documents, either loose or pasted onto the covers. Details of the meetings of the committee of revision are fewer, but usually comprise the signed declarations made after the preliminary meeting of the committee, and the declaration or the extract from the *Dublin Gazette* recording the decision of the final committee. Griffith took a close interest in the details of the appeals.

80 OL/13/19, Co. Galway: 4 baronies heard in July 1845, 6 more in Nov.–Dec. 1845, with the remainder completed by mid-1846; OL/13/9, Co. Cavan, 5 baronies heard in Jan. 1841 and 3 in Apr. 1841. 81 *Returns of date of commencement and final meeting Townland Valuation*, HC 1851 (268). 82 OL/13/8. Baronial hearings were held in Feb. 1844, the preliminary committee of revision meeting in July 1844 and the final committee in May 1847. 83 6 & 7 Will. IV, c. 84, sec. 49. 84 *Return of the several counties, counties of cities, and counties of towns, in Ireland, of which the valuation, under 6 & 7 Wm IV, c. 84, has been completed*, HC 1844 (212). Further returns were made in 1845, 1847, 1847–8, 1849, 1850 and 1851. 85 Documents in books for Donegal (1841), Fermanagh (1844), Louth (1839), Meath (1844) and Westmeath (1843). 86 OL/13/32, page following p. 25 includes Poor Law Valuation; see also books for Galway, Kilkenny, King's County, Queen's County and Wexford.

He chaired all the meetings and many of the books contain notes in his handwriting. Appeals were made in every county, but not in every barony. On the whole, few valuations were appealed, especially when compared with the numbers of appeals made later under the Tenement Valuation.

The reasons for appeal included high valuation, wrong square area, exemption, confusion about boundaries, and mistakes. Appeals against the high price of the valuation account for the majority. In Co. Fermanagh, the complaint of the Hon. John Cole is that 'Garrifly in Killesher is valued at more than anyone would give for it in rent'; Griffith's note states that the townland has been re-valued and no alteration was required.[87] As the valuation was relative, it was necessary to make a comparison with another named place, and examples are noted throughout the books. Appeals were made in every county on grounds of wrong square area. The absence of a standard system of square measurement in existing records was one of the problems of the local taxation system, and an act in 1824 applied statute measure to Ireland.[88] However, occupiers commonly used Irish acres, which are approximately 60 per cent larger than statute acres, and content expressed in the latter was always a larger number.[89] As county cess was based on acreage, this must have appeared an alarming development for occupiers. Property used for public or charitable purposes was valued, but was exempt from local taxation. Premises seeking exemption varied from the observatory in Armagh[90] to the pound in Knock, Co. Mayo.[91] In Newry, Co. Down, a claim to have the land around a school exempted was disallowed, 'the land not being made over by deed to any public body but may be turned from this use at will by the proprietor'.[92] The house of Philip Casement, in the parish of Saintfield in the same county, was exempted, as he was 'parish clerk and schoolmaster'.[93]

The work of the Boundary Survey, which had established the official boundaries from the late 1820s, was a cause of confusion. In some cases, occupiers failed to understand the divisions. In Co. Armagh, the townlands of Creggan Upper and Lower in the parish of Loughgilly were listed in the wrong barony and this was corrected at the appeals.[94] Other townlands and parishes in Co. Armagh made similar claims and were referred to the county committee of revision.[95] Where the Ordnance Survey was found to be correct, the appeal failed, as in Ardquin, Co. Down.[96] Mistakes were also made by the valuation staff both in the field work and in the office work. In Athboy, Co. Meath, two houses were incorrectly valued as one,[97] and in

---

87 OL/13/17, p. 37. 88 5 Geo. IV, c. 74. 89 Statute (or imperial or English) acres need to be multiplied by 0.6173 to convert to Irish acres. Irish acres need to be multiplied by 1.6198 to convert to statute acres. 90 OL/13/5, p. 28. 91 OL/13/32, page facing p. 36. 92 OL/13/14, p. 47. 93 Ibid., p. 4 reverse. 94 OL/13/5, pp 4, 18. 95 Ibid., pp 8, 16. 96 OL/13/14, p. 35. 97 OL/13/34, p. 52.

Taghboy, Co. Galway, the price was admitted as too high perhaps 'in consequence of office mistake' and was corrected.[98] A lapse of time between the field work and the appeal hearings meant that some elements of the work were already out of date, as in the case of a house no longer standing in Hamlinstown, Diamor, Co. Meath.[99]

The act specified strict time limits for submissions. In the book for Co. Kilkenny, there are rough calculations of dates in Griffith's hand checking if an appeal was received within the allotted time.[1] In another case in Kilkenny, he noted 'appeal three weeks late',[2] and in Mayo, after calculating the dates, he wrote 'appeal made eight days too late' and refused to admit it.[3] Yet the book for Co. Clare contains an index of late appeals received up to a certain date, with a further list of applications received after the date, indicating that there may have been some leeway.[4] The response may also have depended on the status of the applicant, and in October 1845 Griffith wrote to the marquess of Clanrickard that, although his appeals were two months late, he was 'most anxious that every error shall be investigated' and directed a new valuation.[5]

In the barony of Iveagh Upper (Upper part), Co. Down, Griffith's notes reflect his desire for agreement: for example 'appellant satisfied with the valuation of his houses on explanation being given' or 'abandoned by appellants who were satisfied'.[6] However, agreement was not universal and in the barony of Ards Lower, Co. Down, occupiers insisted on their disallowed case being re-presented to the committee of revision.[7] The overall impression is that it was difficult to prevail against the valuation, although when it was shown to be justified, alteration was made, as in Kellistown, Co. Carlow, where comparison showed that the check valuation price was lower.[8] The check valuation provided authoritative data for comparison,[9] and where there was grave doubt, a re-valuation was ordered.[10]

Some of the interest of these books comes from additional information. At a time when few names were recorded, appeals concerning houses gave the name of the occupier, although these are likely to be also found in the Townland Valuation original house books and fair-copy field books. The Revd Mr Hawthorne is listed in Tullyherron, Loughgilly, Co. Armagh,[11] and Thomas Jebb claimed that his house in Cootehill, Co. Cavan, was 'valued at £14 and entered against him at £21'.[12] Sir Robert Ferguson MP, who was one of the valuation's most enduring and persistent critics, appealed the

98 OL/13/19, p. 73. 99 OL/13/34, p. 72. 1 OL/13/22, barony of Fassadinin. 2 Ibid., barony of Shillelogher. 3 OL/13/32, p. 27. 4 OL/13/11, late appeals from 31 May to 15 Sept. 1850, and late appeals after the 15 Sept. 1850. 5 OL/2/11, p. 31. 6 OL/13/14, p. 43. 7 Ibid., p. 42. 8 OL/13/8, p. 20. 9 See books for Cos. Galway, Kilkenny and Wexford, as well as King's County and Queen's County. 10 OL/13/38, p. 16. 11 OL/13/5, p. 4. 12 OL/13/9, p. 17.

valuation of his property in the parish of Killea, Co. Donegal.[13] The names of appellants are recorded in a small number of books, which include Griffith's own notes on the barony of Moydow, Co. Longford, where he lists those who withdrew appeals.[14] Some of the names listed do not appear in the field books.[15]

Despite the imposition of statute acres as the standard, other forms of measure were used. Irish acres appear frequently in the books,[16] and also in the indexes and tables of comparative valuations made for staff reference.[17] In Co. Donegal, reference was made to Cunningham acres, a measure used in parts of the north of the country.[18] In Co. Armagh, the acreage in Armstrong's survey is cited.[19] A small number of descriptions of property can be found, such as the mill in Clonkeen, Co. Galway that had no water.[20] In Donoughmore, Co. Donegal, the appeal complained that the northern exposure of the lands was not taken into account.[21] Other documents provide information relating to the grand juries, for which few sources have survived, such as lists of places where road sessions were held in Co. Carlow, or the names of the high constables of baronies in Co. Donegal.[22]

Conclusion

The Townland Valuation appeal books provide information from a relatively early date, including names and descriptions, when few other sources are extant. They are close in date to the tithe applotment books (1823–37).[23] The content of the Townland Valuation was superseded by later work, but the appeals were an important milestone in securing public confidence and in demonstrating that the system worked. The hearings exposed the valuation to public scrutiny and were proof that it could achieve its objective of creating a usable valuation for grand juries. The Townland Valuation became the organizational model for future work. The documents show that Griffith dedicated a great deal of time and effort to the appeals, travelling the country to all of the meetings and mastering the detail of the appeals under discussion. His involvement can be seen in his handwritten notes in every volume. However, the underlying problem was expressed by an appellant in Co. Armagh, who made 'an appeal against valuing in townlands and not affording individuals the power of knowing whether they be duly rated or not'.[24]

13 OL/13/12, p. 1. 14 OL/13/26, p. 3. 15 Examples in OL/13/9/6 barony of Castlerahan, Co. Cavan and OL/13/23/6, King's County. 16 OL/13/9, p. 1. 17 OL/13/11, index of appellants and OL/13/38, p. 7. 18 OL/13/12, p. 1. 19 OL/13/6, barony of Orior Upper. William Armstong had made a highly regarded map of Co. Armagh, using a scale of 40 statute perches to an inch, or 1:7920, see Andrews, *Plantation acres*, pp 382–5. 20 OL/13/19, p. 26. 21 OL/13/12, p. 1. 22 OL/13/8/2 and OL/13/13. 23 See National Archives, titheapplotmentbooks.nationalarchives.ie. 24 OL/13/5, p. 4.

F. TOWNLAND VALUATION PRINTED BOOKS

The Townland Valuation, as agreed at appeals, was printed in a series of small bound books between 1836 and 1850. Multiple copies of these books were printed, and they can now be found in various collections. The National Archives holds Townland Valuation printed books relating to twenty of the twenty-six counties valued under the 1836 act, and a complete set under this act is held by the National Library.[25] The books record the valuation of each barony as agreed at the committee of appeal, and the valuation of the county as agreed at the preliminary committee of revision. A further meeting three years later finalized the valuation, but in the interim it was used for local taxation. The smallest unit valued is the townland, and the names of occupiers or owners are not given. The only names listed are those of members of the committees of appeal and revision. The page for Munterconnaught, barony of Castlerahan, Co. Cavan (plate 11) shows the result of the meeting of the barony committee of appeal. The parish is printed on one small page, and the opposite page includes the abstract for the barony and the declaration of the committee.

The 1836 act prescribed the format of the data, but there was no requirement that this should be presented in a book.[26] The draft valuation circulated before the baronial and county appeals was published in large notices, but the final valuation needed to be used for reference. It is likely that the printed books were made in order to obtain widespread dissemination of the valuation information. The books are in two parts: the valuation of each barony and the valuation of the county as a whole. For each barony there are lists of the townlands and some smaller divisions such as islands in parishes, with their acreage, the valuation of the land and houses and the total valuation. Exempted property is listed at the end of each parish, with its valuation. This is followed by the formal declaration of the committee of appeal, stating the place and date of the meeting and the names of the members and chairman. For county-level appeals, baronies and their parishes are listed under the same headings, with the total value of exemptions in each parish and the declaration of the committee of revision. Similar books were to be printed under the 1846 act but only one book for Co. Dublin is extant.[27]

The pages covering each barony were printed, usually by a newspaper, at a date shortly after the baronial appeal hearings.[28] The barony sections were put together at the meeting of the preliminary committee of revision to produce the book, and alterations made at the final committee of revision

---

25 I am grateful to Dr William A. Smyth for this reference.   26 7 Geo. IV, c. 62, schedule 3.
27 See list OL/14 in the National Archives.   28 OL/14/1/39, Queen's County printed at the office of the *Leinster Express* in Maryborough, 1846.

were entered in manuscript. Two books are present for Co. Wexford, with the second one printed after the final meeting, but these are the only two examples.[29] The results of the final committee of revision were printed in the *Dublin Gazette*, but this document is included in only six of the printed books held in the National Archives.[30] The book for Co. Roscommon illustrates how the entire three-stage process took place. The appeals in the nine baronies were held in five sessions between January 1841 and March 1843, and the valuation as amended was printed on eight separate dates between February 1841 and June 1843 by the *General Advertiser* newspaper in Dublin. The preliminary committee of revision met on 26 May 1843, and its results were printed in June 1843. The final committee met in May 1846 and the alterations were made in manuscript in the book and dated. The *Dublin Gazette* published the final valuation on 9 June 1846.[31]

The exemptions list buildings and other features, such as the graveyards present in almost every parish. Exempted premises tend to be the largest public structures in any locality. Religious buildings range from Roman Catholic chapels, churches, Baptist chapels, Presbyterian meeting houses and Wesleyan Methodist meeting houses found in many parishes, to the Seceders' meeting house and the Covenanters' meeting house in Londonderry,[32] and the preaching house in Ferbane.[33] Official buildings include police and constabulary barracks, gaols, revenue police and excise buildings, custom houses, court and sessions houses, military barracks, ordnance grounds, Martello towers, market houses, fair grounds, coast-guard watch houses and lighthouses, fever hospitals and dispensaries. The newly built workhouses can be seen starting to appear, under various names (poor house, poor law union workhouse).

A wide variety of schools is listed in addition to national schools. The Co. Mayo book lists Westport free school house in Carrowbeg, the Erasmus Smith school house in Killala, a free school house and national school house in Knockaphunta.[34] The town of Birr had a Roman Catholic chapel, a Presbyterian meeting house, a Wesleyan Methodist meeting house, a Quakers' meeting house, in addition to a parochial school house, a free school house, a Presbyterian school house and two national schools. It also had a court house, a gaol, a police barracks, a fever hospital, an old church burying ground, a Quakers' burying ground and a pound.[35]

Under the 1846 act the valuation made in tenements was to be restated in

---

29 OL/14/1/49–50. 30 Cos. Galway, Kildare, Leitrim, Londonderry, Roscommon and Tyrone. See also OL/13, Townland Valuation appeal books, where the extract from the *Dublin Gazette* is included in some books. 31 OL/14/1/40. 32 OL/14/1/32, p. ii. 33 OL/14/1/25, p. 56. 34 OL/14/1/36, pp 50, 57, 77. 35 OL/14/1/25, p. 41.

townlands for county-cess purposes.[36] Dublin (1850) is the only county for which it is known this book was made. The copy in the National Archives is incomplete, as the baronies of Coolock and Rathdown are not present.[37] Under the 1852 act the valuation in townlands was to cease, but abstracts in a similar format of townland, parish and barony continued to be printed until the late 1850s. For copies in the National Archives, see OL/21.[38]

Conclusion

These books were published at the time when the Ordnance Survey maps were near completion, and other statistical data, such as the printed reports of the 1841 census, were being disseminated. Although occupiers are not named, the books contain useful information and can be a good entry point for research on a local area in providing an overview. For each county they present the basic facts of size and relationship of townlands, parishes and baronies, including acreage authoritatively established by the Ordnance Survey. They show the presence and the location of public buildings and services and the individual valuation of exempted premises gives data on their quality and status. The valuation is in itself evidence of relative wealth, and the use of the standardized format allows comparison. The detail behind the printed books is available in the field books and house books. The small number of names may be worthy of attention for family or local history research.

G. TENURE BOOKS

In the Tenement Valuation, a new book was made in which information on tenements was recorded or compiled. This was the tenure book, also known as 'perambulation' book, because the staff 'perambulated' or walked around the boundaries of tenements in the course of the work. The tenure books were made in parishes between 1846 and 1859 and are the earliest documents that systematically record all tenements and the names of occupiers and lessors. The National Archives holds books for all counties in the Republic of Ireland except Queen's County (Co. Laois). Most tenure books were made in respect of rural parishes, but some towns are covered.

The work of valuing in tenements began in 1844 in counties not previously valued and was later extended to other counties. The valuation in tenements was to be used for both poor law and county-cess purposes, and information that was not previously collected in the field work was now

36 9 & 10 Vict., cap. 110, secs 39 and 70. 37 OL/14/2/1. 38 15 & 16 Vict., cap. 63, sec. 2. Copies for some counties are also held in the library of the London School of Economics. I am grateful to Dr William A. Smyth for this reference.

required, including the names of all occupiers and lessors, the location and extent of all tenements, the rent, the tenure and any peculiarities of circumstances. These matters had a bearing on the calculation of the valuation for poor law purposes and the division of poor rates to be paid between landlord and tenant. The work of valuing in tenements was similar to the earlier work and field books, house books and maps continued to be used. However, the data needed to be assembled in a manner that ensured it was complete, as there were many more entries than previously, and it needed to be presented in new formats, that is, in lists of tenements that could be used both for appeals (in the *Primary valuation*) and in the poor law sheets for the poor law commissioners. The tenure book was created to meet these needs (plate 5).

In counties now valued for the first time, the existing poor law lists were obtained in advance of the field work,[39] and all of the documents (field, house and tenure books) were created around the same time with information copied from one to another. From 1848, when the tenement work was applied to counties previously valued in the Townland Valuation, the advance information was compiled from existing valuation documents as well as the poor law lists.[40] Work in the field was always carried out. A small number of notebooks used to make rough lists of the occupiers and their properties are listed with the field books as 'preliminary books'.[41] The surveyor recorded the boundaries of tenements on the field map, and noted in the tenure book the names of occupiers, the tenure and year let, and observations. The square area of tenements was added to the tenure book from the field book. The same surveyor usually measured the houses of the parish in a separate house book and added a summary of the house information to the tenure book. The valuator then examined the parish, made the valuation and responded to queries marked in the tenure book by the surveyor.

The tenure books are printed across two pages, with the county, barony, parish and townland in the header. The format of the tenure books was altered several times over the period of the Tenement Valuation, and in some counties more than one format was used. The format used from 1846 records the lot number, occupiers, immediate lessor, description of the tenement, content of the farm, rent, tenure and year let, and observations. From about 1852, columns were added for the net annual value (land, buildings and total), English (statute) acres reduced to Irish (that is, recalculated in Irish acres), Irish acres, observations and the Ordnance Survey sheet number. Columns for county cess and poor rates were printed in some of these books, and the books used in Co. Monaghan in the late 1850s have columns for measurements of buildings.[42] The basic information of lot number, occupier,

39 OL/2/10, p. 162. 40 OL/6/314, OL/6/320 and OL/6/322 (Co. Kilkenny) contain notes regarding the list of houses already measured in the Townland Valuation. 41 See examples at OL/4/7403 and OL/4/7408. 42 OL/6/1376. This format of book was also used in the re-

lessor and description was usually noted, but the other columns were not always completed, or other notes were entered.

The tenure books survive in good numbers, but not every parish is present and no books are known for Queen's County. Some parishes are spread over several books, especially in the later stages of the work. The appearance varies from perfectly scripted copies to rough books that have suffered in the weather. In some books, pencil notes indicate field work that was later either erased or written over in ink.[43] In general they are easy to read as they were not usually used for calculations or much corrected. Small tenements requiring chain surveys were noted with instructions 'to be surveyed' or 'all to be measured'.[44] The surveys were usually recorded in separate survey books, but in some cases the surveys are at the back of the tenure books.[45]

The actual rent paid by the occupier was now required rather than the valuator's estimate as previously. Abstracts of rent were made in separate rent books for reference. Rent was a delicate subject and Griffith was always anxious that the valuation should not be thought to be based on rent, although rent in towns had been recorded since 1833. The *Instructions 1839* warned staff that this matter had 'a tendency to create dissatisfaction and ill-will on the part of tenants towards their landlords, and distrust and opposition on the part of the landlord relative to the General Valuation'.[46] The official view was outlined in a letter from the office superintendent to a new surveyor in 1846, instructing him to enter in his field book any information in this regard that he hears about a farm: 'It will be a most useful check for us hereafter but you should not appear to inquire too closely, or it might appear the valuation was founded on such inquiry.'[47]

Despite concern about giving the wrong impression, much of this information was collected as the work proceeded. A small number of books for parts of Cork name the sources, such as 'information given by bailiff and occupier John McManus',[48] and 'The above information was given by Patrick Wall of Rundale farm Knockacrump, also by occupier's wife, occupier being absent when I called.'[49] The notes sometimes show the difficulty in getting the information or express doubt about its veracity. In St Finbar's parish in Cork, the valuator wrote: 'Called on Miss Rogers and she refused to tell who her landlord is.'[50] A note by the valuator of the parish of Fertiana and Moycarkey, Co. Tipperary questioned the reliability of his source: 'This is the information I got from the tenant Mick Leahy but will take both and when measured in the office the truth will be found but it is most awful to get the truth from the tenants.'[51]

valuation of Dublin in 1865–7, see pp 113–14 below. **43** See examples at OL/6/92 and OL/6/145. **44** OL/6/305 and OL/6/97. **45** OL/6/320 and OL/6/466. **46** OL/1/2/4, §294. **47** OL/2/11, 27 Oct. 1846, opposite p. 55. **48** OL/6/137, p. 31. **49** OL/6/139, p. 51. **50** OL/6/95, lot 21, Ballintemple. **51** OL/6/458/1, 4 Mar. 1847.

Many tenure books were revised within a relatively short period and this is useful when following changes in holdings or occupation. The information in the tenure books was used to prepare the *Primary valuation* for printing, and in general there is a high degree of correlation between the two. Many books have notes recording the copying and checking carried out for the 'printer's copy'.[52] Some tenure books were used to revise the field books of the Townland Valuation and to make the valuation in tenements of places where it was previously in townlands only. An example of this can be seen in the parish of Fenagh, Co. Leitrim.[53] The tenure books were also used to make the poor law sheets, which were written in the office and sent to the poor law commissioners. The final version of these could only have been made after the appeals, but a copy seems to have been written up shortly after the field work, as indicated by notes on the tenure books.[54] A circular in August 1848 warned staff to do this before leaving the barony and also suggested that the 'perambulation books' did not need to be retained once their contents were copied into the poor law books, advice that, fortunately, was not heeded.[55]

The tenure books contain names of occupiers and lessors, and descriptions of holdings as well as a wide range of information such as the prevailing tenure (type of lease, duration, special conditions), rents paid, changes to tenements, emigration, the non-financial arrangements in place of rent, the operation of common systems, farming and summary information on buildings. There is also valuable information that was not central to the work in hand, such as family relationships, connections with employers or landlords, and occupations.

Rents were both recorded and commented upon. They were expressed in a variety of ways, from the price per acre or the weekly rent to the total price paid in the year; the townland of Ballinvarig, Whitechurch, Co. Cork, records 22s. 9d. an acre for sixty-one acres of land and £3 a year for a house and garden.[56] The valuator in Ardree, Co. Kildare, observed in March 1851: 'Rents in general high and some very high being let by middlemen.'[57] The variety of tenure is also shown, usually with the date of the lease or the 'take'. In Ballinvarig, one lot had a 'lease of 120 years, taken out about 15 years ago' and another a lease for '3 lives or 31 years since 1848'.[58] The same book records a promise of a lease, a lease forever, a lease of 100 years and yearly tenants.[59] Reduction in rents, or 'abatements', are common throughout the books. In Molahiffe, Co. Kerry, a holding was 'given to the present tenant

52 OL/6/2, inside cover. 53 The field book of the Townland Valuation OL/4/6042, p. 1 (1838) lists 5 quality lots. In the tenure book OL/6/975, p. 1 (1854), 17 tenements are listed and the price of each is calculated, making allowance for local circumstances, and copied as a price per tenement into the field book. 54 OL/6/324, p. 1. 55 OL/2/11, opposite p. 91. 56 OL/6/92, p. 15. 57 OL/6/470, p. 1. 58 OL/6/92, p. 10. 59 Ibid., pp 5, 15–16, 20.

£40 less than the former'.[60] In the parish of Carlow, the writer notes: 'Kennedy has a promise of a reduction to £3 an acre.'[61] The complexities of subletting are also set out. The book for the parish of Aglish, Co. Waterford lists Mary Keeffe as holding a house and plot from another occupier, Denis Clancey, and describes how: 'Clancey holds under Dower and he under Captain Stuart immediate lessor under Lord Stuart de Decies, landlord.'[62]

Details are given of arrangements made as an alternative to paying rent, including the use of land and farm work, and there are many examples in parishes in Cos. Kerry and Limerick. The book for Dromin, Co. Limerick lists examples where occupiers have 'freedom' or use of land for their own cows. Notes about cows as the equivalent of land are found in some of the Kerry books,[63] the price of milk in Carrigaline, Co. Cork is given and the value of animals in relation to the land in the same parish is described as: 'Four sheep with lambs or five dry sheep make a sum in this country.'[64] There are frequent examples of rent being paid in labour: 'pays for the house in work at 5d. a day',[65] and 'pays no rent but takes care of plantation'.[66] The book for Carrigaline, Co. Cork records several examples: John Connor held a house and yard 'free as steward', and Thomas Negal had his holding 'free from Mr Power for attending flour mill'.[67] Information on occupations is noted, such as William Higgins in Douglas, Carrigaline, Co. Cork ('dispensary keeper to Dr Lane'),[68] and Joanna Farrell in Dromin, Co. Limerick ('milkwoman').[69]

The books paint a picture of economic conditions in the late 1840s that is stark, with evidence of poor living conditions, eviction and abandonment. Rossaghroe in Doneraile, Co. Cork is described in about 1851: 'This townland is all deserted. There are some miserable cabins still standing but they must soon tumble down.'[70] In Ballyseedy, Co. Kerry, the 'parties who held this have run away and left the land much in arrears'.[71] In Ballymacart, Co. Waterford, the book made in 1848, contains an entry for the house and garden of Mrs Feagan, widow, which is later crossed out with the comment: 'Sir Henry is to throw down Mrs Feagan's house immediately and annex her land to his plantation.'[72] Many references to emigration are found. In Coolbea, Inch, Co. Cork: 'Hodnett, the late occupier went to America about December 1847.' In the same book, a note by Roche described a situation in Ballycrenane, Cloyne where one of the partners in a lot held in common had died and his family had gone to America. His share had reverted to the

---

60 OL/6/278, p. 27.   61 OL/6/1, p. 7.   62 OL/6/464, p. 21.   63 Examples in OL/6/258 and OL/6/263.   64 OL/6/147, pp 10, 23. A 'sum' was the amount of pasture that will support one cow or a proportional number of other stock: *Oxford English dictionary* (compact edition, 1979).   65 OL/6/146, p. 26, Ballynaneening, Templebreedy, Co. Cork.   66 OL/6/145, p. 24, Kilmoney, Ballinaboy, Co. Cork.   67 OL/6/91, pp 1, 57.   68 Ibid., p. 18.   69 OL/6/365, p. 50.   70 OL/6/120, p. 120.   71 OL/6/280, p. 8.   72 OL/6/465, p. 87.

landlord, who took ejectment proceedings against the other partners because he wanted to let the land as one farm.[73] The book for St Mary's, Co. Westmeath illustrates the hardship faced. It describes how in Thatch Island East the hay was lost in 1853, as 'they could not get a boat in time to get it off when the floods came about 31 October'.[74] In the townland of Corralena, a tragedy is noted: an occupier, Catherine Killin 'is gone to America, her children sent her money. Awful deaths on the passage of about a dozen who went from this parish.'[75]

The consequences of hard times for landowners are also shown, with many estates giving the court of chancery as lessor, for example: 'This townland belongs to Robert Leslie esq. (late a minor). The lands are still let under the court of chancery, principally to William Sandes Senior esq., who sublets them again at rack rents',[76] or the book for Caherconlish and other parishes in Co. Limerick, where many holdings are under the court.[77] The book for Killinane, Co. Kerry (1850) describes an accommodation made with the landlords of the parish, including Maurice O'Connell, who 'gives receipts for the whole year's rent to each tenant who pays him half a year's rent. There are four gales of rent due to him in many cases in consequence of depression of the times.'[78]

The book for the parish of Monasteranenagh, Co. Limerick was made in 1848 and contains detailed observations. It illustrates the nature of changes that took place in ownership, emigration and loss of security of tenure for occupiers over a period of fourteen months. In mid-1848 the lessor of the townland of Ballymacscradeen, Mr Cantillon, had allowed temporary abatements of rent because of the difficult conditions. When the book was revised, fourteen months later in August 1849, the lessor of most of the townland was Colonel Vandaleur. Some of the occupiers listed in 1848 were noted as gone to America, the leases of the remaining tenants had been surrendered and all tenancies were now at will. In the other townland in this parish, Monaster South, the immediate lessors had not changed, and the tenancies remained as they were in 1848.[79] In Kildimo, another parish in Co. Limerick, the townland of Ballyrune was described in 1849: 'All the tenants in this townland were ejected on the 1 April 1849. There is no part of the land at present occupied. The court of chancery has given notice of letting it in one or two lots.'[80]

The valuators' notes in the tenure books encompass a wide range of matters that were taken into consideration in arriving at the eventual price, including who built the house, if the occupier held a tenement in another townland and if the tenant carried out improvements.[81] There is also a great

73 OL/6/139, pp 12, 92.   74 OL/6/1552, p. 355.   75 Ibid., p. 3.   76 OL/6/252, p. 1 Kilnaughtin, Co. Kerry.   77 OL/6/324, p. 129.   78 OL/6/261, reverse p. 1.   79 OL/6/468. 80 OL/6/384, p. 47.   81 OL/6/139, p. 2.

deal of information that was collected incidentally, including family relationships, where a tenant is described as 'mother to lessor',[82] or a complicated arrangement where one brother had possession and another paid the rent.[83] The miscellaneous information includes the property in Inistiogue, Co. Kilkenny that had £1 added to the value because of a moat in the garden,[84] the notes in some of the Co. Cork books on the use of shell, sand and seaweed as fertiliser,[85] and the fact that a tenant was the brother of another tenant and was now in the workhouse,[86] or that an occupier in Co. Limerick was 'now in bridewell for carrying off his own crop,' with a further note 'since gone'.[87]

The book for Kilcommon, Co. Mayo contains observations on the vegetation, farming and the situation of tenants. In Lenaregagh, there is evidence of hard times: 'The occupiers falling heavily into arrears, he ejected them this year, they still occupy the houses and have taken the tillage land as conacre.' Exceptionally, the surveyor also observed some successful farming in Bellagelly South in respect of John Swift, who 'has about 6 acres of tillage on this lot though paying only £8 yet I have observed 9 stacks of oats in his haggard which might be estimated to contain 18 barrels. I have learned that he sold £20 worth of butter and over 20 bullocks this year.'[88] The fishery in Stradbally, Co. Limerick was the subject of an unusual arrangement, where in the townland of River Shannon:

> Michael Shea is the only person that fishes that part of the river. He went to law with Sir Richard Deburgo about it as Sir Richard thought to prevent him of fishing, but Sir Richard lost the suit as his title was not perfect. Still Shea has no title only keeps it by *Club law*. He allows no person to fish it but himself.

A further note states: 'This is called commonage of water as no person can show a title to the fishery.'[89] The tenure books occasionally contain a general note on the parish, such as the long description of the parish of Drumreilly, Co. Leitrim in 1855, giving information on the soil, crops, turf, floods, fairs and markets, lack of roads and the market for butter.[90]

Conclusion

The tenure books are among the most accessible of the Valuation Office documents. They cover all tenements and collate the data from the other documents together in one place for the first time, starting in the late 1840s. They feature detail that is of value to the family and local historian, as well

---

82 OL/6/99, p. 22. 83 OL/6/466, p. 1. 84 OL/6/312, p. 3. 85 OL/6/146, p. 69 and OL/6/152, p. 1. 86 OL/6/365, p. 21. 87 Ibid., p. 42. 88 OL/6/432. 89 OL/6/325. 90 OL/6/955.

as material that is of broader interest, such as the data on rent and tenure of the occupiers, and the observations.[91] Some of the tenure books were made during the Famine or within a short period after it and describe a situation that was undergoing major change. The content of the books is similar to that of several other series, but much of the additional information is unique. Relationships between the data in the tenure books and that in the house books, field books and maps of the Tenement Valuation, and with the *Primary valuation*, can usually be established. The tenure books are particularly useful for places where house books have not survived, although they do not contain details of buildings.

The tenure books made in counties that had been valued in the Townland Valuation provide a useful update of earlier information, as they show the short-term changes and can help to narrow down dates. The books give a detailed picture of the economic and social situation in the country in the period immediately after the Great Famine.

H. OTHER SERIES

Certain small series of valuation documents are also of interest to the researcher, but these are random survivals and they relate to only some areas. Some of these series covered the entire country and the documents would have been numerous.

Registry books
Registry books, or registers of calculations, were made in both the Townland Valuation and the Tenement Valuation as part of the office work. They were used to reconcile (or 'assimilate') differences between the official square area of townlands and parishes as printed on the Ordnance Survey maps in statute acres, roods and perches, and the totals of the square area calculated from the field documents during the office work for each unit valued. Measurements taken from the map were known to be less precise than figures established by survey. The square area of each quality lot in the Townland Valuation and tenement in the Tenement Valuation was calculated, and the total figure for the townland needed to tally with Ordnance Survey figure. The figures were made to match by 'assimilation', where the difference was distributed proportionately to all the valuation lots in the townland.

The National Archives holds a small number of registry books from the two valuations. These documents were made for every parish in the country

---

91 See Vaughan, *Landlords and tenants in mid-Victorian Ireland*.

at the time and would have been very voluminous. The surviving samples show how the work was carried out and relate directly to the field books and the calculation books. In the early years the valuators were instructed to carry out the calculations immediately,[92] but the figures in the books show that this work was completed first in the registry books and then entered in the field books. No names are recorded in these books.

In the Townland Valuation, four volumes covering parts of counties Antrim, Londonderry, Kildare, Leitrim, Mayo, Meath and Monaghan were made between December 1830 and approximately 1843. These books have the neat appearance of fair copies, and do not contain rough calculations. The total figures for the townland were entered and the known difference between the figures was redistributed proportionately between the lots, which are listed out. The figures for the lots were then entered back into the original field books and the calculation books, and used to calculate the valuation. This operation was listed on the worksheets in the field books as 'Enter lots into field books' and was the first one carried out.[93]

The extant Tenement Valuation registry books cover some parishes in counties Kilkenny and Meath. In the Tenement Valuation, the square areas of both the entire tenement and each different subdivision by quality in the tenement were calculated. These documents give the Townland Valuation figures on the left and the tenement data on the right. Whatever the content figure for the townland, and regardless of the number of subdivisions or their locations, the total figures needed to match. The townland data was copied from the existing registry books, and the tenement data was obtained from the work done using the office maps. The assimilated figures were copied back into the original field books where they were used to carry out the money calculations of the valuation price both there and in the calculation books. The assimilation work was considered important and was almost always carried out by a senior valuator.[94] The information was written on pre-printed loose sheets that were later bound. Many of the books are undated, but the dates can be deduced from other work in the counties.

List books

The list books are volumes containing summary data for counties, with one or more volumes covering each county. List books were made in both the Townland Valuation and the Tenement Valuation. Only fifteen books survive, covering ten counties, but references in other documents show that they were made in every county. The books were made in a distinctive format, indicating that they were important documents. Most are hardbound

92 OL/1/2/2, §35. This requirement was omitted from the instructions issued in 1839.
93 See OL/8/21/1, Aglish, Co. Mayo, pp 1–2, and field book OL/4/6340, pp 20–3.   94 See Kilkenny books, OL/8/14.

with a marbled paper cover and a tooled leather label on the front. These books were used as a summary of the data on the county, to ensure completeness and to provide basic reference information. In some counties there is a diary of work day by day.

The book is arranged in baronies and parishes and the other information is recorded in columns printed across the double page, showing the townland, content (in statute acres), the field valuation, rent, year last let, proprietor, check valuation, land reduced, houses and total. The completeness of the entries in the books varies. In most cases a figure is given for the rent, but the 'year last let' column only rarely contains dates. The check valuation figures are completed for the most part but check valuations were made only for sample townlands. The figure in 'land reduced' is increased or decreased by a percentage, reflecting the allowance made for circumstances.[95] The list book of 1843 shows the parish of Ardoyne, barony of Forth, Co. Carlow (plate 15). It gives the acreage, the prices of the field valuation by Cuming and the check valuation by Purdon, information on rent and tenure and the name of the lessor. The figures in heavy ink on the right side of the 'proprietor' column are in Griffith's hand, proposing an increase of 6*d*.

Notes on the field books record the fact that the data from the field books was entered in the list book shortly after the completion of the field work, and the final figures were transcribed once the calculations were done. The names of the valuators are frequently recorded on the field valuation price, the check valuation (in abbreviated form) and where there is a diary of work. The latter is useful as a summary guide to the dates on which the work was carried out in each townland and parish, and shows the duration of the work in the county.

Tenement valuation rent books

Under the 1846 act, the valuation was based on the letting value and rent books were made in counties valued in whole or in part under this act.[96] There are 143 rent books. They contain abstracts of rent, provide high-level reference information about the relationship of rents to the valuation and were a check on the valuation arrived at in the field work.

The data relating to sample tenements in townlands and parishes was entered in columns, although not all of the books were printed and they vary slightly. The county, barony and parish are named and the tenement numbers are set out by townland: area, valuation of land, buildings and total, rents before and after 1846, tenure and year taken, check, observations, proprietor and lessor.[97] Some books contain only columns for lot, content,

95 OL/10/12, p. 20 (increase) and p. 78 (decrease). 96 Cos. Carlow, Cork, Dublin, Kerry, Kildare, Kilkenny, Limerick, Tipperary, Waterford, Wexford and Wicklow, as well as King's County and Queen's County. 97 OL/16/116.

valuation of land and houses, total, rents, and the name of the immediate lessor.[98] Not all lots in a townland were not included, but the tenement numbers given can be related to the numbers in the Tenement Valuation field books and tenure books. In most books the names of immediate lessors are noted, but a small number contain names of occupiers.[99] The page for part of the parish of Kilmeen, Co. Cork (plate 16) shows the acreage, the valuation, the rents before and after 1846 (not all completed) and the date of the lease. The names of the middlemen and head landlords are given.

The rent books were compiled from the data in other books when the work there was completed, and few books are dated. Most rent books cover baronies, but some towns are also included, and one book compares rents in towns in Cos. Cork, Tipperary, Kilkenny and Waterford.[1] Griffith showed a strong interest in the rent books, and many have notes and calculations in his hand.[2]

Tenement valuation query sheets

The query sheets are printed forms sent to occupiers of some buildings in Dublin and Belfast during the Tenement Valuation field work under the 1852 act seeking information under the headings: street and house number, names of occupiers and immediate lessors, yearly rent or lease rent, date of the take, fine paid (amount paid on taking up occupation) and taxes paid by the occupier or the landlord. There were also queries regarding other owners, agents, solicitors, representatives or trustees, and about the buildings. The query sheets concern only some houses in some streets. They are arranged in wards of the cities and in streets.

In all 2,022 forms were returned for Dublin, covering wards in the municipal area and dated 1853–4.[3] Many give information that was not requested. The local taxes paid are frequently given, and in one example the amount of ministers' money and parish cess paid in 1854 is listed.[4] Many entries explain how expenses were divided between occupier and landlord. The professions and trades of occupiers are noted: Richard B. Beechey of Baggot Street was a commander in the Royal Navy,[5] and Philip Brady of Cuffe Street was a dairyman with sheds and yards at Liberty Lane.[6] The cost of repairs made in 1843–4 to a house in Gloucester Street is given,[7] and the £150 fine paid on taking up tenancy in a house in Eccles Street is explained as including 'the gasfitting'.[8] On the form for the Whitworth Hospital, instructions were given to the valuation staff to discover the names of the ground landlords, who included Lord Palmerston, the ecclesiastical commissioners and the governors of the Royal Hospital, with the amounts paid to each.[9]

[98] OL/16/102. [99] OL/16/97, OL/16/103 and OL/16/116. [1] OL/16/51. [2] OL/16/103. [3] See OL/17. The printer's imprint shows that 5,000 forms were printed. [4] OL/17/1559. [5] OL/17/799. [6] OL/17/1203. [7] OL/17/2365. [8] OL/17/1543. [9] OL/17/

No valuation house books for Dublin city are extant, and the query sheets are the only manuscript documents from the field work of the Tenement Valuation. They cover a limited number of occupiers and lessors, but they contain some information and possibly some names that do not appear in the printed *Primary valuation* in 1854, as well as the signatures of respondents.

In Belfast, 791 forms were completed, mostly between March and August 1859. The *Primary valuation* was published in November 1860. They relate to a range of premises, from private homes to banks and businesses, and contain similar information to the Dublin forms. They vary from simple queries about names to firm instructions to staff to call at Mr Workman's in Bedford Street and to find out who was the owner of a school in Williams Place.[10] The Army Recruiting Depot at May Street explained that the premises were newly built by the government and had been occupied since 1859 on a lease for twenty years.[11] Their neighbours in May Street, the Trustees of the Music Hall, also completed a form.[12] Many of the replies include details of taxes paid,[13] for example the Revd William Bruce attached details of taxes paid on his premises on Antrim Road on a separate list.[14]

Other valuations
A small number of documents relate to valuations other than the main body of work. These include four notebooks of valuations of railways, canal, mines and collieries over the period 1855–76,[15] and some random documents relating to revisions.[16]

Re-valuation of Dublin, 1865
In 1865 a new valuation bill enabling re-valuation rather than piecemeal revisions was published.[17] In anticipation of the legislation, the re-valuation of Co. Dublin was carried out, but the bill was withdrawn and the re-valuation could not be given legal effect.[18] Copy field books of the re-valuation are extant for electoral divisions in the unions of Balrothery, Celbridge, North Dublin, South Dublin and Rathdown. The thirty-eight books were made between late 1865 and 1868. The units valued are electoral divisions and not parishes. The city of Dublin is not covered by these books.

The book is printed across two pages, with the county, barony, parish, townland and Ordnance Survey sheet reference number in the header. The columns give: reference to map, names of townlands, occupiers and immediate lessor, description, area, net annual value of land, buildings and total, rent and tenure, reputed area of tenement, building measurements in

2273. 10 OL/17/510. 11 OL/17/108. 12 OL/17/110. 13 OL/17/543 and OL/17/724. 14 OL/17/554/1 and /554/2. 15 See OL/15/1. 16 See OL/15/2. 17 *A bill to consolidate and amend the laws relating to the valuation of rateable property in Ireland* (3 May 1865), HC 1865 (135). 18 *Report from select committee on valuation, 1869*, questions 340–6.

yards and tabular value and details. The columns in these books are filled in conscientiously and comprehensively, noting tenements with numbers and giving lower-case italic letters to houses. The names of occupiers and lessors are filled in, and the descriptions are cursory in the manner of the *Primary valuation*. A small number of books have notes in the last column. Most books have an abstract on the last pages showing the new and old valuations and the difference in price for land and buildings for each townland.[19] In some books the old valuation is called 'Poor Law Valuation',[20] referring to the Tenement Valuation under the 1846 act made for the poor law.

These books are the only example of a systematic revision of an area after the completion of the tenement work. The routine revision work included only tenements in which changes had been made and did not concern itself with others, where re-valuation looked at all tenements at the same time. The previous work in Co. Dublin had been carried out in the mid-to-late 1840s under the 1846 act. The North and South Dublin unions were published under the 1852 act in 1854. The re-valuation books provide lists of names and valuations between ten and fifteen years later. While the books are neatly written in the manner of copies, the notes show that field work was carried out, and this was confirmed as part of the otherwise dubious justification of the illegal valuation given by Commissioner J.B. Greene at the 1869 select committee.[21]

In the initial valuation the data in these columns was in separate field books, house books and tenure books. This book appears to attempt to simplify field work and record-keeping by putting all of the data in the same book. Books with similar formats were used as tenure books in Co. Monaghan in the late 1850s.[22] These books contain good information for a period later than the *Primary valuation*.

1. ADMINISTRATIVE DOCUMENTS AND CORRESPONDENCE

Instructions
Seven sets of instructions were issued between 1830 and 1853. The instructions had a major effect on determining the content of the documents, and each is described in chapter 1 above. Reference to the instruction will assist in elucidating the details of the valuation documents.

---

19 OL/15/3/30.   **20** OL/15/3/21.   **21** *Report from select committee on valuation, 1869*, question 339.   **22** OL/6/1376.

Administrative documents

Apart from the correspondence, only very small fragments of administrative documents from the valuation are now extant, consisting of random items, some of which must have existed in much greater numbers. These documents are of interest both for their own content and for what they demonstrate about the organization and management of the work.

Two small books relate specifically to maps made and used in the early 1840s. The first records the copying of town plans in some counties in 1844–8. The second records the movement of documents to and from storage as the valuators used the documents in the field work in 1840–6. A third volume records the movement of books and maps for Co. Roscommon in the tenement work between 1854 and 1856.[23] An attempt was made, probably in the early 1850s, to create an office register for each county of documents in store. Some entries were made in the books for Cos. Antrim and Armagh, but the other books were not used.

Valuation letter books

The correspondence of the valuation was preserved in letter books for the years 1827–1911. In the early part of this period the general letter books consist of incoming letters and copies of outgoing letters, circulars and other correspondence. These documents were bound into books, probably quite soon after they were assembled. From 1860 registers were made in which incoming letters were recorded. From April 1861, damp press letter books came into use, in which copies of outgoing letters were made (incoming letters were not retained). From 1867 the letter books contain lists of dealings with government departments but are not indexed. From the mid-1850s some letter books by specific subject come into use, for example, poor law letter books for correspondence with boards of guardians and the poor law commissioners. There are also some books dealing specifically with buildings such as with Royal Irish Constabulary barracks.

The general letter books between 1827 and 1860 cover approximately the period of the initial valuation. The letters are roughly in date order, but some books overlap in date and in some cases there are gaps. The content of the letter books at this time is extremely varied. Not only were Griffith's other enterprises recorded here, such as the Boundary Survey and his involvement in road-building in Cork and Kerry, but there is also private correspondence about his house in Wales and management of his family's business interests. In the first few volumes these matters figure prominently, as do the constant disagreements with the Ordnance Survey and the deferential epistles written

---

23 OL/1/3/3. Many of the field maps of the Townland Valuation were reused in the tenement work in Co. Roscommon, see OL/11/25.

to the lord lieutenant, chief secretary and important persons in London. From 1830, as the field work was started, the correspondence became focused on the valuation, and while references to other matters are fewer, they are nevertheless present throughout. The early letters are an eclectic mixture of draft legislation and instructions, technical circulars, directions to staff, refusal to sanction increases in pay, intercession in office disputes, instructions about the organization and content of the work, along with a number of long memoranda of self-justification. Many of the letters are drafted or corrected in Griffith's hand, and his close involvement in every aspect of the work is clear, from matters of high policy outlined to the lord lieutenant to reproaches sent to individual members of staff. The letter books also contain copies of the progress reports made to grand juries and some financial data although summaries and figures were also published in returns made to parliament. The interest of these books as a source on staff is described above in chapter 2. In addition to the wealth of detail about every aspect of the valuation, the correspondence also demonstrates Griffith's ability to operate at the highest levels, and his machinations in achieving his objectives. The correspondence surrounding the display of his geological map and other items at the Universal Exhibition in Paris in 1855 is one example of his determination.[24]

A good deal of what is known about the early years of the valuation comes from the letter books, which as contemporary documents have more weight than the self-serving accounts given to the many parliamentary enquiries. This correspondence is fragmentary and while it is likely that many items preserved were selected, there may also be random survivals. The letter books are indexed but not comprehensively. After the mid-1860s, the countrywide valuation consisted only of revision and the work concerned matters such as railways, government property of all kinds including coastguard stations, police barracks and matters such as public-works loans, as well as correspondence with the public.

Conclusion

These series provide background or additional information in specific cases. The instructions are helpful in understanding the documents made in the field. The letter books are useful where relevant correspondence is extant.

---

24 OL/2/14, pp 253, 266, 280, 320. The exhibits comprised the geological map in large and small formats, valuation books and a map for Co. Carlow. A book of instructions, presumably *Instructions 1853*, was also included. Griffith intended to donate the documents to the Geological Society of France.

4

The maps of the valuation

'In winter time it is very hard to preserve maps in the field.'[1]

The National Archives holds approximately 12,000 maps and plans created by the initial valuation between 1833 and 1865. Cadastral surveys commonly created maps that corresponded to descriptions recorded in books, and the Spring Rice Committee referred to models where maps were an integral part of valuations aspiring to high standards.[2] The need for accurate maps was the original imperative behind the extension to Ireland of the mapping work of the Ordnance Survey and it was accepted that the valuation could not be carried out without maps. The lack of a national map was one of the main reasons why the valuation question had not been solved in the past.[3]

The valuation books and maps were created together in an interlinked system that recorded the information and allowed it to be managed and used. The maps represented graphically what was described in the books, fixed the location, made possible the determination of the square area, set out the different qualities of land and allowed the relationships between buildings and land and between holdings to be defined. The books noted who occupied and owned property, the nature of the land and who the neighbours were. The books are the essential key to the data in the maps, as the maps are necessary to understand the size, shape, location and surroundings of the land described in the books. Each without the other can provide only part of the picture.

Griffith acknowledged the central role of the maps when, writing about towns, he described how the maps are 'the assurance that no tenement has been omitted, and likewise are used as a point of reference by preventing mistakes'. The maps demonstrated the superiority of the work of his office over the Poor Law Valuation, where he claimed no maps were made.[4] It was the great good fortune of the valuation that the maps provided were of such excellent quality and accuracy, but it was also a challenge, as it set a high standard that the valuation part of the overall project was expected to match.

---

1 *Report from select committee on valuation, 1869*, question 3297, evidence of Commissioner J.B. Greene. 2 *Spring Rice Report*, pp 5–6. 3 Andrews, *A paper landscape*, pp 1–31 examines the background; see also J.H. Andrews, *Maps in those days: cartographic methods before 1850* (Dublin, 2009) for the movement towards national mapping in other countries at this period. 4 OL/2/13, p. 319.

The use of maps was assumed in all the background rules, beginning with the first section of the first Valuation Act.[5] The instructions include detailed directions on the map work, from what data was to be recorded to how this should be done, the colour of the ink and advice on how to look after the maps.[6] The manuscript books are full of references to the corresponding maps. From the early 1850s, a space for the map reference was printed in the tenure books, and these references were printed on each townland in the *Primary valuation*.

In the early 1830s, there were complaints about errors in the maps and the slow start of the field work was blamed on delays by the Ordnance Survey.[7] Until the printed maps became available, the valuation staff used tracings supplied by the Ordnance Survey from which the data was copied onto the printed maps at a later stage.[8] Despite Griffith's criticism in the early period, he later praised the high quality of the maps.[9] The maps were always considered to be important documents, and a great deal of effort was expended on their preservation in special storage in the office archives in Ely Place, Dublin. The valuation work created two main series of maps, the valuation maps and the valuation town plans.

A. VALUATION MAPS

The valuation of rural areas was carried out using the printed maps made by the Ordnance Survey at the scale of six inches to the mile or 1:10,560. The maps are printed in black and made by county, each of which is covered by a series of non-overlapping, rectangular sheets numbered in a uniform system, with a separate map index.[10] The number of sheets per county varies with the size of the county, with twenty-five for Louth and 153 for Cork. In addition to the basic topographical data, the maps showed the information needed for the valuation work, including houses, the names and boundaries of townlands, parishes and baronies and the number of statute acres in each townland and parish. The printed maps were used as the base maps on which the valuation boundary lines were marked out or 'plotted' and the lots were numbered to correspond to descriptions in the books. Particular houses recorded in the books were also marked on the lots or sketched in, if not printed.

5 7 Geo. IV, c. 62, sec. 1.   6 OL/1/2/4, §15–22; §289–91.   7 OL 2/2, p. 40; OL/2/1, p. 193.
8 OL 2/5, p. 63.   9 OL/2/3, pp 94, 120.   10 The Ordnance Survey 6-inch maps are printed on double-elephant (imperial-size) sheets measuring 1,016 mm x 673 mm or 40 inches x 27 inches. Index maps at various scales were published with each county on a sheet of the same size. See description in J.H. Andrews, *History in the ordnance map: an introduction for Irish readers* (2nd ed., Kerry, Wales, 1993), pp 18–20.

In the Townland Valuation, maps were used with the books in the field work to collect data on the boundaries of lots, the quality of the soil and some houses. This allowed the office work to be carried out. In the final stage, following appeals, the documents of record included a fair-copy field book and a fair-copy map. In practice, this worked well for the Townland Valuation, as it was relatively simple and revision was not envisaged. The Tenement Valuation was more complex, with a greater quantity of data and provision for revision. Also, once the tenement work was extended beyond the original six counties, the work took place in counties where the Townland Valuation was complete. In many counties the maps of the Townland Valuation were reused by the Tenement Valuation and it is now impossible to separate the maps of the two periods of work.

In 1870–83, one edition of the valuation maps was printed.[11] These maps showed tenements in orange on the printed six-inch base map and are a snapshot of the situation for that sheet at the date prepared. The maps do not correspond to the data in the printed *Primary valuation*, published 1847–64, unless no changes were made in the place during the interval of time between when the work was carried out and the book was published. These maps are available on askaboutireland.ie/griffith-valuation. Some of the manuscript maps from which the printing was carried out are held in the National Archives.

Each map was made for a specific purpose and contains unique information. When a final map became worn or overfilled, it was 'cancelled' or made non-current by copying the most recent layer of data onto a new base map and withdrawing the old map from use. In some cases the date of cancellation was noted, but not always. The use of coloured inks is important in identifying copies, as it was the practice to make copies in a different colour, for example, to copy in red ink maps originally drawn in black and vice versa.

Volume of maps and variation

The twenty-six counties of the Republic of Ireland are covered by 1,590 Ordnance Survey printed six-inch sheets. There are approximately 11,000 valuation maps because there are several copies of each sheet. The maps are now arranged in one series by county and by sheet number. Each sheet number comprises a set of all of the maps for that number, with an average of six or seven. The sets include field maps, office maps and fair-copy maps for the Townland Valuation and the Tenement Valuation. Within each set, the maps are arranged by barony and in the sequence in which they were made and used. The National Archives holds valuation maps for every county in the Republic of Ireland and five maps for Northern Ireland.

11 Andrews, *History in the ordnance map*, p. 56.

Multiple copies of each sheet were made because: (1) different kinds of maps were made (field maps, office maps and fair-copy maps, see below for details); (2) data for two valuations was recorded on the maps; and (3) the work was organized by barony. The field work in each barony was carried out by a separate team who had copies of all of the sheets covering their barony. They marked up the parishes in their barony on the map, with the result that only the data for one barony is shown on each sheet. This means that if, for example, three baronies are shown on one sheet, three separate valuators each made an original field map relating to their own barony only. This arrangement was also followed in work on the office maps. In the Townland Valuation there is only one copy of the last map, the fair-copy map. In the Tenement Valuation the last map, the fair-copy map, was drawn in poor law unions in every county, usually with each poor law union on a separate copy.

The example of sheet 100 of Galway illustrates how the maps were reused, how the sets were formed and how the reuse of existing maps affected the arrangement of the documents. The tenement work in Co. Galway made wide use of the existing Townland Valuation maps. Sheet 100 covers parts of two baronies, Clonmacnowen and Longford, the remaining parts of which are on, respectively, eight and twelve further sheets.[12] The poor law unions that extend over sheet 100 are Ballinasloe and Portumna. A single geographic area is covered by sheet 100, but the boundaries of the baronies are different from those of the poor law unions. In the Townland Valuation, five copies of sheet 100 were used: an original field map and an office map for each of the two baronies, and one fair-copy map that shows the two baronies together. There are eight Tenement Valuation maps: an original field map and an office map for each of the two baronies, and two fair-copy maps for each of the two poor law unions. In theory this means there should be thirteen copies of sheet 100, all with different data. However, instead of making two new field maps and two new office maps for the two baronies, the Tenement Valuation reused the Townland Valuation maps by overlaying the new tenement data on the existing townland data. The Tenement Valuation made four new fair-copy maps, two for each of the two poor law unions. This made nine maps in total. Re-using the maps created a saving of four maps.[13] Scaled up to the entire Co. Galway, this represented a not inconsiderable economy of at least 250 maps.

12 *Townland Index, 1901*, barony of Clonmacnowen, sheets 61, 73, 74, 86, 87, 88, 98, 99 and 100; barony of Longford, sheets 88, 98, 99, 100, 101, 106, 107, 108, 109, 117, 118, 126 and 127.
13 OL/11/11/782–90. The 9 maps are: (1) Townland Valuation fair-copy map (for baronies of Clonmacnowen and Longford); (2) barony of Clonmacnowen, Tenement Valuation original field map (drawn on Townland Valuation original field map) and (3) Tenement Valuation office map (drawn on Townland Valuation office map); (4) barony of Longford, Tenement Valuation original field map (drawn on Townland Valuation original field map) and (5) Tenement Valuation office map (drawn on Townland Valuation office map); (6) and (7) two copies of union of

The maps of the valuation 121

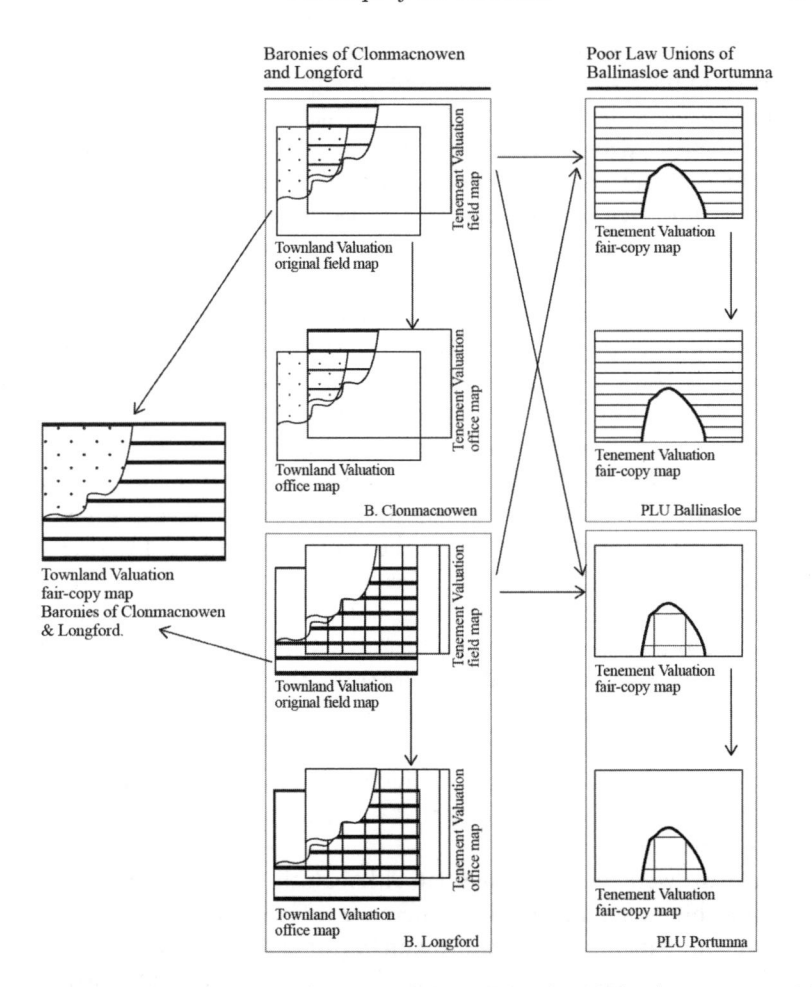

4.1 Diagram showing how sets of maps made in the Townland Valuation were reused in the Tenement Valuation.

The maps were made at the same time as the books to which they refer, but most do not bear a date and many were revised at later dates. The Ordnance Survey issue date is noted in the bottom right-hand corner but this shows only the date before which the work cannot have taken place. It is likely that most maps were used within a relatively short time after this date. For example, in Co. Westmeath the townland work took place in 1838–41 and the tenement work in 1852–4. The maps used in the townland work were issued by the Ordnance Survey in 1837–8 and those used in the tenement

Portumna, Tenement Valuation fair-copy map; (8) and (9) two copies of union of Ballinasloe, Tenement Valuation fair-copy map.

work in 1849–50. A map with an issue date in the late 1840s can only have been used in the tenement work, and this identifies the undated office maps as copies made in the late 1840s of the Townland Valuation maps originally made in the late 1830s. Further dates were written on the maps by the valuation staff and can represent any number of possibilities, including when work was completed or when data was copied to or from this map.

In some cases the maps are difficult to decipher because of the reuse of the Townland Valuation maps in the tenement work. They need to be read with care to ensure that the divisions and data from each period are correctly identified on the original field maps. The townland lines and writing are commonly in black ink and the tenement additions in red ink, but there are exceptions. This can be verified by comparing the boundaries of the quality lots on the fair-copy maps of the Townland Valuation with the reused map, and by comparing the boundaries on the fair-copy map of the Tenement Valuation with the same reused map to identify which line is which. The reuse of maps is noted in the lists in the National Archives. In general, the final maps (Townland Valuation fair-copy maps and Tenement Valuation fair-copy maps) are legible, as they were well drawn and were intended as the maps of record. The working maps can be challenging to read, but many contain pencil notes and detailed information that may not be on the fair-copy maps. In most counties a direct sequence of information from one map to the next can be established (for example, where the lots of the Townland Valuation are copied to a map on which the Tenement Valuation is then plotted), but in other counties there is no data that is common to the two periods of work.[14]

The maps were usually stored flat, although those used in the field work were probably rolled for carrying. There are six examples of field maps that were cut into small sections and mounted on cloth so that they could be folded to approximately A5 size. These maps were made in the early stages of the work in the 1830s, and the practice appears not to have continued.[15]

Maps of the Townland Valuation

The Townland Valuation created field maps, office maps and fair-copy maps. The latter was to be the permanent record of the soil of the entire country, and little alteration was expected. There is now no county in which all copies of the three maps of the Townland Valuation are extant, although there are examples in some sheet numbers.[16]

---

14 See Carlow, Donegal, Kilkenny and Monaghan. In Queen's County there is only one map with common data. 15 OL/11/1/1–4 (Co. Antrim); OL/11/4/385 (Co. Cavan) and OL/11/8/1 (Co. Down). 16 See National Archives lists for Cos. Clare, Galway, Kildare, Leitrim, Louth, Mayo and Meath.

Townland Valuation field maps
The valuator worked through each barony, parish by parish, a townland at a time. He marked his map in black ink, usually using broken lines to show the boundaries of lots, frequently circling the lot numbers. Some maps contain notes, including names of occupiers, prices, land, geology, crops, seaweed and 'lines of percentage'.[17] Houses likely to be over the £3 or £5 threshold were marked, although many were later crossed out as the calculations showed them to be exempt. The Townland Valuation field maps correspond to the original field books. In most counties, each barony is shown on a separate field map. The field map covering the townland of Crannagh, Kilmacdaugh, Co. Galway (plate 1) shows the lots divided by broken lines and numbered, and a house that was valued and then crossed out.

Townland Valuation office maps
An office map is one that was used in the office and not in the field. Some are labelled 'office sheet' or 'house sheet'.[18] The *Instructions 1830* set out the rules for how they were to be copied from the field map (using fine red lines and the same numbers) onto 'a second copy of the Ordnance map of the parish, which is never to be taken into the field'. The office maps were used to compute the content or square area of lots, using one of two methods: by triangles or by parallel lines drawn through the map at a distance of twenty perches.[19] The *Instructions 1833* further specified that these maps were to be 'preserved for the office'.[20] Almost all of the Townland Valuation office maps are ruled with printed parallel blue lines. The lines may have been printed in the office in Dublin.[21] In some cases the lines cover only the area of the map where work was taking place, suggesting that they were ruled as required. In theory, the office maps contain the same information as the field maps from which they were copied but houses are not noted. Some show lines of percentage around towns, and many contain names or notes. The Townland Valuation field books also correspond to the office maps. Each barony is shown on a separate office map.

In most counties, these maps were reused in the tenement work, but a few examples of the unaltered originals survive.[22] In some counties there are no office maps extant, although they must have existed originally.[23] With the exception of three maps in Mayo, the work on the office maps everywhere is

17 Concentric lines marked around towns showing the percentage increase due to proximity. 18 OL/11/21/101 and OL/11/21/600. 19 OL/1/2/1, §47. 20 OL/1/2/2, §290. 21 I am grateful to Zoë Reid, senior conservator at the National Archives, for drawing my attention to the stationery ruling machine in the National Print Museum, Beggars' Bush, Dublin 4. 22 See Clare, Kildare, Leitrim, Louth, Mayo, Meath, Roscommon, Westmeath and Wicklow where 7 or fewer examples exist. 23 See Carlow, Cavan, Donegal, Kilkenny, King's County, Longford, Monaghan and Queen's County.

undated, but the Ordnance Survey issue dates show them to be contemporaneous with the field maps.[24]

Townland Valuation fair-copy map

The Townland Valuation fair-copy map was drawn as the map of record once the appeals were complete. All baronies are drawn together and the maps are filled to the edges. The maps show quality lots. Houses that the office calculations put over the £5 threshold are numbered, but are infrequent. The maps were finely drawn by draftsmen in the office in Dublin with attention to detail and clarity. In most counties, the numbers and boundary lines are in red ink and parish boundaries are shaded in purple. Few of these maps were subsequently altered.[25] The Townland Valuation fair-copy maps correspond to the fair-copy field books.

There are no Townland Valuation fair-copy maps extant in Cos. Carlow, Clare, Roscommon, Sligo, Westmeath and Wicklow. The reason for this is not known. From 1834, as each barony was completed, copies of the maps and books were made available in the office of the county treasurer and at the Townland Valuation appeal hearings, and this obligation was removed only in 1852.[26] The National Archives holds an additional copy of the fair-copy maps, signed by Griffith, for counties Cavan and Longford. This may be a copy made for the county treasurer in accordance with the 1836 act and it is authenticated by the commissioner.[27]

Maps of the Tenement Valuation

The Tenement Valuation started in 1844 and was legislated for in 1846 and 1852. The amount of data now collected was much greater than before, as there were more tenements than quality lots. Each tenement was broken into subdivisions by quality, and every house was recorded. The meticulous attention required in calculating the content and value of every tenement, however small, was described by Griffith in March 1848: 'The detail of the office work is enormous and liability to error in such a multitude of calculations so great that it is necessary to have each item calculated a second time by a different hand.'[28]

From this time every individual tenement, from gardens to large farms and vast areas of mountains, was recorded on the map, showing its location, size and shape, as well as every dwelling house, outhouse and other building. Using the corresponding book, it is possible to identify on the map the location and boundaries of farms, the quality of each subdivision of the land

---

24 OL/11/21/571, OL/11/21/797 and OL/11/21/831.   25 OL/11/21/835 and OL/11/21/850: these maps were marked up with tenements.   26 4 & 5 Will. IV, c. 55, sec. 7 and sec. 9. This was confirmed in sec. 35 of the 1836 act.   27 6 & 7 Will. IV, c. 84, sec. 15. See lists in OL/11 in National Archives.   28 OL/2/12, p. 21.

and its position, and the houses inhabited by specific individuals. These maps have an immediacy because the houses were noted and the boundaries were drawn as they were seen on the ground by the valuation staff.

In the Tenement Valuation, the same information was collected on all tenements throughout the country and the outcome of the work was the same, but the manner in which the documents were used varied. There are broadly two categories of maps. The first was made in counties valued for the first time where the work was done from the beginning. The second was made in counties that had been valued under the Townland Valuation and where some data had already been collected on maps.

Maps of the Tenement Valuation in counties valued for the first time
Counties valued for the first time under the Tenement Valuation were Cork, Dublin, Kerry, Limerick, Tipperary and Waterford. The work created field maps, office maps and fair-copy maps and was carried out by a valuator and a surveyor working together. Some maps relating to appeals are extant for Co. Tipperary only.

TENEMENT VALUATION FIELD MAPS
The field maps are also called 'perambulation maps', as the boundaries of tenements were perambulated, or walked around, before being recorded. In this period, two copies of each map were created in the field work, one made by the surveyor and one by the valuator for each sheet of the barony concerned. The surveyor's duty was to mark every tenement over one acre on his map and to carry out chain surveys of tenements under five acres in extent. He also collected the names of occupiers in the tenure book or field book and measured houses and buildings in a house book. Houses were usually given temporary numbers on the map, later changed to letters. An office circular in late 1846 explained that the surveyor should 'first perambulate a townland – that is make all the boundaries of the tenements – then begin his numbers, at the north or top of the townlands, continuing downwards from left to right and then from right back to left again'.[29] The numbers on houses were to be written so as to distinguish them from the numbers of land. Some maps were extensively renumbered. The surveyor's documents were given to the valuator on completion.[30]

The valuator valued the land and the houses. He used a new copy of the surveyor's map and the surveyor's field book or a copy. In some cases the same tenement numbers were used and in others new numbers were given. The valuator marked (usually with broken lines) the different qualities of land on the map, which already showed the tenement boundaries with solid

29 OL/2/11, pp 51–3. 30 OL/1/2/6, §5.

lines. This showed the subdivisions by quality. In the field book he described the subdivisions separately, as each was valued at a different rate. At first, various notations were used, including numbers and italicized letters, and from 1853 a system using index numbers added to the tenement number became standard – for example, 5^1, 5^2 and 5^3 for three different qualities in lot 5.[31] Many of the original numbers were rewritten with index numbers at later dates. Following the work in the field, the data on the two maps was reconciled, the maps were cross-corrected and the numbers were made to agree. Many of the field maps are worn, and the data is crowded and corrected multiple times. The Tenement Valuation original field maps relate to the Tenement Valuation field books, house books and tenure books.

TENEMENT VALUATION OFFICE MAPS

The office work for the Tenement Valuation was similar to that for the Townland Valuation, but more extensive. Office maps from this period remain only for Co. Tipperary, and there are two examples for Co. Cork. The data on the office maps was copied from the field maps. Some of the office maps are ruled with lines, but most are not. The content of each tenement and each subdivision by quality was calculated. The system of index numbers for subdivisions was also used on the office maps. Some of these maps were renumbered and some contain notes or names. Houses were not normally marked on the office maps. These maps correspond to the Tenement Valuation field books and tenure books.

TENEMENT VALUATION FAIR-COPY MAPS

The Tenement Valuation fair-copy maps were the final drawing of the tenements that had been valued. There are frequently two successive copies of this map, and the first one usually corresponds to the *Primary valuation*. These maps are drawn in poor law unions. The tenements are numbered within townlands, and where there is more than one house in a tenement, it is noted with a lower-case italic letter, although this was not always applied. Where tenements held by a single individual are in separate parcels of land, they are noted with capital letters (for example, 1A, 1B and so on). In practice, many of these maps were revised at later dates. Some of the second fair-copy maps were drawn in preparation for the printing of 1870–83, and some may correspond to the cancelled books held in the Valuation Office.

Maps of the Tenement Valuation in counties previously valued

A number of different methods were used in the tenement work in counties previously valued by the Townland Valuation. In some, existing maps were

31 OL/1/2/7, §27.

reused and in others new maps were made. See appendix F, table of main map types.

From 1848 the Tenement Valuation was extended to other counties where, in every case, Townland Valuation maps had already been made. Despite claims by Griffith and others at the 1869 select committee that the valuators in the Tenement Valuation were not allowed to see the Townland Valuation work,[32] the practice of re-using maps was widespread and was confirmed by Henry Duffy, who described how the 'maps were given to the tenement surveyors, to save the expense of a new set, and they marked the boundaries on them. Then the same maps were given to the valuators.'[33] In other counties, little use was made of the Townland Valuation, except for reference.[34] Original field maps, office maps and fair-copy maps were made as part of this work.

Although the information now required was more detailed, the original work on the value of agricultural land could be reused. In sixteen counties, at least some of the Townland Valuation field maps and office maps were reused in the tenement work.[35] The tenement information and the townland information were plotted together on the same map, but they were in different-coloured inks and can usually be distinguished. The extent of reuse varied from one county to another, and in some counties a combination of methods was used. Some field maps and office maps contain additional information, including names, field prices, notes on land, farming and geology.

TENEMENT VALUATION FIELD MAPS

The work was carried out by the surveyor and valuator as before, but this time their work created one field map only. New field books were not made in these counties. Tenements were noted in the tenure books and additional houses in house books. In general, the field maps correspond to the tenure books. Three different methods of making the field map were used:

> (1) Reused Townland Valuation maps: The surveyor took the original field map of the Townland Valuation, on which the quality lots were already shown, into the field and marked on it the boundaries of the tenements, thereby creating the subdivisions by quality. He noted information in the books and numbered the entries to correspond to the map. He also marked the houses on the map with numbers or letters and sketched in houses that were not printed. The same map was then given to the valuator, who went

[32] *Report from select committee on valuation, 1869*, questions 1518–26. [33] Ibid., questions 2027, 1990–7. [34] Ibid., question 1998. [35] Cos. Cavan, Clare, Galway, Kildare, Leitrim, Longford, Louth, Mayo, Meath, Roscommon, Sligo, Westmeath, Wexford and Wicklow, as well as King's County and Queen's County.

over the land and valued the additional houses and checked the information on the subdivided tenements. The tenement data was usually written in red ink and overlaid on the black-ink markings of the townland work. In some counties a great deal of data was overlaid, corrected and renumbered (see plate 1).

(2) Copied Townland Valuation maps: The quality lots from the Townland Valuation field map were copied onto a new Ordnance Survey base map. This was used in the field by the surveyor to carry out the work, after which the map was passed to the valuator, as described above. These maps are undated, but the Ordnance Survey issue dates show that they were made at the time of the tenement work.

(3) New printed maps: In this arrangement new field maps were made using a new Ordnance Survey base map. The work was as described above, with the surveyor plotting the tenements directly onto the map before passing it to the valuator. Only the tenement boundaries are shown on these maps and not the subdivisions by quality.

TENEMENT VALUATION OFFICE MAPS

In the majority of cases, the existing office maps of the Townland Valuation were reused in the office work of the Tenement Valuation. Out of a possible total of nearly 1,600, only sixty-nine now exist in their original state without Tenement Valuation data.[36] Here the tenement boundaries from the field work were drawn over the existing quality lots, creating the subdivisions by quality in each tenement. The Townland Valuation office maps were already ruled with lines. Houses were not usually noted on office maps. In cases where the Townland Valuation maps were not reused, new office maps were made by copying the townland map and superimposing the tenement boundaries. Some of the copy office maps made by the Tenement Valuation are ruled and some are not.

Further variants of the office maps were also made, including maps in Co. Donegal that contain the tenement boundaries only and not the subdivision by quality, and the arrangement in Mayo where the office map contains the tenement boundaries only and the subdivision by quality is shown on a separate map. In some counties, such as Monaghan, a direct connection

---

36 These maps were made for 20 counties now in the Republic of Ireland. These counties are covered by 807 printed Ordnance Survey sheets. The estimate is based on 2 copies of each sheet and is low.

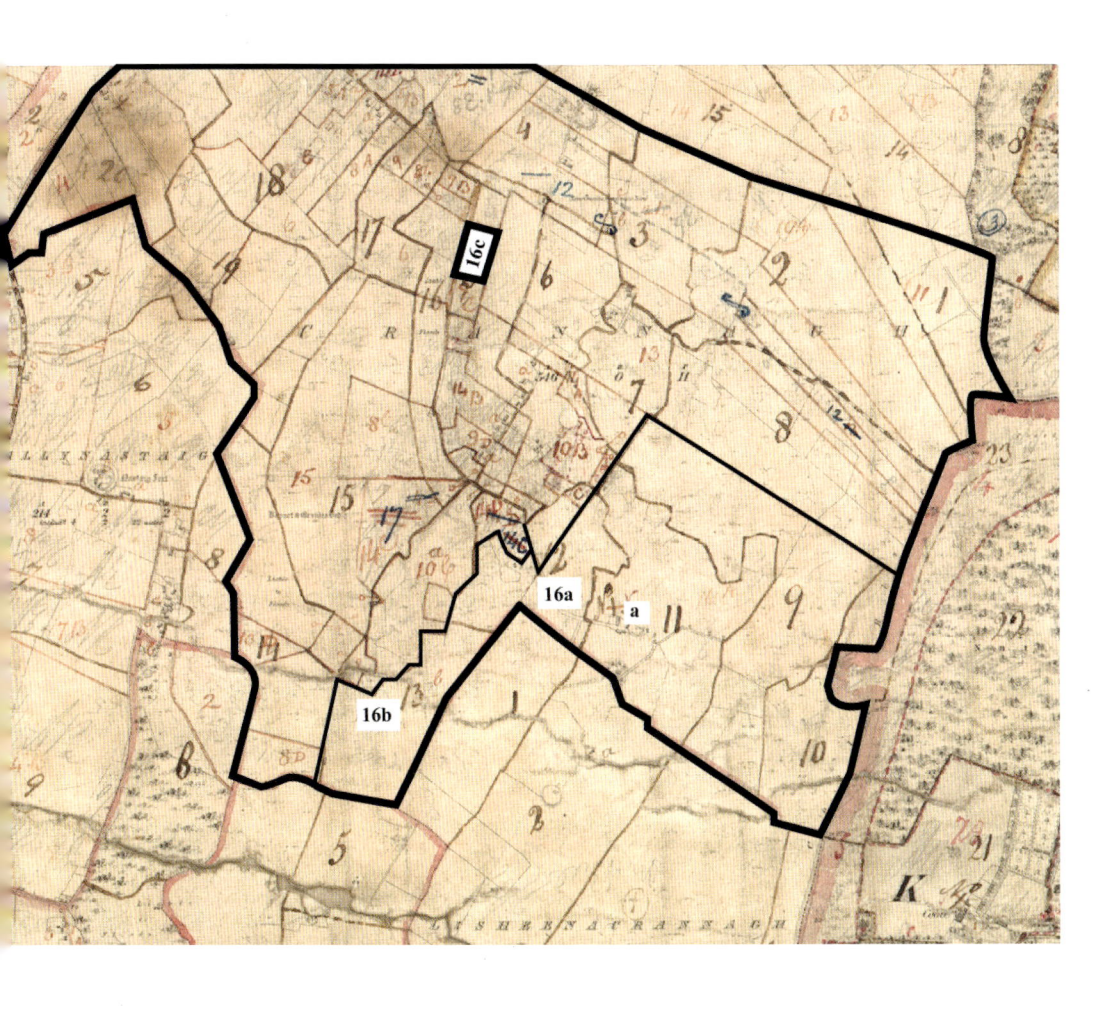

1   Tenement Valuation original field map (drawn on Townland Valuation original field map), Co. Galway, sheet 122, townland of Crannagh, parish of Kilmacduagh, OL/11/11/958 [1842].

Townland of Crannagh

No. of Lot.	Description of Lots.	Quantity A. R. P.	Value per Statute Acre, with slate, lime, sand manure, etc. in an ordinary situation.	Amount of Land. £ s. d.	Amount of Houses and other profitable buildings thereon. £ s. d.
5	Bog & arable, chiefly arable	102 1 16	8	45 18 1	26 7 10
	Clay slate, dry, soils mostly deep, friable, stony and mostly stiff Nº Mellow				
	Ill-managed				
	Also waste at houses	21 1 08	1 2 0 0	6 9 0	1 0
6	Dry stony clay soils on grey gravel— also, rocky arable and gatey & moist pasture. Also waste at houses	22 2 36	7 0 0 10 0 0	15 19 3 0 0 0	11 7 4
		4 0 0 1 0 0	7 0 6 0 6 0	2 1 6 0 0 0	1 6 0
7	Rocky pasture, but Potatoes but less tillage. Also rocky & waste. Also waste at houses	9 3 25 1 0 0	0 12 10 6 0 4 3	0 9 11 0 8 0	4 4 4 3
8	Rocky pasture, but some Grass and lees rotted— and a little Mellow arable. Also rocky Mellow arable. Also waste of river	30 1 25 4 0 0 1 2 0 0	6 9 9 7 0 0 0 0	9 17 7 2 8 0 0 0 0	5 14 0 1 8 0
	Carried forward	196 3 30		96 13 4	55 13 4

Townland of Crannagh

No. of Lot.	Description of Lots.	Quantity A. R. P.	Value per Statute Acre, with slate, lime, sand manure, etc. in an ordinary situation.	Amount of Land. £ s. d.	Amount of Houses and other profitable buildings thereon. £ s. d.
	Brought forward	196 3 30		96 13 4	55 13 4
9	Rocky pasture, mostly dwarf gorse, little tilled. Also, waste, river soils	35 1 18 1 0 0	7 0 0 3 6 0	13 5 2 0 6 0	7 15 0 3
10	Natural Meadow. Spontaneous heavy grass, but little tilled. Also waste of river	15 3 02 1 0 10 0 0	20 0 10 0 0	16 11 0 0 0 0	9 9 1
11	Dry stony clay soils on thin gravel. Also rocky pasture. Also waste at houses	28 2 10 1 2 0 3 0 1	0 16 0 0 3 0 0 3 0	24 6 14 0 7 6 0 14 0	5 7
12	Rocky pasture, Bushy but Landlord's part of Franie and overhold. Franie and overhold. Also, thin & arable	17 3 04 1 0 0	2 16 0 12 0	2 4 5 0 12 6	1 6 8 0 7 0
13	Stony clay & arable. Chiefly soil and Mellow. Also, rocky pasture	26 2 01 4 2 0	12 7 3 0 2 6 1 6	16 11 3 0 1 3	9 12 2 0 6 9
	Carried forward	330 . 0 35		£171 2 5	98 1 6

2 Townland Valuation original field book, townland of Crannagh, parish of Kilmacduagh, Co. Galway, OL/4/5485, p. 9 (1842).

Houses in Townland of Curragh

No.	Name and Description	Quality Letter	Length	Breadth	Height	Number of Measures	Rate per Measure	Amount £ s d
1st x	James Carr Esq							
	Dwelling	1+	28	20.0	12.0	52	6¾	2.6
	Outhouse		2.d	25.06	27.0	40	3¾	10.7
	Cowhouse		1.st	8.76	08.06	14	3	11
	Cowhouse		1.st	18.2.69	07	32	3½	11
	Barn		2d	30.0	7.0	7½	3½	1.2
					Rotation	Coffey	5.1.7	
							4.2.3	
2	Michael Carr Esq £2							
	Dwelling		1st	30.0	19.0	7.6	72	0.2	3
	Barn		2d	25.0	17.0	7.0	43	4½	16.5
	Fields		2.d	35.0	16.0	6.0	56	3½	17.0
						Rotation	4.0	
						Coffey	2.11	

Houses in Townland of Kilmacow

No.	Name and Description	Quality Letter	Length	Breadth	Height	Number of Measures	Rate per Measure	Amount £ s d
1st x	Patrick Farly	£2						
	Dwelling		2.d+	36.0	23.0	10.0	52	10¾	3.13.5
	Barn		2.d+	22.0	9.6	7.0	42	4	14/o
	Fields		2.d+	33.0	16.0	6.0	30	4½	11/0
						Rotation	5.5.1	
						Coffey	3.1.1	

No.	Name and Description.	Quality Letter.	Length.	Breadth.	Height.	Number of Measures.	Rate per Measure.	Amount £ s. d.	Name and Description.	Quality Letter.	Length.	Breadth.	Height.	Number of Measures.	Rate per Measure.	Amount £ s. d.

Houses in Townland of **Crannagh** | Houses in Townland of **Ballynultagh & Rockpark**

9 Ba	John Faly No roof							15 1 0 0	Martin Carr No roof							2 0 0 1 0 0
10 Ba	Patk Diviny No roof							20 1 0 0	Patk Quinn No roof							20 1 0 0
12 Ba	John Linnane No roof							10 0 15	Bridget Regan No roof							20 1 0 0
14 Ba	John McLoughlin House							5 12								
16 Ba	James Ryan No roofs							40 2 0 0	**Rockpark** Martin Lally House							15 0 7
									Michl Lally House							15 0 7

10th & 12th Decr 53
Thos. Holt
Surveyor

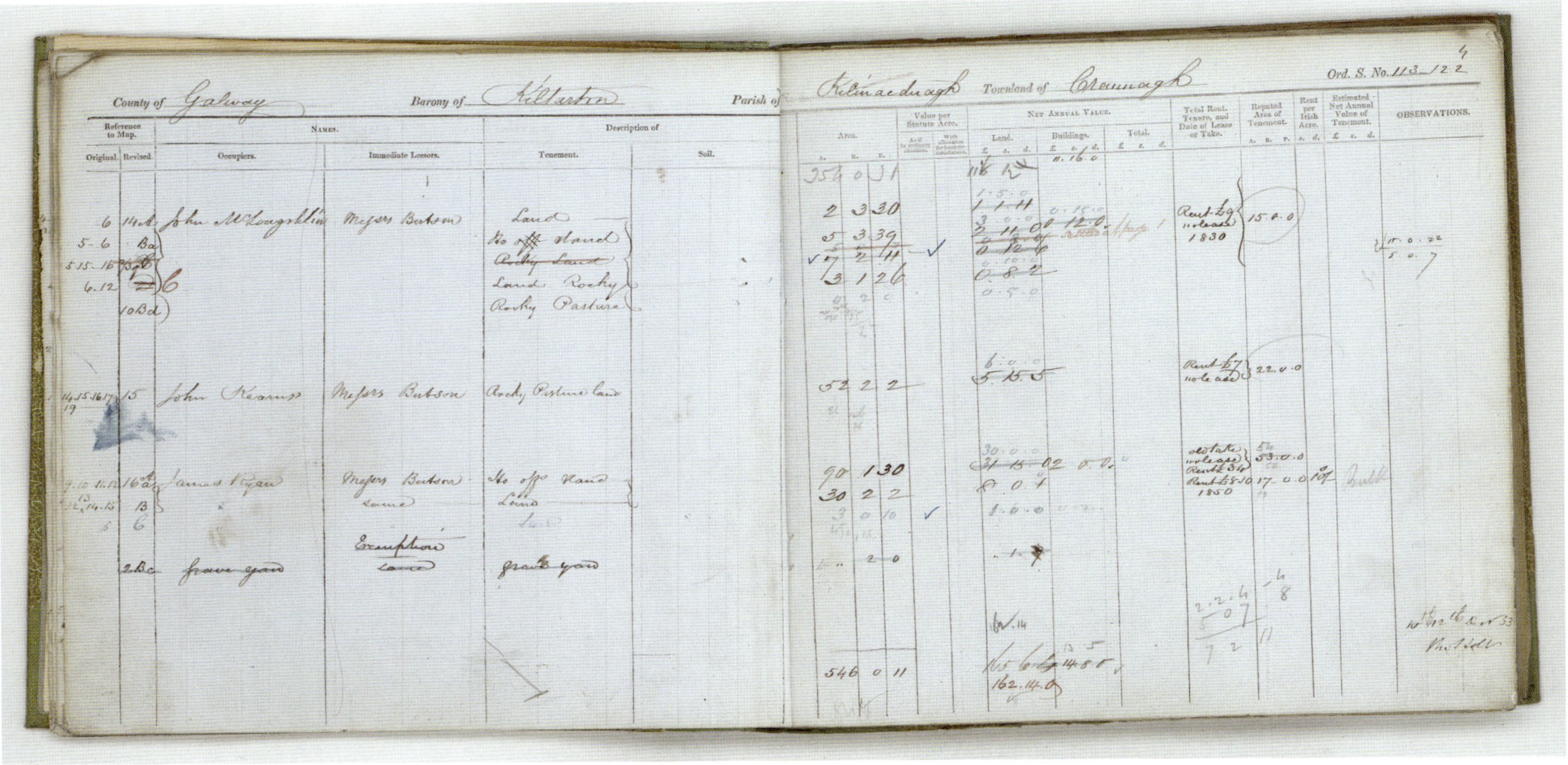

5 Tenement Valuation tenure book, townland of Crannagh, parish of Kilmacduagh, Co. Galway, OL/6/796, p. 4 (1853).

6   Valuation town plan, Ballina, Co. Mayo, OL/12/21/8 [1841].

Houses in Town of Ballina

Townland of Ballina

No.	Name and description	Length	Breadth	Height	Quality Letter	Number of Measures	Rate per Measure	Amount of House	Gross Amount	Valuator's Estimate	Yearly Rent	Value of Garden	Lease Rent	OBSERVATIONS
5	11 Patrick Loftus Esqr — Justice house and shop	12.6 10.6	8.0	9.0	1b	31	2.4	3	11		10.0.0				is small just to happy but things too late altogether Rooms inconvenient
	House & Store	12.6 10.6	8.0	9.0		41	11		10	1					
	Private Apartment	17.0 12.0	17			40									Stores New one life upwards 60 yrs
	Garden 60ft														
														None £7	
12	Steven Loftus Esqr Grocer House and shop	21.0 31.0	27.0	10b		28	2.02	7	12	7	45.0.0				Small garden house rather slight inferior. One extra as good. Rent Hall unfurnished — lately erected
	Do to John Kelly	16.0 20.0	9.7			31	2.0	3	2	0					From £60 to £70. A Grocer House
	Shop Shed	10.0 8.6	13			18	1.24	1	1	23					Do Do Ground Stored & Lights
	Open	5.6 12.0	10			13	6		2	6					
									11	10				None £14	
13	James Bryan (Publican) House & Shop	15.0 22.0	25	1 Cr		33	16	2	7	6	10.11.0				Lease of Ease bought the freerent too much lower than supposed rate
	reparation in back	15.3 6.0	21	1 Cr		20	14	1	6	8					his Cap & Corner Lane profitable
	Allen Store	15.0 12.6	4.0	1 Cr		20	17	2	11	3					Rent £14
									19	1					

TOWN OF Ballina

Townland of Ballina

Bridge STREET.

Bought [prices]

No.	NAME OF OCCUPIER AND DESCRIPTION OF TENEMENT.	Relative Value by Tables.	Rent by the Year.	Rent by Lease.	OBSERVATIONS.	Estimated Value	Relative Value, multiplied by	Relative Value with Percentages.	Value finally settled.	Value, deducting one-third.
1	Michael Smith, house	130—2—6	22—0—0	17—12—0				16—2—0		
2	John Avery, house	130—2—0—0	15—0—0	14—8—0	Small shop	15—0—0	5/4	13—0—0		
3	Robert Gordon, house	104—2—0—0	14—0—0	13—4—0	Small shop					
4	James Walsh, house	104—1—17—0	15—0—0	12—0—0	Small shop	10—10—0	6—0	11—2—0		
5	Thomas Owen, house	104—0—3—0	14—0—0	8—0—0	Small shop	18—0—0	3—0 2—0			
6	Denis Walsh, house and yard	104—5—0—0	19—0—0		Small shop	18—0—0	3—0	17—17—0		
7	James Ward, house Office and yard	204—1—15—0	12—0—0	9—12—0	Small shop	10—0—0	3—0	9—1—0		
8	George Logy, house and yard	104—2—12—0	15—0—0	12—15—0	Small shop	12—0—0				
9	William Walton, house	204—1—4—0	10—0—0	8—0—0	Small shop	7—10—0	6—0	7—4—0		
10	Patrick Gray, house	204—1—1—0	12—0—0	8—0—0	Small shop	7—10—0	6—0	6—6—0		
11	James Culye, house Office and yard	104—3—9—0		17—0—0		18—0—0	3—0 2—0			
12	Steven Lyster, house Office and yard	104—7—10—0 104—3—17		30—0—0		457—0—0				
13	James Stephens, house	104—2—14—0	20—0—0	16—0—0	Public house	16—16—0	3—0	12—12—0		
14	William Jordan, house Office and yard	104		16—0—0		15—0—0	3—0	14—18—0		

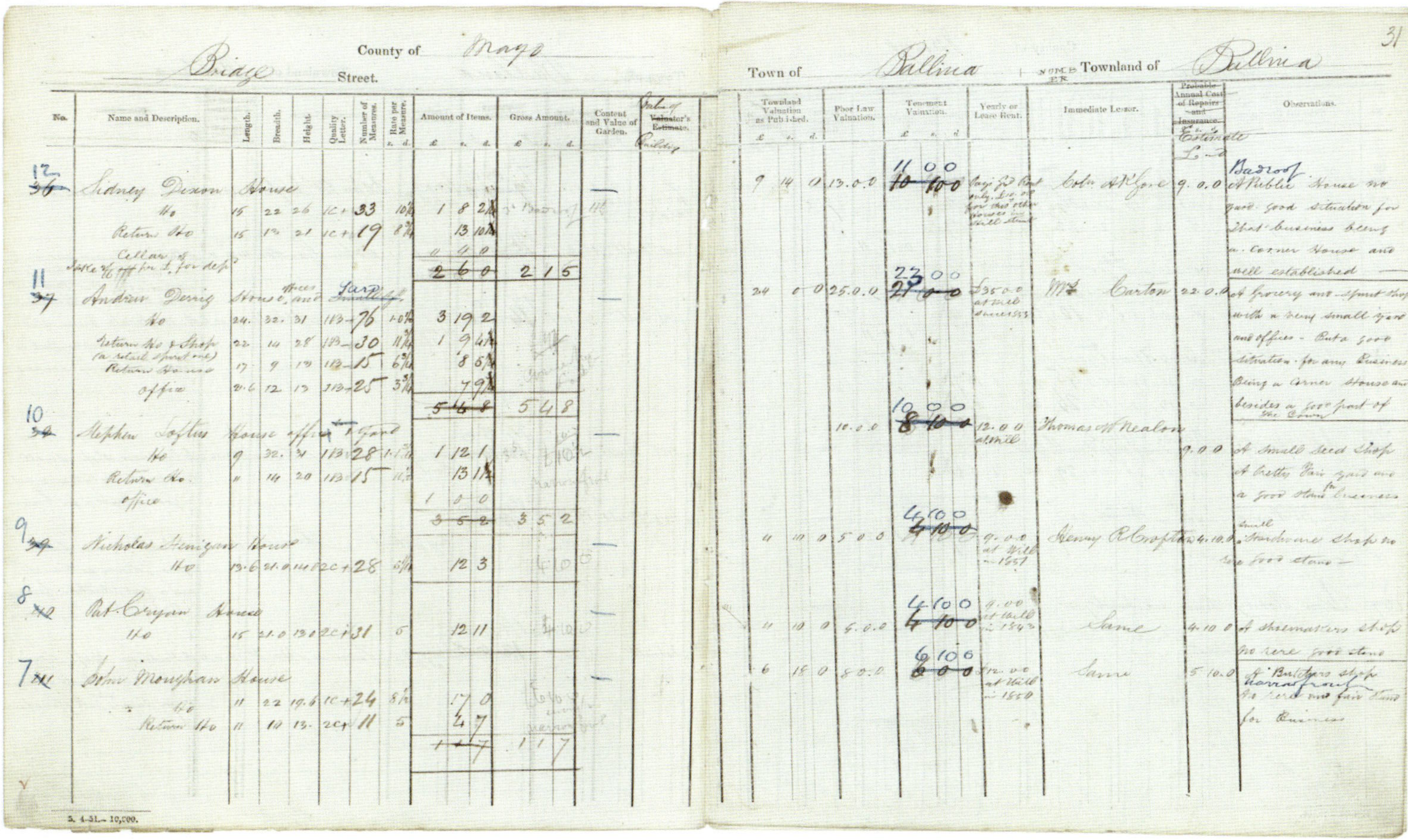

9 Tenement Valuation house book, Ballina (town), Co. Mayo, OL/4/3115, p. 31 (1854).

10 Townland Valuation appeal book, barony of Castlerahan, Co. Cavan, OL/13/9 (1840).

BARONY OF CASTLERAHAN, (Continued.)

TOWNLANDS AND PARISHES.	Quantity.	Annual Value of Land.	Annual Value of Houses deducting one-third.	TOTAL.
	A. R. P.	£ s. d.	£ s. d.	£ s. d.
MUNTERCONNAGHT.				
Baliaghdorragh,	325 2 37	186 19 3	10 19 0	197 18 3
Behernagh,	771 1 36	358 2 10	18 6 0	376 8 10
Carrick,	557 0 11	271 19 1	4 5 0	276 4 1
Corronagh,	369 0 6	173 4 5	8 8 0	181 12 5
Croughan,	442 1 6	226 8 2	14 7 0	240 15 2
Crossafehin,	218 2 32	134 4 6	9 15 0	143 19 6
Eighter,	718 2 31	432 11 2	36 5 0	468 16 2
Island,	369 1 25	220 17 3	12 7 0	233 4 3
Islands in Lough Ramor,				
Beherna Island,	0 1 20	0 0 0	0 0 0	0 0 0
Cock Island,	0 2 20	0 0 0	0 0 0	0 0 0
Corlea Island, North	0 2 23	0 0 0	0 0 0	0 0 0
Corlea Island, South	0 1 11	0 0 0	0 0 0	0 0 0
Corronagh Islands, No. 1,	0 1 23	0 0 0	0 0 0	0 0 0
No. 2,	0 0 29	0 0 0	0 0 0	0 0 0
No. 3,	0 3 28	0 0 0	0 0 0	0 0 0
No. 4,	0 0 21	0 0 0	0 0 0	0 0 0
Corronagh Sand Bank,	0 0 11	0 0 0	0 0 0	0 0 0
Cow Island,	0 2 14	0 0 0	0 0 0	0 0 0
Crane Island,	0 1 37	0 0 0	0 0 0	0 0 0
Crossafehin Islands No. 1,	0 3 13	0 0 0	0 0 0	0 0 0
No. 2,	0 0 35	0 0 0	0 0 0	0 0 0
Fort Frederick Island,	0 0 11	0 0 0	0 0 0	0 0 0
Garret's Island,	0 0 24	0 0 0	0 0 0	0 0 0
Illanakirka Island,	0 0 37	0 0 0	0 0 0	0 0 0
Knockatemple Island,	0 2 9	0 0 0	0 0 0	0 0 0
Knocknagartan, North	0 0 31	0 0 0	0 0 0	0 0 0
Knocknagartan, South	0 0 13	0 0 0	0 0 0	0 0 0
Mare's Island,	0 0 36	0 0 0	0 0 0	0 0 0
Porter's Islands, No. 1,	0 1 10	0 0 0	0 0 0	0 0 0
No. 2,	0 2 20	0 0 0	0 0 0	0 0 0
Ryefield Island,	0 1 30	0 0 0	0 0 0	0 0 0
Ryefield Sand Bank,	0 0 9	0 0 0	0 0 0	0 0 0
Ryefield Stony Island,	0 0 22	0 0 0	0 0 0	0 0 0
Scrabby Island,	0 0 37	0 0 0	0 0 0	0 0 0
Sloe Island,	0 2 18	0 0 0	0 0 0	0 0 0
Stony Island,	0 0 25	0 0 0	0 0 0	0 0 0
Knockarnbeen,	316 2 37	152 8 10	0 0 0	152 8 10
Knockatemple,	495 2 29	257 7 8	4 10 0	261 17 8
Knocknagartan,	251 3 10	127 14 0	0 0 0	127 14 0
Knocknaveagh,	422 3 31	240 0 11	4 15 0	244 15 11
Lerganboy,	272 2 8	129 15 0	0 0 0	129 15 0
Ryefield,	923 0 1	315 7 3	43 7 0	358 14 3
Total,	6465 0 6	3418 0 4	167 4 0	3585 4 4
EXEMPTIONS.				
Knockatemple, Church and yard,	0 3 0	0 8 5	11 0 0	11 8 5
—— Roman Catholic Chapel and yard,	0 3 20	0 9 7	8 3 0	8 12 7
—— Grave-yard,	0 2 0	0 4 0	0 0 0	0 4 0
Total of Exemptions,	2 0 20	1 2 0	19 3 0	20 5 0

BARONY OF CASTLERAHAN, (Concluded.)

ABSTRACT OF THE PARISHES.

PARISHES.	Quantity.	Annual Value of Land.	Annual Value of Houses, deducting one-third.	TOTAL.	Total, exclusive of Exemptions.	
					Content.	Value.
	A. R. P.	£ s. d.	£ s. d.	£ s. d.	A. R. P.	£ s. d.
Bailieborough,	40 3 10	25 7 3	0 0 0	25 7 3		
Exemptions,	0 0 0	0 0 0	0 0 0	0 0 0		
Castlerahan,	10292 2 13	5765 2 5	682 0 0	6447 2 5		
Exemptions,	9 3 30	6 5 10	123 12 0	129 17 10		
Crosserlough,	11718 1 12	6118 5 3	351 9 0	6469 14 3		
Exemptions,	11 1 33	4 16 8	73 4 0	78 0 8		
Denn,	1711 3 14	911 11 8	20 6 0	931 17 8		
Exemptions,	0 0 9	0 0 0	0 0 0	0 0 0		
Killinkere,	12073 2 6	5774 11 0	166 3 0	5940 14 0		
Exemptions,	4 2 30	2 6 6	49 19 0	52 5 6		
Loughan or Castlekeeran,	3612 3 4	1625 15 11	34 3 0	1659 18 11		
Exemptions,	0 1 0	0 2 6	0 0 0	0 2 6		
Lurgan,	10543 1 33	4998 10 9	637 10 0	5636 0 9		
Exemptions,	10 0 1	5 16 2	79 17 0	85 13 2		
Mullagh,	12869 0 32	6145 18 1	332 5 0	6478 3 1		
Exemptions,	3 2 32	1 5 4	37 12 0	38 17 4		
Munterconnaght,	6465 0 6	3418 0 4	167 4 0	3585 4 4		
Exemptions,	2 0 20	1 2 0	19 3 0	20 5 0		
TOTAL,	69279 3 5	34804 17 8	2774 7 0	37579 4 8	69237 2 10	37174 2 8

COUNTY OF CAVAN, TO WIT. } At a Meeting of the Committee of Appeal for the Barony CASTLERAHAN, held at the Sessions-house, at Virginia, on Friday, the 8th of January, 1841; pursuant to public Notice from the Commissioner of Valuation.

The Appeals having been considered and adjusted, the Valuation of the Barony, as amended, amounts to Thirty-seven Thousand One Hundred and Seventy-four Pounds, Two Shillings and Eight Pence.

Dated, Sessions-house, Virginia, this 8th day of January, 1841.

RICHARD GRIFFITH, Commissioner of Valuation.

ABRAHAM BRUSH,
ROBERT SARGENT, } Members of the Committee
CHARLES MORTIMER, } of Appeal.
GEORGE SHAW,

11 *Townland Valuation* printed book, parish of Munterconnaght, barony of Castlerahan, Co. Cavan, OL/14/3, pp 8–9 (1841).

VALUATION OF TENEMENTS.
PARISH OF MULLAGH.

No. and Letters of Reference to Map.	Names — Townlands and Occupiers.	Immediate Lessors.	Description of Tenement.	Area.	Rateable Annual Valuation — Land.	Rateable Annual Valuation — Buildings.	Total Annual Valuation of Rateable Property.
	CLOGHBALLY, UPPER—continued.			A. R. P.	£ s. d.	£ s. d.	£ s. d.
21				21 1 2	0 3 0	—	
22				9 3 11	0 2 0	—	
23	Trustees Marquis of Headfort,	In fee,	Land, bog,	51 3 14	0 4 0	—	1 15 0
24				43 3 32	0 4 0	—	
25				21 1 0	0 2 0	—	
26				204 1 31	1 0 0	—	
			Turbary of lots 21, 22, 23, 24, 25, and 26,	—	—	—	6 0 0
			Total of Rateable Property,	927 1 8	325 5 0	14 0 0	345 5 0
			Exemptions—None,				

PARISH OF MUNTERCONNAUGHT.

No.	Names	Immediate Lessors.	Description of Tenement.	Area.	Land.	Buildings.	Total.
	BALLAGH-DORRAGH. (Ord. S. 43.)						
1	James Minagh,	Trustees Marquis of Headfort,	House, offices, and land,	27 1 26	17 15 0	2 0 0	19 15 0
2	John Reilly,	Same,	Land,	0 3 4	0 10 0	—	0 10 0
3	James Porter,	Same,	Herd's house and land,	24 1 15	15 0 0	0 10 0	36 0 0
4		Same,	House, offices, and land,	26 3 35	18 15 0	1 15 0	
5	Thomas Togher,	Same,	Herd's ho., off., & land,	11 2 16	8 0 0	0 15 0	17 10 0
6		Same,	House, offices, and land,	10 3 2	7 10 0	1 5 0	
7	Bryan Cadden,	Same,	Herd's ho., offs., & land,	16 2 5	12 15 0	1 5 0	14 0 0
8 a	James Gray,	Same,	Herd's ho., offs., & land,	17 3 28	13 15 0	0 10 0	14 5 0
— b	Owen Togher,	James Gray,	House,	—	—	0 10 0	0 10 0
9 a	Peter Reilly,	Trustees Marquis of Headfort,	Herd's ho., offs., & land,	41 2 20	29 10 0	1 0 0	30 10 0
— b	Joseph Gillick,	Peter Reilly,	House,	—	—	0 5 0	0 5 0
— c	Michael Lynch,	Same,	House,	—	—	0 5 0	0 5 0
— d	Owen Lynch,	Same,	House,	—	—	0 10 0	0 10 0
— e	Charles Reilly,	Same,	House,	—	—	0 5 0	0 5 0
— f	Margaret Purcell,	Same,	House,	—	—	0 5 0	0 5 0
10	Mary Togher,	Trustees Marquis of Headfort,	House and land,	6 1 26	3 15 0	0 5 0	4 0 0
11	Charles Browne,	Same,	Land,	14 3 34	11 5 0	—	11 5 0
12	Thomas Reilly,	Same,	House, offices, and land,	28 2 6	21 10 0	1 15 0	23 5 0
13 a	John Condron,	Same,	House, offices, and land,	17 1 30	13 10 0	2 0 0	15 10 0
— b	Patrick and Catherine Reilly,	John Condron,	House,	—	—	0 10 0	0 10 0
14	Hugh Porter,	Trustees Marquis of Headfort,	Land,	4 0 30	2 10 0	—	22 5 0
15			Herd's house and land,	27 3 22	19 0 0	0 15 0	
16	Patrick Rahill,	Same,	House, offices, and land,	29 2 9	18 10 0	1 5 0	19 15 0
17	Trustees Marquis of Headfort,	In fee,	Land (bog),	9 3 5	—	—	7 0 0
18			Herd's house, offices, land, and quarry,	9 0 4	4 10 0	2 10 0	
			Total of Rateable Property,	325 2 37	218 0 0	20 0 0	238 0 0
	BEHERNAGH. (Ord. S. 43.)		Exemptions—None,	—	—	—	—
1	James Skelly,	Trustees Marquis of Headfort,	House, offices, and land,	16 1 26	9 10 0	1 5 0	10 15 0
2 a	Honoria Brestle,	Same,	House, offices, & land,	16 2 14	5 0 0	1 5 0	6 5 0
2 b	Mary Brestle,		House, offices, & land,		5 0 0	1 0 0	6 0 0
3	Honoria Brestle,	Same,	Land,	12 3 30	3 0 0	—	3 0 0
	Mary Brestle,				3 0 0	—	3 0 0
4			Land,	2 3 25	1 5 0		
5 a	Matthew Farrelly,	Same,	House, offices, & land,	15 3 8	10 0 0	0 15 0	8 5 0
5 b	Peter Farrelly,		House, offices, & land,			0 10 0	4 3 0
5 c	Thomas Farrelly,		House, offices, & land,			0 10 0	4 3 0
6			Land,	8 0 20	3 11 0		

12 *Primary Valuation, County Cavan, union of Cootehill,* 1857, parish of Munterconnaught (barony of Castleraha Co. Cavan, p. 59.

13 Tenement Valuation appeals (1846 Act), parish of Killabban, barony of Ballyadams, Queen's County, OL/19/24/1, p.13 (1850).

VALUATION OF TENEMENTS.
PARISH OF MOYRUS.

No. and Letters of Reference to Map.	Townlands and Occupiers.	Immediate Lessors.	Description of Tenement.	Acres A. R. P.	Rateable Annual Valuation. Land. £ s. d.	Buildings. £ s. d.	Total £ s. d.	Total Annual Valuation of Rateable Property. £ s. d.
4	DERRYVEALA WALSHA—*continued.* Redmond Joyce.	Provost and Fellows of T.C.D.	Herd's house and land.	21 2 36	4 0 0	0 2 0	4 2 0	4 10 0
6	Martin Joyce.	Redmond Joyce.	House and garden.	0 0 9½	—	0 7 0	0 7 0	0 7 0
			Total.	1434 3 28	16 19 0	0 9 0	17 8 0	17 8 0
1	ILLION, EAST. Michael Joyce.	Directors of the Law Life Assurance Co.	House, offices, and land. Water.	1513 3 5 17 0 37	9 15 0 —	0 10 0 —	10 5 0 —	10 5 0
			Total.	1531 0 2	9 15 0	0 10 0	10 5 0	10 5 0
	LEE ISLAND (*Ord. S. 31.*) Directors of the Law Life Assurance Co.	In fee.	Land (of no agricultural value).	1 2 32	—	—	—	—
1	ILLION, WEST. (*Ord. S. 31/32, 43/44.*) Thomas Rothwell. Redmond Joyce.	Redmond Joyce. Provost and Fellows of T.C.D.	House, offices, & land. Land. Water.	658 3 5 28 0 39	8 8 0 1 14 0 —	0 7 0 — —	8 15 0 1 14 0 —	8 15 0 1 14 0
			Total.	663 0 4	10 2 0	0 7 0	10 9 0	10 9 0
1	LEHANAGH, NORTH. (*Ord. S. 38 & 24.*) Michael Conroy.	Redmond Joyce. Michael Conroy.	House, office, & land. House and land. Water.	605 0 15 57 0 39	4 6 0 1 19 0 —	0 5 0 — —	4 11 0 1 19 0 —	
			Total.	662 1 7	6 5 0	0 5 0	6 10 0	
	SHANNAKEELA (*Ord. S. 38 & 24.*)	Directors of the Law Life Assurance Co. Directors of the Law Life Assurance Co.	House, offices, & land. (mountain)	1700 3 20	0 10 0	—	0 10 0	1 10 0
1 a	Margaret Joyce.				0 10 0	—	0 10 0	0 10 0
b	Myles Joyce. John Joyce (Dick).	Same. Same.	" " "		0 15 0	—	0 15 0	0 15 0
2	Thaddeus Chaney.	Same.	" " "		0 10 0	—	0 10 0	0 10 0
3	Martin Lynch.	Same.	" " "		0 10 0	—	0 10 0	0 10 0
4	Patrick Carney.	Same.	" " "		0 10 0	—	0 10 0	0 10 0
5	Thomas Joyce.	Same.	" " "		0 10 0	—	0 10 0	0 10 0
6	John Joyce (Ned).	Same.	" " "		0 10 0	—	0 10 0	0 10 0
7	Barbara Mangan.	Same.	" " "		0 10 0	—	0 10 0	0 10 0
8	Mark Chaney.	Same.	" " "		0 10 0	—	0 10 0	0 10 0
9	Thaddeus Chaney.	Same.	" " "		0 10 0	—	0 10 0	0 10 0
10	Patrick Carney.	Directors of the Law Life Assurance Co.	House, offices, & land.	28 0 24	3 0 0	0 10 0	3 10 0	3 10 0
11	Martin Lynch.	Same.	House, office, & land.		2 10 0	0 10 0	3 0 0	3 0 0
12	John Joyce (Ned).	Same.	House and land.	47 1 26	1 6 0	0 3 0	1 9 0	1 9 0
13	Thomas Joyce.	Same.	House and land.		1 4 0	0 7 0	1 11 0	1 11 0
14	John Joyce (Ned).	Same.	House and land.		1 0 0	0 3 0	1 3 0	1 3 0
15	Barbara Mangan.	Directors of the Law Life Assurance Co.	House, office, and land. House, office, & land. House, office, & land.	4 1 38 20 1 2 6 1 2	0 18 0 1 10 0 —	0 4 0 0 5 0 —	1 2 0 1 15 0 —	1 2 0 1 15 0
16	Mark Chaney. John Joyce (Dick).	John Joyce (Dick).	Land.					1 14 0
6 a		Provost and Fellows of T.C.D.						
b	Margaret Joyce.							
11		Directors of the Law Life Assurance Co.	Land.	24 0 28	0 15 0	—	0 15 0	
	Myles Joyce.	Margaret Joyce.	House, offices, & land.					5 10 0
	Margaret Joyce.							

15 List book, barony of Ardoyne, Co. Carlow, OL/10/1 (1843)

Barony of Duhallow, County of Cork — Parish of Kilmeen

No. of Lot	Area A. R. P.	Valuation Of Land £ s d	Valuation Of Buildings £ s d	Total £ s d	Rent Before 1846	Rent After 1846	Tenure and Year taken	Check	OBSERVATIONS	Proprietor	Lessor
		Glentohan									
1	242.2.6	23.12.0	9.9.0	33.1.0	37.1.0	16.10.0	1827?		This lot has been open Mountain about &c	Right Hon. the Earl of Cork	Right Hon. Earl of Cork
2	692.2.3	29.5.10	3.2.0	32.7.0		25.0.0	1852				
3	356.1.0	9.14.9	0.18.0	10.12.9	16.0.0		1823				
4	250.2.32	11.5.3	2.0.0	13.5.3	12.0.0	6.0.2	W 1851				
	1508.3.1	41.10.3	5.7.0	46.19.3	58.0.0						
		Glencagh									
5	1052.2.34	55.11.9	4.14.0	60.1.5.9		32.0.0	1858 W			Wilfred the Earl of Cork	Richard Longfield Esq
4	77.2.6	19.6.0	3.7.0	22.13.0	27.0.0		1838 W				
5	153.2.37	16.7.0	0.10.6	16.17.6	12.0.0		1852?				
6	441.1.23	11.12.10	2.18.0	14.10.10	16.10.0		1829 W				
7	76.2.22	8.18.11	1.10.0	10.8.11	14.0.0	10.0.0	1829			Richard Longfield Esq	Richard Longfield Esq
8	77.0.25	22.7.0	3.15.0	26.0.10	25.0.0		1857 W				
9	163.2.27	14.7.3	2.16.0	17.3.7	22.0.0		1852 W				
Total	2121.0.14	128.19.0	14.14.0	143.11.6	1403.10.0				Denis and John Coneghan are Middlemen and Cork Renters		
		Glentanedowney									
1	4.6.7	16.4.0	6.2.16.0	13.0.0	6.0.0		1833			Denis Donehan Greeman Boulaghn Buffe	Denis Donehan Esq Greeman Boulaghn Buffe
2	57.2.11	9.4.11	1.13.0	11.8.11	12.0.0	10.0.0	1842				
3	9.10.1.23	3.3.10	1.15.0	4.18.10		5.13.9	1832				
Total	72.2.11	9.4.11	11.15.0	11.11	100.0						

cannot be established although it must have existed at the time. In some counties, only a small number of office maps have survived.[37] In others there are no office maps (for example, in Carlow, Kilkenny and Monaghan), but the tenement field work in these counties plotted the tenements directly onto new printed maps without earlier data and, as they were not cluttered, it may have been possible to do the calculations without transcribing them to new sheets, although reference would still have been needed to the quality lots of the Townland Valuation field maps.

TENEMENT VALUATION FAIR-COPY MAPS

The fair-copy maps of the Tenement Valuation show the final version of the tenements. These maps are known as 'union' maps because they were made in poor law unions, even where the related *Primary valuation* volume was published by barony. The fair-copy map was drawn with care by an office draftsman as the map of record. The boundaries of tenements are drawn in red ink, the boundaries of townlands and parishes are shaded in colour and the names of townlands are highlighted. These maps show the location and extent of every tenement and, in theory, show houses denoted by letters.

There is considerable variation within the fair-copy maps. Some of them correspond to the *Primary valuation*, but with others it is difficult to find a correlation, in which case they may relate to cancelled books (still in the Valuation Office). It is not known if the maps were drawn before or after the appeals but this would not have caused anything more than minor differences. Many were revised, some were redrawn at a later date and some have remained unaltered. In theory, these maps remained valid until they were 'cancelled'. In many counties, there are two copies of each map, some dated and some not. Revisions were made on many of these maps but unless they can be related to changes made as a result of appeals, they must correspond to alterations made in the cancelled books. Copies of the maps drawn from the early 1870s in preparation for the printed valuation map (1870–83) are present in some cases.

Conclusion

The maps are an excellent source of information and are fundamental to understanding the other archives of the valuation. They identify the exact sites of houses and the location, extent and other features of farms occupied by named individuals, show the relationship of buildings to the land, put the tenements in the context of their community and provide a wide range of data on the quality of land. They document changes in occupation and ownership at a period of transformation, and in some counties, for example

---

37 Co. Longford, 4; Co. Meath, 2; Queen's County, 1.

Tipperary, they illustrate the large-scale changes that took place over a short time.

This is a very large collection of maps but it is not complete. In certain counties entire types of map, such as Townland Valuation fair-copy maps, are not present, and in other cases there are random gaps. In most cases it should be possible for the researcher to identify some maps that relate to their subject. The table in appendix F shows the main types of map that exist for each county.

Some maps note names on the tenements and many have pencil notes of the field prices. Occasionally other information is given. In Dunowla, Kilshalgan, Co. Sligo, a note records the place where 'Nicholl shot the golden eagle'. The event is not dated but the map was made in approximately 1855.[38] In Co. Tipperary the scene of the murder of Gustavus Thibault in the parish of Killeenasteena in June 1862 is marked.[39] The location is shown in the graveyard of Glebe, Glandore, Co. Cork of 'the outrage at the funeral of a man who was murdered at Ross when 2,000 people assembled to prevent the clergyman reading the funeral service in November 1862'.[40] A pencil sketch on the back of a field map shows the landscape from Croagh Patrick and Clew Bay to Killary Harbour; the artist is not known and this map was used in both valuations.[41]

The maps can present a number of difficulties for the researcher, including the large numbers, the variations and the manner in which the information was added in layers. It is necessary to identify the books that correspond to a particular map, to find the specific data on the map and to interpret the data. The account above indicates in general what books and maps should correspond, and the lists in the National Archives give details of the maps in each county. It can be helpful when looking at the valuation maps to have a copy of the Ordnance Survey six-inch map for the area, or a sketch of the position of townlands, as well as the names of parishes and townlands. The data can usually be interpreted by matching the descriptions in the field books, house books and tenure books with the map. In general the researcher needs to be aware of inconsistencies in the recording.

An explanation for the poor condition of the some of the maps was given by commissioner J.B. Greene to the select committee in 1869, when he described the difficulties met by the revising valuator in looking after the map. He:

> is obliged to take it with him in wet weather or dry. He has to get over the ditches with it in his hand; besides that the changes that

38 OL/11/26/163, sheet 24.   39 OL/11/27/600, sheet 68. This murder is referred to in Vaughan, *Landlords and tenants in mid-Victorian Ireland*, p. 144.   40 OL/11/6/1045, sheet 142.
41 OL/11/21/58, sheet 85.

have to be made are numerous, and have to be recorded on the map, so that, in about four years, we get a new set. As soon as a county or the portion of a county gets worn out, we give it to the draftsman to make another map.[42]

He explained that because of the expense of replacement: 'We try to make the maps last as long as we can by patching and repairing.'[43]

B. VALUATION TOWN PLANS

The valuation town plans show houses and other buildings in towns valued in both the Townland Valuation and the Tenement Valuation. More than 1,400 valuation town plans are held in the National Archives, relating to more than 850 towns and villages in the Republic of Ireland. Town plans were made from the beginning of the valuation in conjunction with the manuscript house books and the complete data is available only when the books and plans are read together. The books name occupiers and describe and measure each house and building, and the corresponding plan shows its outline shape, exact location, and the surrounding environment. The valuation town plans are the only large-scale plans of some towns made in the nineteenth century, particularly the smaller towns.

The cadastral work in towns required base plans on which the specific properties valued would be plotted or marked, similar to the process of marking tenements in rural areas on the printed base maps made by the Ordnance Survey. This required plans at a large scale because the detail could not be shown at the six-inch scale of the printed maps. This was known from the outset but it was not immediately obvious what the scale should be, although the Spring Rice Committee in 1824 recommended a scale of twelve inches to the mile.[44] The mapping of towns first became a difficulty during the work in Co. Londonderry, and in some cases the valuators redrew the towns by scaling up the printed six-inch maps to four feet to the mile or 1:1,320. However, this method was found unsatisfactory and in late 1832 it was agreed that the Ordnance Survey would provide plans at a scale of five feet to the mile or 1:1,056.[45] The Ordnance Survey made manuscript coloured town plans as the work on the six-inch mapping took place in each county.[46] These town plans were retained by the Ordnance Survey, are now held by the National Archives as part of the archives of the Ordnance Survey

---

42 *Report from select committee on valuation, 1869*, question 512.   43 Ibid., question 1297.
44 *Spring Rice Report*, p. 8.   45 Andrews, *A paper landscape*, p. 83.   46 Andrews, *History in the ordnance map*, p. 19, map showing OS survey dates by county; and p. 27, map showing dates of OS manuscript town plans.

and cover 102 towns in the Republic of Ireland.[47] Copies were made as base plans for the valuation work. In Dublin city, the plans printed in 1847 and 1864 were used. The Ordnance Survey produced plans at a variety of scales until approximately 1836 and from that date at 1:1,056.[48]

The valuation town plans consist of working plans (base plans on which the work was plotted), and a small number of reference plans. The latter were not used in the work. Many of the reference plans are drawn at the smaller scale of 1:2,112, but the working plans are at the 1:1,056 scale. Little is known about how the base plans were made, and this matter would benefit from detailed further study. Some valuation base plans are copies of the Ordnance Survey set, but the exact relationship is not known and the discrepancy in numbers raises questions (850 towns on valuation town plans and 102 on Ordnance Survey town plans). The vast majority of the plans bear no first date. A number of town plans are signed by Griffith.[49] This may indicate that the plans were made by the Ordnance Survey and were received at this date by the valuation, but it may also show the copy was made by the valuation. There are also instances where the valuators or surveyors making the house books in a town drew a plan at the 1:1,056 scale (possibly scaled up from the six-inch map) on small sheets of paper that they pasted together. A full-sized plan was later produced in the office. Examples of this can be seen in Glandore, Co. Cork, where the surveyor William Scott drew a plan of the town.[50] In Enniskeen, also in Co. Cork, there are two plans drawn by two valuators around the same time.[51] This suggests that they found themselves working in the town without a plan and had to improvise in the short term. J.H. Andrews understands that valuation staff may have made the plans of some small towns as the detail on the valuation plans and the six-inch printed maps is not the same.[52]

The valuation town plans are drawn with delicacy, have neat numbering and some have elaborate lettering or decorative north signs. Public buildings, such as courthouses, churches and police barracks are frequently named, and industrial buildings such as mills, breweries or distilleries also have captions. Houses and garden plots are outlined in black, and each separate property is numbered. Revisions of the town plan are usually made in black ink and are more roughly sketched in. It should be possible to date the additions from the house books. Many of the revisions were made at the time of the Tenement Valuation when houses previously exempt, or new buildings, were included. The later development of the towns can also be traced with the building of Catholic churches, schools and courthouses, and the positioning of post offices and banks on prominent streets. The section of the town plan of

---

[47] See OS/140, Ordnance Survey manuscript town plans. [48] Andrews, *History in the ordnance map*, p. 56. [49] OL/12/4/15, Cavan town, 1841; OL/12/9/5–6, Balbriggan, Co. Dublin, 1848. [50] OL/12/6/69. [51] OL/12/6/62–3. [52] Andrews, *History in the ordnance map*, p. 56.

Ballina, Co. Mayo (plate 6) shows the shambles, the gasworks and a sawmill added at a later date to the original plan.

On the Ordnance Survey town plans in the National Archives the towns are usually drawn in the centre of a standard large map sheet, with north at the top, some with several small towns on the same sheet and the buildings are not always numbered.[53] On the valuation copies, some of the towns were repositioned on the sheet in a manner more convenient for the work, placing the drawing at a different angle from the original Ordnance Survey plan and including a north sign.[54]

The valuation of the towns took place at the same time as the work in the surrounding rural areas. Most of the plans are undated, but the start date is inferred from other documents. The plans were used by the valuation staff as the base plan on which to mark out buildings and associated lots, numbering them to correspond to the entries in the house books, in the same manner as the printed base maps were used in rural areas. It appears that the valuator took the plan into the field and many are now in a worn condition.[55] The use of town plans is not mentioned specifically in the instructions until 1839, but some plans were made before this date.[56]

The plans are now arranged in counties and towns. Researchers should note that the name of a town may not be the same as the name of the parish where it is situated (see *house books*, p. 74). Most towns are covered by one plan, but this depends on the size or shape of the town. In some cases several small towns are drawn together on one sheet and large towns are spread over several sheets. The cities of Dublin, Cork, Limerick and Waterford, where there are multiple sheets, have index plans. Where there is more than one copy of a town plan covering the same area, they usually relate to successive periods. Revisions of the plans were made, but it can be difficult to pinpoint the dates on which alterations were made.

Plans were 'cancelled', or made non-current, when they became worn or overcrowded, or when revisions were carried out and the latest layer of data was transferred to a new copy.[57] The periods for which the town plans were maintained as live documents varied. To some extent it depended on the number of alterations made, but the fact that they were in manuscript may also have been a factor in their longevity, as making copies required

---

53 The Ordnance Survey town plans and valuation town plans were usually drawn on double-elephant size sheets of paper measuring 1,016 mm x 673 mm (40 inches x 27 inches). **54** See Johnstown, Co. Kilkenny on OL/12/14/23 (reference plan) and OL/12/14/24 (working plan). **55** OL/12/6/78, Kanturk, Co. Cork. This plan was folded in four, with the name of the town written on the folds, indicating that it was carried around. In the office the plans were stored flat. **56** See OL/12, Co. Donegal. The plans are largely undated in Donegal, but the work in towns there took place from 1833. **57** *Report from select committee on valuation, 1869*, question 1291–301.

redrawing both the base plan and the most recent layer of valuation data and this was very labour intensive. The life of the plans could be as short as five years, for example the plans of some towns in Co. Tipperary were received in 1849 and cancelled in 1854. The next plans for the same towns were current for more than fifty years until cancelled in 1907.[58] It is common for plans made in the 1830s and 1840s to be cancelled only in the early twentieth century. The absence of development in many towns in the second half of the nineteenth century can be seen in the small number of alterations made over a long period.[59]

Beginning in the 1860s, the Ordnance Survey published large-scale printed maps for towns but only the larger towns were covered.[60] For example, in Co. Longford sixteen towns are covered by valuation town plans and only Longford town was later printed (1893). In Co. Louth only Dundalk (1892) and Drogheda (1872) were printed, and there are nineteen towns with manuscript valuation town plans.[61] The printed town plans came into use as plans were replaced. Printed plans were made at 1:1,056 scale by enlargement from the 1:2,500 printed maps, and for some small villages the printed 1:2,500 maps were used directly. Many of the alterations to the plans were made at a date later than the last manuscript books held in the National Archives and the *Primary valuation* and do not correspond to any documents held there. They are likely to relate to the cancelled books that are held in the Valuation Office.

Rules for numbering houses in towns first appeared in the *Instructions 1839* and were further elaborated in the *Instructions 1853*.[62] The numbering was to start at a public building on the main street and to proceed in a prescribed manner towards the edge of the town, completing one side of a street before moving to the other. In theory, the same numbers were put on the plan and in the book. In some but not all cases this still works perfectly. The numbering was not related to any real numbers that might exist on the buildings, although occasionally reference is made to local numbers.[63] The printed *Primary valuation* for the cities of Belfast, Cork and Dublin listed the number in the street as well as the tenement number.

In general, a correlation can be made between the working copies of the town plans and the manuscript house books, and in some cases the quarto books, but time and careful observation are required to identify the related data across the series. In some cases the relationship cannot be determined.

58 See plans of Ballina and Portroe, Co. Tipperary, OL/12/27/3 (1849–54), OL/12/27/4 (1854–1907). 59 William J. Smyth, 'The roles of cities and towns during the Great Famine' in Crowley, Smyth & Murphy (eds), *Atlas of the Great Irish Famine*, pp 240–54. 60 Gertrude Hamilton (ed.), *A catalogue of large scale town plans prepared by the Ordnance Survey and deposited in PRONI* (2nd ed., Belfast, 1981). 61 Andrews, *A paper landscape*, pp 335–6; see also list of OL/12 in National Archives. 62 OL/1/2/4, §166–8; OL/1/2/7, §210–12. 63 OL/5/3390 (Portlaw, Co. Waterford) and OL/7/120 (Holy Trinity, Cork city).

The numbering of entries is important in matching the data on the plan and in the books. The numbering on the working plans was made by valuation staff and usually corresponds to the numbering in the house books of either the Townland Valuation or the Tenement Valuation. Many of the numbers were altered more than once. It may also be possible to relate the town plan to the quarto book where additional information may be available, using the house book to establish the link. As noted, almost all of the working plans have numbering and amendments that are connected to later cancelled books, held in the Valuation Office.

The town plans were made in broadly the same manner in both valuations. The change from the Townland Valuation to the Tenement Valuation did not affect towns as it did rural areas, as most houses in towns were above the £5 threshold and already had been valued. In the Townland Valuation the town plans show houses over the valuation threshold, measured in the house books and numbered to correspond to the plans. Houses under the value were noted as exempt or if the buildings were adjoining they were drawn in a block and not numbered. Many town plans were revised in the Tenement Valuation, and as the previously exempt buildings were now included as well as new buildings, the plans were usually renumbered to correspond to the new books. Some were later further updated until their cancellation. In counties valued for the first time under the 1846 act, the town plans were made as part of the tenement work in the normal manner, and all houses were valued.

Conclusion

The town plans provide an overview of the towns where the relationship between the different parts can be understood at a glance. Matters such as the width of the streets, the location of commercial and official buildings, the market place, the presence of industry, the bridges and the roads leading to other towns are all made visible at once and defined in relation to each other. On occasion they contain notes, such as the spot marked on the lake outside Dunmanway, Co. Cork where Sir Richard Eyre Cox drowned in 1783.[64]

The town plans are a valuable resource for towns of all sizes, from small villages to large cities. Finding specific information requires using the plans in conjunction with the house books and, if possible, the quarto books. In addition to identifying precise houses, it is possible to see the town as a whole. The plans contain successive layers of data and show development of the town over the course of the nineteenth century, including courthouses, police barracks, schools, banks and churches. The reference plans are carefully drawn, but contain little beyond the outlines and do not relate directly to the books.

64 OL/12/6/58.

5

The *Primary valuation*

The *Primary valuation* or *Griffith's valuation* is a series of printed books that list property, occupiers and lessors of land and houses in Ireland at dates between 1847 and 1864. The 251 books were published under the Tenement Valuation Acts of 1846 and 1852. The term 'primary valuation' had a specific meaning as the draft or preliminary valuation that was drawn up for the purpose of allowing public scrutiny, appeal and eventual alteration. It first appeared in relation to the Townland Valuation in the *Instructions 1839*[1] and was used in the 1846 Tenement Valuation Act.[2] After that date 'primary' refers only to the Tenement Valuation and always with the meaning of the preliminary valuation.[3] Griffith's authority as commissioner of valuation is cited on the title page of each volume. Although he simultaneously held several high-profile government appointments during his long career, including chairmanship of the Board of Works (a much larger organization), it was the valuation that he created and directed for nearly forty years with which his name became synonymous.

The *Primary valuation* provides the first standardized snapshot of property, occupancy and ownership for the entire country from the time immediately following the Great Famine. Although it represents only a small proportion of the total volume of archives created by the valuation, the *Primary valuation* is the best-known of all of the valuation documents and holds a prominent place in the public imagination.[4] It was printed in multiple copies and widely disseminated. Many archives and libraries hold copies and examples can still be found for sale. It has been digitized and indexed and is available online free of charge.[5] It is highly legible and its content makes it both useful to researchers, ranging from the family historian to the academic analyst, and fascinating for more casual perusal.

The fact that the *Primary valuation* books were printed makes them appear definitive and authoritative, although the reason for printing was to

1 OL/1/2/4 §13; see also OL/2/7, p. 221. 2 9 & 10 Vict., c. 110, schedule form A, 'Primary valuation of tenements'. 3 The books published under the 1846 act have 'Primary Valuation' on the title page and headers. This was omitted after 1852, but the term continued to be used in the notice included in the books warning that this was the primary valuation and that the valuation after appeals would be made in manuscript only. 4 The *Primary valuation* books represent approximately 6 per cent of the books of the initial valuation (up to 1865) in the National Archives, excluding maps and administrative documents. 5 See askaboutireland.ie/griffith-valuation.

ensure sufficient copies for public circulation. The 1846 act applied originally to only six counties and, although it could be extended to other counties, it was uncertain at the time how matters would develop and there is nothing to suggest an intention to publish a series of books covering the whole country, as eventually transpired. Public dissemination of the draft valuation lists was required from the 1826 act, and printing was mandatory from 1836, but there were now two important differences between the Townland Valuation and the Tenement Valuation. The first was the fact that the *Primary valuation* books were published by the Government Stationery Office as part of a uniform-looking set, in sober, official, blue covers, and most were substantial volumes. The equivalent document in the Townland Valuation, the draft valuation list, consisted of a large notice for each barony, usually printed by the local newspaper, and the valuation was published in book form only at the final stage.[6] Secondly, in contrast to the Townland Valuation, in which individual occupiers were not named and were only directly affected when the valuation was applotted to show their liability for tax (a process that was at a remove from the valuation), the Tenement Valuation now not only named all occupiers for the first time in print, but stated their individual valuations publicly and treated everyone, great and small, in the same manner.

The appearance of the books was an important part of the message that they were issued by central authority and reflected the key characteristics of the valuation, which was scientific, systematic, universal and uniform. Inside the books, the data was presented in the same manner, in neat printed columns of names and figures, confirming the rigorous standard that applied at every stage, from the valuator's work of collecting the information in the field, to the office work of collating, copying, calculating, checking, settling the price and preparing for publication. The *Primary valuation* was a milestone document: it confirmed the position of the valuation as the national authority, with the status of its progenitor mirrored in its name. Its immediate purpose was as a draft pending appeals, but it was an essential stage in the work that became the basis of all later valuation. The content of the books was based on the field work and office work.

The *Primary valuation* books were published as the work in each area was completed. The unit of publication was not specified in the acts, and books were issued in either baronies or poor law unions.[7] Between 1847 and 1852

---

6 See OL/13, Townland Valuation appeal books. Copies of these notices are folded into the appeal books (see plate 14). The format was prescribed in the 1826 act, see 7 Geo. IV, c. 62, schedule 1. See OL/14 for the printed *Townland valuation*. 7 Ninety-five books were published by barony under the 1846 act. Under the 1852 act, 16 books were published by barony (this was the completion of the work in Cos. Cork, Kerry, Limerick and Tipperary). From April 1853, only poor law unions were used for the remaining 140 books published. In counties where

the books were published by barony, for a period in 1852–3 they were issued in one or the other unit and from 1853 they were only in unions. In the small number of cases where baronies crossed county boundaries, the entire barony was covered in one book.[8] Poor law unions were much larger than baronies, with many extending into more than one county.[9] In general, a separate book was published for the part of a union in each county. The union of Ballyshannon spanned parts of Cos. Donegal, Leitrim and Fermanagh and was published in three separate books at different dates.[10] The union of Boyle was in Cos. Roscommon and Sligo and was published in two books with the same date. There were exceptions to this practice.[11] The books were usually set out in civil parishes and townlands in alphabetical order, or in streets in cities and towns; books published from the late 1850s are arranged by townland within electoral divisions, but the tables of contents give the parish name and other information.

The format of the text of the *Primary valuation* was prescribed in the 1846 and 1852 acts.[12] The data is in columns across one page: the number of the tenement, occupier's name, immediate lessor's name, brief description of the holding, the square area of land occupied in acres, roods and perches and the valuation price of land and buildings, in pounds, shillings and pence sterling. All tenements were valued and those exempt from taxes, such as churches or schools, are listed at the end of each townland. After the 1852 act some new properties were included, such as canals, railways and fisheries, and rent derived from exempt property became liable for rates, noted as 'half rent'.[13] The number of entries in the books varied widely, as did the sizes of townlands.[14] The rules in the various instructions related to the manuscript documents, and many of the same conventions were used in the printing.

The 1846 act used the definition of 'tenement' in the 1838 Poor Law Act, where a tenement was a hereditament that was liable for rates, including houses and land.[15] The term 'occupier' means the person in occupation of

work had already begun when the change took place, both baronies and poor law unions were used (Cos. Clare, Dublin, Kildare, Louth, Meath and Wicklow, and King's County). **8** *Townland Index, 1851* lists 10 baronies that are in more than one county. **9** *Townland Index, 1871*. By 1871, there were 163 poor law unions of which 69 were in more than one county. **10** *PV, Co. Donegal, union of Ballyshannon* (Dublin, 23 Feb. 1858), *PV, Co. Leitrim, union of Ballyshannon* (Dublin, 20 Feb. 1857) and *PV, Co. Fermanagh, union of Ballyshannon* (Dublin, 1 July 1862). **11** *PV, Co. Galway, union of Clifden* (1855). The union of Clifden is in Co. Galway but this book includes on 5 pages the parish of Inisbofin, Co. Mayo, pp 109–14. **12** 9 & 10 Vict., c. 110, form A; 15 & 16 Vict., c. 63, form 1. **13** OL/1/2/7, §45, examples throughout; see *PV, Co. Dublin, union of Dublin South* (1854), p. 171: Trustees of Damer's Fund, immediate lessors of the Essex Street Unitarian School in Dublin; *PV, Co. Cavan, union of Bawnboy* (1857), p. 21: half annual rent of petty session house in Swanlinbar, Co. Cavan. **14** The variations in the size of townlands were very great. The townland of Glenwood, Kilcrumper, Co. Cork contains 36 acres. The townland of Glinsk, Kilcommon, Co. Mayo contains 2,050 acres. **15** See 9 & 10 Vict., c. 110, sec. 9 and 1 & 2 Vict., c. 56 (Poor Law Act), sec. 63; the definition in the *Instructions 1853* is

the tenement. In its simplest form, 'immediate lessor' means the person from whom the occupier holds the property and can refer to either the owner or a person who holds the property from another, but it can have other meanings. Real estates or freeholds of inheritance are described as 'in fee', and where anything less than freehold is concerned the name of the immediate lessor is given. Tenements described as 'free' mean that the person holds by right of possession and no landlord is recognized.[16] The term 'waste' means the area adjoining or under houses, the yards of houses or roads that are not included in the square area of the land to be valued.[17] The words 'in chancery' appear frequently, meaning that the estate is under the jurisdiction of the court. Some of these entries can be linked to cases in the Encumbered Estates Court and its successors.[18]

Each tenement was numbered within the townland. The numbering reflected the complexities of the different kinds of tenure. Three sets of characters were used: arabic numbers, capital letters and lower-case italic letters. In general, a separate number was given to each tenement. Where a person held more than one tenement under different leases or from different landlords, each was numbered separately. Where a tenement was held by several persons it was treated as one entity unless the parts were clearly defined. A capital letter was added to the number for each detached part of a tenement.[19] Where a tenement was made up of detached portions, the *Instructions 1853* required them to be arranged in numerical order, but the existing system of using capital letters for the detached portions was continued in use.[20] The practice of listing detached portions of a tenement together on one line is first seen around 1849, as for example '7ABC James Morris' in Ballywalter, Callan, Co. Kilkenny, with one figure of 36 acres for the square area and one figure of £27 for the valuation.[21] From about 1850 detached parts were usually each noted individually, with their area and valuation, as in the example '16A John Loughlin', with the parts B, C and D, also occupied by Loughlin, on separate lines.[22] Small tenements were distinguished if more than one acre in extent or grouped together if less. Each

'any rateable hereditament that may be holden or possessed for any term, tenure, or agreement, not less than from year to year'. See OL/1/2/7, §10. 16 Ibid., §41; see examples *PV, Co. Galway, union of Tuam* (1855), p. 99; and *PV, Co. Kilkenny, barony of Fassadinin* (1849), p. 15. 17 OL/1/2/7, §170–1. 18 NAI, LEC 46/40 (1857), LEC 56/14 (1859) and LEC 134/24 (1878): the property of Robert Westropp in Caherhurley, Kilnoe, Co. Clare; land in this townland was put up for sale by the Encumbered Estates Court in 1877, by the Landed Estates Court in 1859 and by the Land Judges Court in 1878. The list of tenants in the 1857 sale documents correlates to a fair degree with the *Primary valuation* list. The documents for 1859 contain many of the same family names. 19 *PV, Co. Cork, barony of Fermoy* (1851), p. 7: the townland of Ballyhay in the parish of Ballyhay is divided into 10 lots. Number 2 is shown with 2 capital letters to consist of 2 separate parcels of land, held on a single lease but the parcels are not contiguous. Number 7 is similar. 20 OL/1/2/7, §25. 21 *PV, Co. Kilkenny, barony of Callan* (1849), p. 2. 22 *PV, Co. Galway, union of Ballinasloe* (1856), p. 52.

proprietor's tenements were listed in sequence, detached parts of tenements were kept in sequence and common land was listed after farms.[23] Cases where an occupier held tenements in more than one townland were usually cross-referenced, but this may not have been universally applied.[24] The tenements listed in the *Primary valuation* usually correspond to the first Tenement Valuation fair-copy maps.

Italicized letters were used in three cases in the *Primary valuation* and on the maps: (1) for holdings too small to be shown separately on the maps and that were grouped together; (2) for land other than agricultural land, such as orchards or quarries; and (3) for lots containing both the farmer's house and cottiers' houses where they were all given letters.[25] Where there was only one house in a lot, it was not usually given a letter. Common land was shown with all occupiers named and their valuations listed but only the total acreage was entered. Land held in common was frequently poor quality or mountain land and described as 'land (mountain)'[26] or 'land (common)'.[27]

The *Primary valuation* books are one of the most important sources of names in the nineteenth century and their significance has grown since searchable databases became available online. The books give the names of the occupiers and of the immediate lessors of property. The recording of names largely follows the rules set out for the manuscript documents. At first this required noting only the first name and surname, but more elaborate rules were published in the *Instructions 1853*. The full name of each occupier was recorded, although in the printing the first name was sometimes abbreviated to fit in the space. Where the first name was not known, a dash was entered.[28] In joint occupancy or ownership, the names of both parties were entered.[29] Gentlemen 'of property, learning or the law' were to have 'esquire' annexed to their names, and ladies of like rank, Mrs or Miss; medical doctors, 'knights, baronets etc should have their proper titles'. The early books contain many deliberate distinctions, such as in the barony of Fermoy, where James Foote esq. and H.D. Spratt were listed, one with title, one without.[30] The women superiors of religious houses were given the courtesy title of 'Mrs', as in Mrs Galwey, superioress of the Sisters of Charity in Waterford[31] or Mrs Eleanor Connolly, head of the nunnery in Carrick-on-Suir.[32] The denomination of a clergyman can be deduced, such as Revd Michael Ready PP in Carrowmore, Moynoe, Co. Clare,[33] and in some cases,

23 OL/1/2/7, §10–16, 22–6. 24 *PV, Co. Cork, barony of Fermoy* (1851), p. 7. 25 OL/1/2/7, §16, 18 and 26. 26 *PV, Co. Galway, union of Clifden* (1855), p. 14. 27 *PV, Co. Galway, union of Tuam* (1855), p. 49. 28 *PV, Co. Cork, barony of Fermoy* (1851), p. 99, gives several examples. 29 For example, see Mary Cullinan and Catherine Jones, occupiers, in Castleblagh, Ballyhooly, Co. Cork, *PV, Co. Cork, barony of Fermoy* (1851), p. 12 and Wm and Matilda Shanley, Bolton Street, Dublin, *PV, Co. Dublin, union of Dublin North* (1854), p. 141. 30 *PV, Co. Cork, barony of Fermoy* (1851), p. 21. 31 *PV, Co. Waterford, county of the city of Waterford* (1851), p. 49. 32 *PV, Co. Tipperary, barony of Iffa and Offa East* (1850), p. 34. 33 *PV, Co. Clare, union of Scarriff*

their office is given, for example, Rt. Hon. and Most Revd Richard Whately DD, archbishop of Dublin.[34] Careful attention is paid to titles of rank, such as Sir W.W. Becher, Bt. and Viscount Doneraile.[35] Some occupiers held multiple titles, such as Very Revd Viscount Mountmorres[36] or Rt. Hon. and Most Revd Lord John G. Beresford.[37] Military rank is included, for example Lieut.-Col. Wm Temple French[38] and adding 'RN' to the entry for Capt. Frederick Lowe clarifies that he is a naval man.[39] Office is also noted for members of parliament and resident magistrates, as Thomas Meagher esq. MP, and his neighbour, Joseph Tabuteau esq. RM, in Waterford city.[40]

Distinguishing persons with identical names in the same townland required the addition of an 'agnomen' or nickname.[41] This can provide information on names, family or other relationships and professions. In cases where the same name, without a distinction, occurs more than once in a townland it may be the case that a person held more than one tenement. Many of the distinctions by name were based on the traditional practice of adding the name of another family member. Two examples from Co. Cork give William O'Leary (Jer.) and William O'Leary (Con.).[42] In Shankeela, Moyrus, Co. Galway, 'Dick', 'Ned' and 'Peggy' were added to the names of three men called John Joyce.[43] In Killeany on Inishmore island, Co. Galway, there were Mary Conneely (Bawn) and Mary Conneely (Cath.).[44] A large number of these distinctions were recorded in Keel East, Achill, Co. Mayo using descriptive terms such as 'young', 'baun', 'trumpet', 'tailor', 'boat' and 'rake'.[45] In some cases professions were given, as in the cases of Michael Lavelle ('weaver'), Martin Moran ('shoemaker'),[46] Daniel O'Brien ('polisher') and Thomas Ryan ('carpenter').[47]

While the *Primary valuation* is a most valuable source for names, it is not a complete list, as not all occupiers are included. Apart from the fact that only the occupier's name is noted and not the names of other family members, there are two principal cases where the names were not recorded. The first relates to occupiers of buildings comprising multiple dwellings. Houses let in apartments or lodgings were described as 'lodgings' and the name recorded in the occupier column was that of the immediate lessor.[48] The large number of names that were excluded is illustrated by an example in Bow Street,

---

(1855), p. 52. 34 *PV, Co. Dublin, union of Dublin South* (1854), p. 3. 35 *PV, Co. Cork, barony of Fermoy* (1851), pp 22, 23. 36 Ibid., p. 79. 37 *PV, Co. Cavan, union of Bawnboy* (1857), p. 7. 38 *PV, Co. Cork, barony of Fermoy* (1851), p. 99. 39 *PV, Co. Clare, union of Scarriff* (1855), p. 7. 40 *PV, Co. Waterford, city of Waterford* (1851), p. 102. 41 OL/1/2/7, §31. 42 *PV, Co. Cork, barony of Fermoy* (1851), p. 99, Downing North, Kilcrumper. 43 *PV, Co. Galway, union of Clifden* (1855), pp 79–80. 44 *PV, Co. Galway, union of Galway* (1856), p. 157. 45 *PV, Co. Mayo, union of Newport* (1855), p. 35. 46 Ibid., p. 27 (Lavelle) and p. 72 (Moran). 47 *PV, Co. Clare, union of Scarriff* (1855), p. 15. 48 OL/1/2/7, §34: 'For any house let in separate apartments or lodgings, the immediate lessor is to be entered as the occupier, with the observation "in lodgings".'

Dublin. Fifty-four buildings are listed in the 1854 book, twenty-eight of which are described as 'lodgings'. The same names are noted in the occupier and lessor columns for most of these houses and include one lessor who held nine houses. These were modest houses, mostly valued under £10. The *Primary valuation* shows that houses numbered 4 and 5 were 'lodgings'.[49] In the 1901 census and street directory these houses are described as 'tenements' and the census lists fourteen heads of household resident there, where two names were given in the *Primary Valuation*.[50]

The second exclusion of names concerns tenements held in connection with employment or 'place', such as by gardeners or herdsmen. The early *Primary valuation* books do not make these distinctions but give the name of the person who occupied the property.[51] From 1850, generic descriptions such as 'caretaker's house' or 'herd's house' start to appear in the books with the name of the lessor instead of the name of the occupier, and after 1852 they are routine.[52] The *Instructions 1853* specifically required that the name of the immediate lessor and not the occupier be recorded in these cases.[53] Thus the personal names of stewards, dairymen, woodrangers, labourers, cottiers and others were edited out before printing although they continued to be recorded in many of the manuscript documents well into the mid-1850s. The *Primary valuation* book for Scarriff Union, Co. Clare contains many such entries. In the townland of Lakyle, Clonrush, Revd Alex. P. Hanlon is listed as occupier of 'nine labourers' houses', total valuation £3 15s., with no land attached.[54] In Aughinish, Ogonnelloe, Simon G. Purdon, who had a house valued at £30 at Rahena Beg and was the landlord of most of the parish, was listed as occupier of a lot consisting of cottiers' houses and woods.[55] The persons who lived in these houses were not named in the *Primary valuation*.

The presence of a name in the *Primary valuation* can have different meanings. Matters that need to be considered include whether the person actually lived in the place where their name was listed, whether they were an occupier or a lessor, or both, and the status of the lessor. Apart from the cases outlined above, the occupier was the person who lived in the house and

---

49 *PV, Co. Dublin, union of Dublin North* (1854), pp 179–80. Fifty-four lots are listed, of which 42 are dwellings and 28 of these are 'lodgings'. Apart from the night asylum and three vacant properties, names are listed in respect of 50 houses. 50 Census 1901 Dublin 48/91, N form and B1 form; *Thom's official directory of the United Kingdom of Great Britain and Ireland for the year 1901* (Dublin, 1901). 51 For examples, see *PV, Co. Kilkenny, barony of Crannagh* (1849), and *PV, Co. Tipperary, barony of Ormond Upper* (1850). 52 For examples, see *PV, Co. Dublin, barony of Balrothery East* (1852), p. 58; *PV, Queen's County, barony of Clarmallagh* (1850), pp 6,9, 12, 24, 3 1, 33; *PV, Queen's County, barony of Upperwoods* (1850), pp 17, 63; *PV, Co. Tipperary, barony of Iffa and Offa East* (1850), pp 50, 57, 141. 53 OL/1/2/7, §12. See OL/1/2/4, §140,153–5 for earlier guidance. 54 *PV, Co. Clare, union of Scarriff* (1855), p. 78. 55 Ibid., pp17–19, 25.

farmed the land. Although the immediate lessor was the person from whom the occupier held the tenement, the name of the real owner may never appear, because there can be one or more levels of subletting. Subdivision and subletting of land was common practice, despite efforts to prevent it. For example, on the Lansdowne estate in Co. Kerry, this was strongly discouraged and most occupiers held directly from Lord Lansdowne, but subdivision was known to take place and the *Primary valuation* book for Kenmare parish shows examples of subletting.[56]

It is possible in some cases to see a complete trail of letting arrangements, but this becomes more complicated as the number of levels of subletting increases. In the simplest version, the immediate lessor was the owner of the property and let it to the occupier directly, for example in Ballyeighter, Aughrim, Co. Galway, Lord Clonbrock let six lots directly to seven occupiers (see fig. 5.1).[57] In a more complicated but common version found throughout the books, a property was held from an immediate lessor by an occupier who retained part for himself and sublet parts to others. An example in Inchnagree, Doneraile, Co. Cork, consisted of 262 acres and the immediate lessor was James Hill. It was let in two fairly equal lots to John Morrissy and the representatives of Arundell Hill, who then sublet the houses only, making a total of seven lots (see fig. 5.2).[58] Where further subletting took place, it can be difficult to establish the exact situation. An arrangement involving three levels of relationships can be seen in the townland of Slievebrickan, Tomregan, Co. Cavan, where the entire townland was held by Dorothea Griffith from the representatives of John C. Jones. Although Griffith was listed as the occupier of three tenements (herd's house, land and bog), she did not live in the townland and the real occupier of the herd's house was not named. Griffith was the immediate lessor of the other tenements, including three leased to Terence Donohue, who then sublet a house to John Donohue (see fig. 5.3).[59]

Similar arrangements affected the definition of ownership in towns, from the humblest cabin to the grand houses of Dublin that were not freehold. For example, Griffith always referred to his house at 2 Fitzwilliam Place as his property, but the immediate lessor was the Rt. Hon. Sidney Herbert, a member of the Pembroke family whose estate still includes large parts of south Dublin.[60]

Ground used for agricultural purposes was described as 'land', dwellings were described as 'houses', other outbuildings as 'offices' and a list of build-

---

56 Gerard J. Lyne, *The Lansdowne Estate in Kerry under W.S. Trench, 1849–72* (Dublin, 2001), pp 4–10; *PV, Co. Kerry, barony of Glanarought* (1852), pp 10–12. **57** *PV, Co. Galway, union of Ballinasloe* (1856), pp 8–9. **58** *PV, Co. Cork, barony of Fermoy* (1851), p. 65. **59** *PV, Co. Cavan, union of Bawnboy* (1857), p. 5. **60** *Report from select committee on valuation, 1869*, question 1429; *PV, Co. Dublin, union of Dublin South*, p. 143.

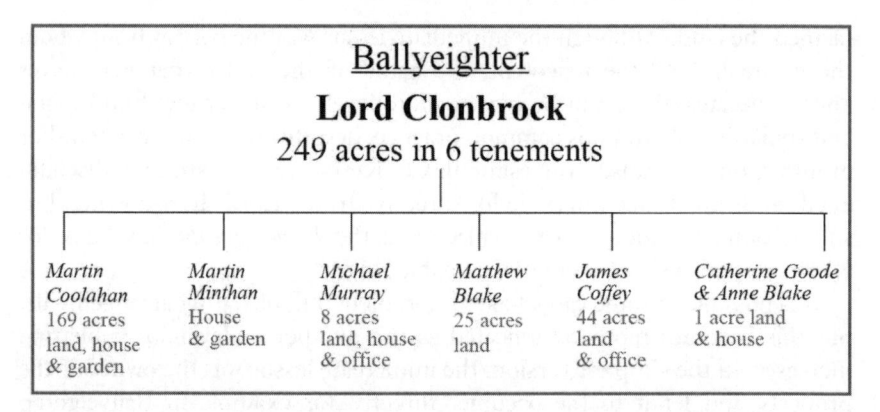

```
                        Ballyeighter
                       Lord Clonbrock
                    249 acres in 6 tenements
    ┌──────────┬──────────┬──────────┬──────────┬──────────┐
  Martin      Martin     Michael    Matthew    James      Catherine Goode
  Coolahan    Minthan    Murray     Blake      Coffey     & Anne Blake
  169 acres   House      8 acres    25 acres   44 acres   1 acre land
  land, house & garden   land, house land       land       & house
  & garden               & office              & office
```

5.1 Simple letting arrangement.

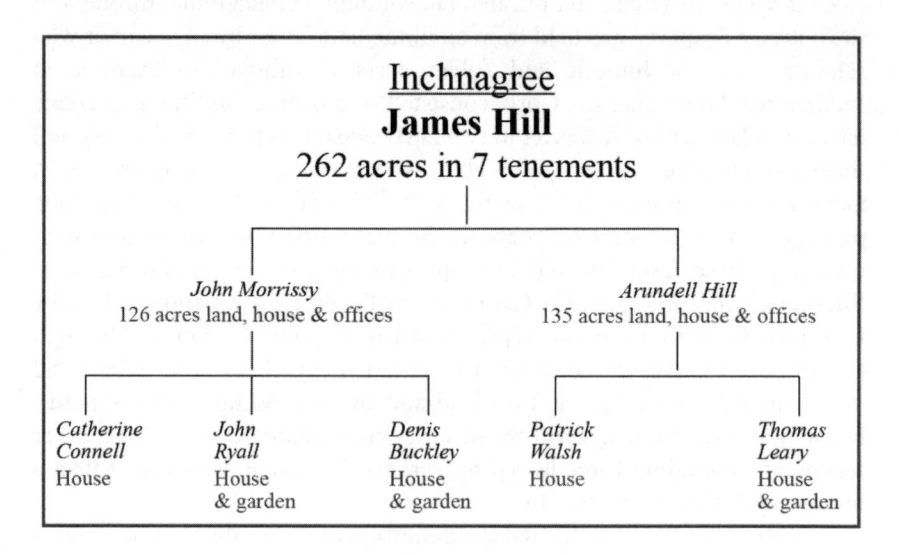

```
                          Inchnagree
                          James Hill
                    262 acres in 7 tenements
          ┌──────────────────────────┴──────────────────────┐
      John Morrissy                              Arundell Hill
  126 acres land, house & offices        135 acres land, house & offices
   ┌──────┬──────┬──────┐                    ┌──────────┬──────────┐
 Catherine  John    Denis                  Patrick              Thomas
 Connell    Ryall   Buckley                Walsh                Leary
 House      House   House                  House                House
            & garden & garden                                   & garden
```

5.2 Letting arrangement with subletting.

ings that were to be 'more particularly described' was given in the *Instructions 1853*.[61] The terse description 'house, office and land' was used for most tenements and treated all entries in an egalitarian manner, mostly on one line, using standardized words to depict situations of great contrast. The 132 acres in the townland of Ballintober, Killallaghtan, Co. Galway, was in four tenements, each described as 'house, offices and land'. The total value of the houses was £5 10s.[62] Properties in the Georgian squares of Dublin, where most houses were described not very differently as 'house, offices and small

61 OL/1/2/7, §43–4. 62 *PV, Co. Galway, union of Ballinasloe* (1856), p. 87.

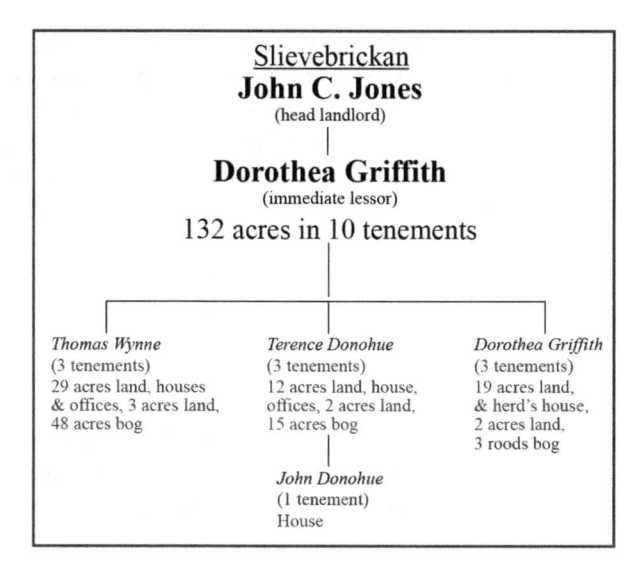

```
┌─────────────────────────────────────────────────────────────┐
│                       Slievebrickan                         │
│                       John C. Jones                         │
│                       (head landlord)                       │
│                             │                               │
│                     Dorothea Griffith                       │
│                      (immediate lessor)                     │
│                   132 acres in 10 tenements                 │
│                             │                               │
│        ┌────────────────────┼────────────────────┐          │
│   Thomas Wynne         Terence Donohue       Dorothea Griffith │
│   (3 tenements)         (3 tenements)         (3 tenements) │
│   29 acres land, houses 12 acres land, house, 19 acres land,│
│   & offices, 3 acres land, offices, 2 acres land, & herd's house, │
│   48 acres bog          15 acres bog          2 acres land, │
│                             │                 3 roods bog   │
│                        John Donohue                         │
│                        (1 tenement)                         │
│                        House                                │
└─────────────────────────────────────────────────────────────┘
```

5.3 Letting arrangement with several levels of subletting.

garden', were valued at over £100 each.[63] The property in Dublin with the highest value was dealt with in a few words: 'Trinity College buildings and park, £4,750',[64] and the other great public buildings were similarly noted, such as 'Bank of Ireland [in College Green], buildings, offices and yards attached, £3,800',[65] or 'Dublin Castle, government offices, official residences, grounds and yards, £2,800'.[66]

The books show rural areas made up of houses, land, gardens and yards, but they also include orchards, osieries,[67] woods and plantations, mountain land, bog and commonage, houses in ruins and under construction, quays and landing places, mills and collieries, towing paths, canals and railways, lighthouses, salmon fisheries, eel weirs and oyster beds. The towns and villages have buildings of all kinds: constabulary barracks, prisons and lunatic asylums, workhouses, hospitals and dispensaries, court and sessions houses, schools, graveyards, chapels and churches of many denominations, workshops and manufactories.

The perusal of the entire book for a parish, a town or other geographic area presents a picture of the built environment, social conditions and economic activity. The book for the union of Ballinasloe covers both the rural areas and the town.[68] It includes small holdings, houses with low valuations, a small number of houses of middle value, schools, churches, chapels and

63 *PV, Co. Dublin, union of Dublin South* (1854), p. 118, Merrion Square East and South; p. 144, Fitzwilliam Square South.   64 Ibid., p. 70.   65 Ibid., p. 162.   66 Ibid., p. 33.   67 A plantation of willow used in making baskets.   68 *PV, Co. Galway, union of Ballinasloe* (1856).

graveyards, forges, the Midland Great Western Railway and the Grand Canal, a quarry, plantations, police barracks and dispensaries, fair greens, many herds' houses, and the magazine, tower and garden of the Board of Ordnance at Esker. In the town of Ballinasloe there are a number of schools, a lying-in hospital, a gasworks, an agricultural hall, an 'old brewery', a convent, a hotel, a tan yard, a fair green, a market house, a shambles, a Roman Catholic chapel in progress, a police barracks, a sessions house and bridewell, a dispensary and the workhouse which, as usual, is the most valuable building of the entire union and which, with a valuation of £250, must have been one of the larger examples of its kind.

The book for Waterford city was published in 1851 when the city had a population of 36,628.[69] It describes yards for coal, timber and slate, an old sail-cloth factory, a starch factory, lime kilns and salt works, iron foundries, steam mills, Waterford Gas Company, a tan yard, a coach factory, breweries, beer cellars and a dockyard. There were many bacon cellars and stores, a weighhouse, market and stores for butter, a fish market and store, corn stores and kilns, two delph stores, a glass house, a feather store, spirit and bonding stores, and the custom house. There were several banks, the hotel and coach house of Charles Bianconi, and the offices of the Waterford Steam Packet Company and the Chamber of Commerce. Many of the commercial premises had high valuations, indicating large sizes. There were old and new courthouses, county gaols and infantry barracks. There was a billiard room and a club house. The houses varied a great deal, from those valued at under £1 to the Bishop's Palace at Cathedral Square, valued at £110. The city had a large number of premises occupied by charities, from Fanning's poor house (valued at £118) to Carroll's poor house (valued at £5), a lying-in hospital, auxiliary workhouses, a large leper hospital (later the Waterford Infirmary), and a fever hospital. There were schools, including national schools, a Blue Coat free school, the commercial school and the Christian Brothers free school. The presence of the Society of Friends can be seen in the meeting houses, burial grounds, school and property in the city owned by the Trustees of Newtown School.[70]

The books contain few references to business concerns. Manufacturing premises, mostly mills, breweries and distilleries, were identified, but no mention was made of professions other than what can be deduced from the names listed. Not a single public house was included, and so few shops that they appear to be errors. The book for Clonmel mentioned almost no shops,[71] and the larger city of Waterford included a very small number.[72] However, in Dublin the development of department stores is heralded in the

69 *Census of Ireland, 1851, part I, vol. II, Co. Waterford* (Dublin, 1852), p. 373.   70 *PV, Co. Waterford, Waterford city* (1851).   71 *PV, Co. Tipperary, barony of Iffa and Offa East* (1850), pp 119, 123, 134.   72 See example *PV, Co. Tipperary, barony of Ormond Upper* (1850), p. 85.

'warerooms' found around the city. The premises of Cannock, White and Company at 12–14 Henry Street is the present site of Arnotts department store, and number 14 Henry Street was owned by John Arnott.[73] The warerooms of Todd, Burns and Company at the corner of Jervis Street and Mary Street became the department store of that name.[74] It is difficult to explain why some activities were specified and not others when commercial designation had a bearing on the valuation.[75] The Dublin city books contain many references to bakeries, and several are listed in Galway, but none are mentioned in Waterford.[76] Monuments or historic buildings were of no interest apart from their eligibility for tax. Ancient structures such as Dun Aengus on Inishmore island[77] are not mentioned, but Trim Castle merited inclusion in a reference to two acres of 'land surrounding Trim Castle'.[78] In Waterford city, the medieval Reginald's Tower was valued as normal because it was still in use as the constabulary barracks.[79] No trace of the Irish language appears in the books, and the long lists of occupiers of places where Irish was the normal spoken language, such as the parish of Moyrus, Co. Galway, are rendered in English.[80]

All houses are included in the *Primary valuation*, and their valuation prices provide good indications of their quality and condition. In her study of the area around Newgrange, Co. Meath, Geraldine Stout relates house types to the sizes of farms. She includes photographs of existing houses that would typically have been valued at 10s., £2 10s., £6 10s. and £65 in 1850. This can provide researchers with an idea of what a house with a particular valuation in a rural setting might look like.[81]

In the Townland Valuation most houses were omitted because they were worth less than £5. A breakdown of the figures in the *Primary valuation* quantifies a situation of general poverty and poor living conditions. In the samples examined below, most houses were valued below £5, with large numbers below £1. The rural areas of the union of Bawnboy, Co. Cavan in 1857 (excluding the towns of Swanlinbar and Ballyconnell) had only fourteen houses valued at £10 or over out of the estimated total of 2,000 houses, and of those the most valuable were two houses worth £40. In the

---

73 *PV, Co. Dublin, union of Dublin North* (1854), p. 66.   74 *PV, Co. Dublin, union of Dublin North* (1854), p. 69. Todd Burns functioned as a department store until the premises were taken over by Penneys in 1969.   75 *PV, Co. Limerick, barony of Connello Upper* (1852), p. 97; OL/5/1235, p. 41, Michael Irwin (licensed), 'add 1/8 for business', with a further note 'no business now done in this'.   76 *PV, Co. Dublin, union of Dublin North* (1854) and *PV, Co. Dublin, union of Dublin South* (1854); *PV, Co. Galway, union of Galway* (1856), pp 9–35; *PV, Co. Waterford, Waterford City* (1851).   77 *PV, Co. Galway, union of Galway* (1856), lot 2 of townland of Kilmurvey. This is a large lot held in common between several occupiers.   78 *PV, Co. Meath, union of Trim* (1854), p. 77.   79 *PV, Co. Waterford, Waterford city* (1851), p. 58.   80 *PV, Co. Galway, union of Clifden* (1855), pp 39–80. See also J.H. Andrews, *Atlas of Ireland* (1979), p. 87.   81 Geraldine Stout, *Newgrange and the bend in the Boyne* (Cork, 2002), pp 146–63; G. Stout, 'The bend of the Boyne,

union of Scarriff, Co. Clare (1855), the number of houses in the rural areas is estimated at over 2,000; only twenty houses reached a valuation of between £5 and £10 and a further eighteen, £10 or more. In many townlands the total valuation of all houses did not reach £10.[82] In both Bawnboy and Scarriff, the buildings with the highest values are the workhouses, at £118 and £100, respectively.[83] Many of the other high-value buildings in these two books were public buildings, such as constabulary barracks and chapels.

Another feature of the lists of names is the large number of occupiers and the very small number of lessors. In many cases, the same lessor is listed for entire townlands or parishes, with only small patches in other hands. By and large, individual persons are listed as the owners of property, and few institutional landlords are listed. Exceptions include the canal and railway companies, which generally owned the property connected with their operations, Trinity College Dublin, owner of large estates throughout the country, and the Law Life Assurance Company, which bought the Martin estate in Co. Galway in 1853 and owned a large proportion of the union of Clifden.[84] Many of the institutional landlords were bodies associated with churches, such as vicars choral of Christ Church Dublin, listed as lessor of the complex in Dublin described as 'King's Inns, Prerogative Court, registry offices, law library, gate-lodges, garden and lawn'.[85] The dependence of charities and churches on income from property can be seen throughout the books. The trustees of the church in Lusk, Co. Dublin owned several premises in the nearby village of Balrothery, as did the trustees of Wilson's Hospital.[86] In Dublin city, the rector and churchwardens of St Catherine's Parish held a brewery and mill valued at £340 in the James' Street area.[87] Some surprising names appear, including Lord Palmerston, who was one of the lessors of the complex in North Brunswick Street, Dublin that included the Richmond Asylum and the North Dublin union workhouse, and who became prime minister less than a year later in 1855.[88] The extent to which the families of the developers of eighteenth-century Dublin continued to occupy houses in the streets they had built can be seen with the Sherrard family still owning part of Sherrard Street, and similar cases in Eccles Street and Jervis Street.[89]

Co. Meath' in F.H.A. Aalen, Kevin Whelan and Matthew Stout (eds), *Atlas of the Irish rural landscape* (Cork, 1997), pp 299–315.   82 *PV, Co. Cavan, union of Bawnboy* (1857); *PV, Co. Clare, union of Scarriff* (1855).   83 *PV, Co. Cavan, union of Bawnboy* (1857), p. 29; *PV, Co. Clare, union of Scarriff* (1855), p. 64.   84 Thomas Colville Scott, *Connemara after the Famine*, ed. Tim Robinson (Dublin, 1995). See *PV, Co. Galway, union of Clifden* (1855).   85 *PV, Co. Dublin, union of Dublin North* (1854), p. 251.   86 *PV, Co. Dublin, barony of Balrothery East* (1847), pp 15–16.   87 *PV, Co. Dublin, union of Dublin South* (1854), p. 305.   88 *PV, Co. Dublin, union of Dublin North* (1854), pp 181–2.   89 Ibid., pp 166–7, 246 and 69.

USING THE *PRIMARY VALUATION* AS THE STARTING POINT FOR RESEARCH

The *Primary valuation* is a useful starting point for research. It is searchable online, using either a personal or family name or a place-name. Once this is identified the researcher can work backwards in time through the manuscript books and forward through appeals and beyond to the cancelled books. (See appendix I.)

Despite the usefulness of the summary information in the *Primary valuation* books, the presentation of a large amount of data in a small space means that it is truncated and detail is omitted. The detail can be found in the manuscript documents. This would allow the researcher to determine the precise location and boundaries of the tenement, the quality of land and, in some cases, the kind of farming carried on, as well as the type, size, quality and position of the house where the occupier lived, and the same information about the neighbours and surrounding area.

The different information in the *Primary valuation* and in the manuscript books is summarized below:

	Primary valuation	**Manuscript documents**
Land	Standardised description	Detailed description of composition of soil.
	Total acreage	Breakdown of the acreage of each quality of land in the tenement with the rate per acre of each.
	Total valuation	Valuation of each quality of land in the tenement and total.
Buildings	Standardised description	For each building in the tenement: description, measurements, quality, materials, condition and rate per measure.
	Total valuation	Valuation of each building and total.
Names	Occupiers and lessors at the date of the field work	Range of names associated with the tenement, including information on former occupiers and corrections and revisions showing changes.
Locations	Tenements numbered in townlands and shown on maps	Some names omitted in the printed books. Maps show exact locations of tenements and houses in townlands.

5.4 Data in *Primary valuation* and in manuscript books.

The valuation price provides an indication of the quality of land, but apart from words such as 'mountain' or 'plantation', little can be determined about its nature or the kind of farming carried on. The qualifying terms used for some houses (for example, wood ranger's house, sheep house) may allow inferences to be drawn. For example, in the parish of Caherconlish, Co.

Limerick, there are references to dairies and dairymen's houses.[90] The occupiers of land held in common are listed in the *Primary valuation*, with the lessor and the amount of valuation of each occupier, but the proportion held by each person is not stated. This information can be found in the manuscript books.[91] The *Primary valuation* covering the townland of Garroman, Moyrus, Co. Galway lists eleven occupiers of over 1,200 acres of common land. The manuscript tenure book gives the proportions of the total held by each occupier.[92]

Fuller descriptions of buildings are also found in the manuscript books. A premises in Kiltoghert, Co. Leitrim occupied by the National Board of Education is described in the *Primary valuation* as 'house, offices and land';[93] the entry in the house book is 'Model farm house or agricultural school'.[94] The extent of the difference between the printed *Primary valuation* and the manuscript books can be seen in a comparison of entries relating to Roundstone, Co. Galway. The *Primary valuation* describes lot 14 as a 'house, offices, yard and garden' occupied by Denis Kelly. The house book of 1854 describes lot 14 as a hotel, stores and stables, with the comment: 'Small enclosed yard and garden which is well kept, also a small garden in front. The only hotel here principally kept up by tourists and sportsmen. Good business for four months.' In the *Primary valuation*, lot 27 consisted of a house, small garden and yard. The house book described a 'publican and grocer, also post office' and gives the length of frontage of the post office on the street.[95] The manuscript book for the nearby town of Clifden, made in 1853, was corrected to provide the text for printing and shows how all the detail relating to shops, businesses and professions was edited out. Thus the butcher, stationer, pawnbroker, haberdasher, watchmaker, shoemakers, tailors and several publicans were crossed out and the standard 'house, yard, offices' substituted.[96]

Two examples from Co. Sligo illustrate the additional information in the manuscript books, both from 1855. The *Primary valuation* lists Richard Leheny as occupier of a house in the village of Aclare, and the house book describes the premises as 'shop for the sale of spirits, porter and ale. This public house does a good business on Saturdays.'[97] In the town of Ardnaree

---

90 *PV, Co. Limerick, barony of Clanwilliam* (1852), examples on pp 23, 27.   91 See examples in parish of Abbeygormacan, Co. Galway in *PV, Co. Galway, union of Ballinasloe* (1856), p. 101, and *PV, Co. Galway, union of Clifden* (1855), p. 21 and throughout this book.   92 *PV, Co. Galway, union of Clifden* (1855), p. 41; OL/6/723, pp 2–5. The proportions are given in fifty-sixths or 112ths.   93 *PV, Co. Leitrim, union of Carrick-on-Shannon* (1856), p. 80.   94 OL/5/4023, p. 79. 95 *PV, Co. Galway, union of Clifden* (1855), p. 59; OL/5/2791, pp 5, 8.   96 OL/5/2742. The Townland Valuation house book for Clifden (1844) contains detailed notes, see OL/5/2743. 97 *PV, Co. Sligo, union of Tobercurry* (1857), p. 107; OL/5/3235, lot 15.

the Rt. Revd Thomas Feeney was occupier of a house and yard valued at £8. The valuator observed that the house was used as a classical school: 'It is neither public or charitable as all the pupils pay high for education in it. A great portion of the house is occupied by priests.' A second book for Ardnaree names these premises as 'Diocesan school'.[98]

Where the names of certain occupiers of tenements are omitted in the *Primary valuation*, they can frequently be found in the manuscript house books. In Gortymadden, Abbeygormacan, Co. Galway, James Smith and James Breslin are given in the printed book as the occupiers of two herds' houses, but the 1853 house book lists Michael Fahey as herd to James Smith and John Connor as herd to James Breslin.[99] In Grange West, Caherconlish, Co. Limerick, a tenement listed in the *Primary valuation* as a dairyman's house is described in the manuscript house book as occupied by James Conway, 'caretaker, lives in the house'.[1] After 1853, the name of the lessor was to be noted in place of the occupier. In many, but not all, cases the name of the real occupier continued to be recorded in the manuscript book and was excised before printing. In Lissananny Beg, Emlaghfad, Co. Sligo, James Jackson is listed in the *Primary valuation* as lessor of a herd's house. Both the house book and the tenure book in 1855 name Thomas Connolly as occupier, but the entry was corrected to 'herd's house' before printing.[2] Useful related names may also be found in the earlier Townland Valuation house books. A house in Cregg, Drumcliff, Co. Sligo was occupied by William Gallagher at the time of the Townland Valuation in 1839. The house book was revised in 1855 and Gallagher's name was erased and replaced with 'Thomas Ward's herd'. The quality of this house had deteriorated and the valuation was reduced.[3] Other similar cases can be seen in Sligo.

While the *Primary valuation* contains general information about buildings, it gives no indication of what a house looked like. The example in the table below shows how the data from the manuscript house book can expand on the entries in the *Primary valuation* in the townland of Ballynacloona, Kilmurry, Co. Tipperary.[4] The shape, size and materials of the houses and other buildings can be ascertained from the house book, using the codes from the instructions and the measurements in the house book (see appendix G).[5]

---

98 *PV, Co. Sligo, union of Tobercurry* (1857), p. 147; OL/5/3237, 158 Abbey Street; OL/5/3236, p. 16. This building was not exempted. 99 *PV, Co. Galway, union of Ballinasloe* (1856), p. 102; OL/5/1026, p. 39. 1 *PV, Co. Limerick, barony of Clanwilliam* (1852), p. 23 and OL/4/6059, p. 120. 2 *PV, Co. Sligo, union of Boyle* (1858), p. 45; OL/4/6749, p. 170 (house book); OL/6/1521, p. 4 (tenure book). 3 OL/4/6739, p. 176 (house book); OL/6/1510, p. 55 (tenure book); *PV, Co. Sligo, union of Sligo* (1858), p. 76 (no. 19a). 4 *PV, Co. Tipperary, barony of Iffa and Offa East* (1850), p. 65 and OL/5/1531, pp 10–17 (1846). 5 OL/1/2/4 (1839), §131–7 and OL/1/2/7 (1853), §174–90.

Primary Valuation					House book							
Lot no.	Occupier	Lessor	Buildings	Valuation buildings	Quality	Description	Length	Breadth	Height	Size in measures	Rate per measure	Gross valuation
3ABCa	Thomas Ryan	William Barker	House, offices	£11 7s. 0d.	1A-	House, porch, addition + 12 other buildings	36 8 30	21 2 21.6	15 9 8	75 1 64	1s. 6½d. 1s. 1½d.	£5 15s. 7d. 1s. 0d. £2 18s. 8d. £10 3s. 2d. Total £18 18s. 5d.
Aa	Alice Carberry	Thomas Ryan	House	5s. 0d.	3C	Dwelling	21	14	6	30	2½d.	6s. 3d.
Cc	Michael Barclay	Thomas Ryan	House	12s. 0d.	3C+ 3C+ 3C+ 1C+	Dwelling, porch, stable + piggery	39 6.6 14 8	14.6 24 11 5.6	6 6 5.6 4.6	56 1 15 4	3½d. 3½d. 2d. 2¼d.	16s. 4d. 3d. 2s. 6d. 9d. Total 19s. 10d.

5.5 Data on houses in *Primary valuation* and manuscript house books.

This manuscript house book was made in September 1846 and revised in January 1850. The *Primary valuation* was published in October 1850. Three examples from this townland relate to the occupiers Thomas Ryan, Alice Carberry and Michael Barclay. In the *Primary valuation* Thomas Ryan occupied a house and offices valued at £11 7s., leased from William Barker. In addition to his dwelling, the house book lists, for Ryan's tenement, twelve other buildings, including farm buildings, servants' sleeping quarters and a car house. The letter code 1A- was given to the house and most of the buildings, showing they were slated and built of stone or brick with lime mortar, with ordinary finish. If more than twenty years old, better-finished buildings would be given this rating. Three of the farm buildings (cow house, dairy and potato house, not shown) had the code 3C+, showing they were thatched, with either stone walls with mud mortar, dry stone walls pointed or good mud walls and were in good repair. A fourth farm building (also not shown) was given 3C, meaning it was of the same quality but out of repair. The house measured 36 feet (11 metres) wide by 21 feet (6.5 metres) deep, and was 15 feet (4.6 metres) high to the bottom of the eaves, so was likely to have two storeys. The footprint was 71 square metres and, if in two storeys, the floor area was 142 square metres including the walls. The house book figure was reduced by one-third to give the valuation of £11 7s.

Ryan sublet several other tenements in the townland, including a house valued at 5s. to Alice Carberry. That this was a single-storey rectangular thatched house, made of stone or mud walls, with a total floor area of 28 square metres. It was old, not in repair and was classified as 3C, the second lowest score for a house. Michael Barclay's tenement is described in the *Primary valuation* as 'house, offices and garden' valued at 12s. The house book, where the name is written 'Bartley', shows that it was a single-storey rectangular thatched house of 35 square metres, made of stone or mud walls and in good repair. His piggery was classified as 1C+, and was built of stone or brick with a slate roof and was old but in repair.

PUBLICATION AND CHANGES IN THE BOOKS

The *Primary valuation* books appeared piecemeal over a period of seventeen years. The first books published were seven baronies in Co. Dublin in 1847, and the last was the union of Armagh in December 1864. Over this period, six further valuation acts came into force, and while minor changes were made, the core data remained the same throughout. The text for printing was supplied in 'printers' copies' made from the manuscript tenure books,[6] but no example of these documents is extant and there are no known instructions to the printers. The large amount of data and the permanent preoccupation with economy would have been factors in determining the size of the pages and the style of print.

Although printing of the valuation lists was routine since the mid-1830s, it took a little time for the production of the *Primary valuation* books to be organized in a satisfactory manner. In 1845, in anticipation of the tenement work, Griffith wrote to the secretary of the poor law commissioners, expressing doubts about the printing and suggesting that 'perhaps lithographed copies might be made at a less expense than ordinary printing'.[7] In 1847, the books were printed by two Dublin firms, Alexander Thom and Gunn & Cameron. In 1848–9 further books were printed by Thom. However, Treasury rules required using the Government Stationery Office and the contract was awarded to the Dublin firm of G. & J. Grierson, which printed the majority of the books issued between 1850 and early 1852.[8] Griffith was not happy with the rate of progress, and in April 1850 wrote to William Wake in the Stationery Office that Grierson could not provide the output required: 'My opinion is that Mr Thom should have at least half of the printing. If matters are not arranged in a satisfactory manner I must on public grounds bring the matter before the Treasury.'[9] The pressures can be observed in the fact that different kinds of paper were sometimes used in the same book.[10] In December 1851, Griffith again wrote to Wake saying that Grierson was unable to print more than about one hundred pages a week, about half of what was required, but that he had already spoken to Mr Thom, who had 'abundant means' to do the other half.[11] In 1852 the printing

---

6 OL/6/2, inside cover. 7 OL/2/10, pp 229–30. 8 OL/2/6, p. 210. 9 OL/2/12, p. 392.
10 *PV, Co. Waterford, barony of Coshmore and Coshbride* (1851), has blue paper for pages 1–40, and cream paper on p. 41 and again from p. 77 (printed by Grierson, 1851); *PV, Co. Waterford, barony of Decies-without-Drum* (1851), is on pale blue paper to p. 100 and from there brighter blue (printed by Grierson, 1851); *PV, Co. Cork, Municipal Borough of Cork* (1852), is on blue paper up to p. 64, pale blue paper pp 65–220, and then blue paper again pp 221–85 (printed by Grierson).
11 OL/2/13, pp 272–3. The *Primary valuation* shows that Grierson was a smaller business than Thom. Its works in Essex Street, Dublin were valued at £57 for 2 buildings, according to *PV, Co. Dublin, union of Dublin South* (1854), p. 172. Thom's premises in Abbey Street was valued at a total of £180, which made it one of the most valuable concerns in that large street, according

was shared between Grierson and Thom and, in addition, fifteen books were lithographed.[12] From 1853, Thom did all the printing.

The publication of the *Primary valuation* was an extraordinary achievement. The names of occupiers and lessors, the descriptions of the property, the square area of every piece of land and the valuation of every tenement in the country were printed in a standardized format, at a time when the population was at its highest. Compared with the Townland Valuation, the printing of the *Primary valuation* was challenging in both the quantity and complexity of data: for the Townland Valuation, there was one large printed notice for each barony (see plate 10), and one slim printed volume for each county (see plate 11); in contrast, in all counties except Carlow, the *Primary valuation* comprised a separate book for each barony or poor law union. For Cork this amounted to twenty-four books, and for Louth there are four books. The *Townland valuation* gave summary figures for acreages and values of townlands, parishes and baronies. Each *Primary valuation* book printed individual entries for thousands of names in townlands, parishes and larger units, with further exacting data in more columns. For example, the barony of Crannagh, Co. Kilkenny, covers eight small pages of the *Townland valuation*,[13] and sixty-eight large and densely filled pages in the *Primary valuation*.[14] The difference can be seen in the example of Ballaghdorragh, Munterconnaught, Co. Cavan (plate 12) where there are more than twenty separate and detailed entries, including names. In the printed Townland Valuation book, one line covered this townland (plate 11).

There are minor variations in the early books. Those published under the 1846 act give the valuator's name and the date of the work at the end of each parish and some give lists of exemptions for examination by the sub-commissioners for appeal.[15] Deviations from the usual methodology were noted: where the valuation was made by replotting the Townland Valuation into tenements, this fact was recorded at the end of each parish.[16] The refer-

to *PV, Co. Dublin, union of Dublin North* (1854), p. 57. 12 *PV, Co. Cork, barony of Bear* (1852); *PV, Co. Cork, barony of Cork* (1852); *PV, Co. Cork, barony of Kinsale* (1852); *PV, Co. Cork, barony of Muskerry East* (1852); *PV, Co. Cork, barony of Muskerry West* (1852); *PV, Co. Cork, barony of Carbery East, West Division* (1852); *PV, Co. Cork, barony of Bantry* (1851); *PV, Co. Kerry, barony of Corkaguiney* (1852); *PV, Co. Kerry, barony of Dunkerron South* (1852); *PV, Co. Kerry, barony of Iveragh* (1852); *PV, Co. Limerick, barony of Connello Lower* (1852); *PV, Co. Limerick, barony of Connello Upper* (1852); *PV, Co. Limerick, barony of Glenquin* (1852); *PV, Co. Limerick, barony of Shanid* (1852); and *PV, Co. Tipperary, barony of Iffa and Offa West* (1852). A manuscript document could be reproduced by lithography without the laborious setting of type. As writing clerks were employed in the office and copies were already being made for the printer, it is likely this could have been done without much difficulty. There is no record of the printer who carried out the lithographic printing. 13 OL/14/1/21, pp 12–19. 14 *PV, Co. Kilkenny, barony of Crannagh* (1849). 15 See examples *PV, Co. Limerick, barony of Kenry* (1850) and *PV, Co. Cork, barony of Carbery East, East Division* (1851). 16 Example *PV, King's County, barony of Clonlisk* (1851), p. 2: 'arranged in tenements and valuation revised by direction of the Commissioner'.

ence of the printed Ordnance Survey map on which the townland was located was only routinely included from the middle of 1850.[17] Each book has a table of contents – but as is the case with the layouts of the covers, title pages and headers, there are variations throughout. The books were usually published with blue paper covers, printed with the act, the title '*Primary valuation*', the barony or poor law union and corresponding areas, information about appeals and the date and place of publication. The covers of the lithographed books bear similar information. After 1854 a further notice was added in red print warning that the *Primary valuation* was liable to appeal, was not to be used 'as the settled valuation' and that the final lists would be issued only in manuscript.[18]

Despite a generally high standard, the books contain some inconsistencies, and minor typographical errors are present.[19] As a rule, superfluous information was omitted, but it occasionally escaped editorial excision, such as the entry in respect of three houses adjoining Guinness' brewery in Dublin: 'taken down to widen the street'.[20] Under the 1846 act a number of books of alterations and revisions were printed following the appeals, and one book was issued under the 1852 act, but this was not continued.[21] These books are described under *appeal books*.

CONCLUSION

The *Primary valuation* is a summary of what property existed, who occupied and owned it, its extent and its valuation price. The relationship between tenements, occupiers and owners and the link to farms and common land can be seen at a glance. It is accessible, easy to use and informative and provides a snapshot of society, infrastructure and buildings. The compression of the information for large areas facilitates access and allows them to be viewed in their entirety. It was made to a uniform standard and the books are comparable, although made over a period of seventeen years and the valuations made between 1846 and 1852 were based on the fair letting value and not on the scale of prices. It is an excellent point of entry for research of all kinds in valuation and other archives, whether earlier or later. The summary nature of the *Primary valuation* means that it is short on detail, but where further information is required, the manuscript books are available.

17 First printed in the barony of Kilculliheen in Co. Waterford in April 1849.   18 For example, *PV, King's County, union of Parsonstown* (1854).   19 *PV, Co. Tipperary, barony of Iffa and Offa East* (1850), p 137, 'Gand Jury'; *PV, Co. Kerry, barony of Corkaguiney*, p. 11, 'dispencary'.   20 *PV, Co. Dublin, union of Dublin South* (1854), p. 304.   21 *Report from select committee on valuation, 1869*, questions 920–2: Commissioner J.B. Greene explained that the valuation was issued only in manuscript because of the cost of printing a second time.

At first view, the books can appear dense and seem to contain descriptions so standardized as to be meaningless. J.H. Andrews has remarked that the beautiful engraving of the Ordnance Survey six-inch maps transformed an untidy countryside into a work of art.[22] Similarly, the *Primary valuation* could be described as an abstraction of the countryside, with its systematic ordering of occupiers in townlands, parishes and counties in orderly, quantifiable rows of words and figures. It records the social, cultural and economic life of the country in broad brush strokes, but having the data relating to each place set out on the same page is most useful. It is now most frequently used as a genealogical research tool because of its listing of names, but its most valuable aspect may be as an entry point or as a signpost to further sources for research beyond the minimal entries. The investigation of the background detail using the very large series of manuscript documents will almost certainly yield rich rewards. The *Primary valuation* is the tip of a very large iceberg of information, most of which is made up of manuscript documents.

---

22 Andrews, *A paper landscape*, p. 134.

6

Appeals against the *Primary valuation*

The principle of appeal was established with the Valuation Act of 1826, and the Tenement Valuation Acts of 1846 and 1852 continued this, allowing appeals against the *Primary valuation*. The appeals were the last stage of work in establishing the valuation and the appeal documents are the last series of archives of the initial valuation. They provide the link between the archives made in the initial valuation and the updated valuation in the manuscript cancelled books, created as the documents of record, and still held in the Valuation Office. The appeal procedures under the two acts were different and the documents are in two series.

A. APPEALS UNDER THE 1846 ACT

The 1846 act created a massive expansion in eligibility to appeal, and it became possible for individual occupiers and lessors to appeal without cost and without legal assistance. This turned out to be one of the most unworkable aspects of the act, although it created documents that are among the most interesting and informative in the archives. The response of occupiers and owners in appealing in large numbers created dismay in the office, and the expense and experience of dealing with the workload demonstrated that another method was required.[1] One of the main changes brought in with the 1852 act was a new procedure for simpler and cheaper appeals.

Appeals under the 1846 act were heard in ninety-five baronies and documents for seventy-five of these are held in the National Archives,

---

1 OL/2/13, p. 100, Griffith to the chief secretary, Somerville, 19 Feb. 1851, explaining that as it is free, all occupiers appeal 'taking the chance of a reduction in the amount of the valuation of his tenement, as he conceives that the appeal can do him no injury. Hence the amount of appeals *which end in nothing* because there were no substantial grounds put forward for appeal, but as the county must pay the expense which in the county of Cork would probably exceed £5,000, it is time to put an end to the system.' A new valuation bill was introduced in February 1851, but did not pass. See also OL/2/13, pp 104–5, Griffith to sub-commissioner John Kelly, 26 Feb. 1851: 'Mr Buck will have informed you of the difficulty in which I am placed in consequence of the enormous expense of the sub-commissioners' court as compared to the cost of the valuation; and I find with much regret that the costs of you and Mr Buck's court exceed considerably that of any of the others, all of whom are now using their best endeavours to diminish the expense by deciding on the evidence in conjunction with the information previously observed.'

relating to Co. Carlow and parts of Cos. Clare, Cork, Dublin, Kerry (one document only), Kildare, Kilkenny, Limerick, Tipperary, Waterford, Wicklow and Queen's County.[2] The 1846 appeals also took place in parts of King's County and Co. Meath, but no documents from these appeals are known. Where only part of a county was appealed under the 1846 act, the remainder was appealed under the 1852 act.

The number of appeals against the Tenement Valuation varied from one place to another. In 1869 the new commissioner of valuation, J.B. Greene, described the 'incredible number of appeals; from one or two baronies in Tipperary alone we had over 5,000 appeals', and claimed that 'there were parties who trafficked in the appeals and got them up'.[3] By 1869 the predominant memory of the 1846 appeals was their high cost and the fact that the majority had failed, but the documents themselves show that many alterations were made as a result. The rate of appeals in Co. Tipperary was exceptionally high and in 1851 a specific return was made to parliament, noting that most originated in the office of 'one attorney who who had caused placards to be posted over the district, headed in large characters "Rents, Poor's Rates, Taxes"'.[4] As in the Townland Valuation, every effort was made to minimize the number of appeals by seeking consensus in advance. In June 1846, before publication of the *Primary valuation* for the barony of Nethercross, Co. Dublin, arrangements were made for owners to compare the draft lists with their own records and, in cases of difference as regards square area, to have the tenements re-surveyed.[5]

The first appeal hearings were held in Nethercross in September 1847, but the appeal books for this barony have not survived. The last hearings were in the barony of Shanid, Co. Limerick in August 1852. The second Tenement Valuation Act was passed on 30 June 1852 and *Primary valuation* books issued after that date were subject to the new system. Appeals in six baronies, where the process had been started before the new act and that had hearings scheduled for July and August 1852, proceeded under the old system.[6]

---

2 Listed in OL/19 and two microfilms MFA/16 and MFA/19. 3 *Report from select committee on valuation, 1869*, questions 368–73. 4 *Return stating the date of the completion of the field valuation in each barony in the Co. of Tipperary; of the number of parishes where revisions were held previous to the issuing of the primary valuation, with the names of the parishes where revisions were held more than once*, HC 1851 (403), pp 2–3 (hereinafter cited as *Return of completions and revisions in Co. Tipperary*, HC 1851 (403)): over 17,500 appeals were lodged in 8 of the 12 baronies of Co. Tipperary. 5 OL/2/11, p. 43. 6 Appeal books for 4 of these baronies are in the National Archives: OL/19/3/1, Co. Carlow, 6 July 1852; OL/19/6/3 Carbery East, West Division, Co. Cork, 27 July 1852; OL/19/17/4 Connello Lower, Co. Limerick, 20 July 1852; OL/19/17/23, Shanid, Co. Limerick, 24 Aug. 1852.

Arrangements for appeals

The appeals were carried out by barony and related to a printed *Primary valuation* book, the title page of which gave the venue and first date of the hearings. A model appeal form was included in the book. The completed forms were returned, first to the local board of guardians and then to the commissioner's office in Dublin where preparations for the hearings were made. Notices advertising the hearings were printed in numbers that indicate wide dissemination.[7] The appeals were heard by two sub-commissioners appointed by the lord lieutenant from among the senior valuators and further appeal could be made to the court of quarter sessions.[8]

The appeals were organised in a manner that confirmed their official status. A formal application was required, evidence was taken on oath and they were usually held in the local court house or sessions house. Alternative venues included a hotel, a private house and the Salmon Leap Inn in Leixlip, Co. Kildare.[9] The duration of the hearings depended on the numbers appealing, which varied from twenty-nine in the barony of Rathdown, Co. Wicklow, heard in one day,[10] to 362 in the barony of Maryborough East, Queen's County, heard over seventeen days, including one day when the sub-commissioner noted 'heard 86 appeals this day'.[11] The large numbers in Co. Tipperary can be seen in the book for the barony of Clanwilliam, where the hearings took six days more than the thirty days originally planned.[12] There is a reference in Co. Kilkenny to allowing a further day for hearing 'complaints who did not appeal'.[13] The sub-commissioners had the power to summon witnesses, but there is no indication that they used it.

At the hearings, the appellants were sworn. The sub-commissioners heard the evidence, asked questions, and sought the views of third parties. They wrote notes, usually numbering the entries to correspond to the *Primary valuation*. The appellants explained the background to the appeal and compared their valuation with that of similar holdings. They expanded on the circumstances, rent or tenure, and gave all manner of extraneous information. Some appellants withdrew their appeals or failed to appear.[14] The notes show that both field books and field maps were consulted at the hearings.[15]

---

7 OL/19/24/1, notice inside front cover. The imprint shows that 100 copies were printed; OL/19/29/1, 75 copies; OL/19/24/2, 50 copies. All printed by Alex. Thom in Dublin. 8 The court of quarter sessions was also known as the assistant barrister's court. 9 OL/19/13/4, hotel; OL/19/27/16, Mrs Hill's house in Toomyvarra, Co. Tipperary and OL/19/13/2. 10 OL/19/32/1, note on table of contents. 11 OL/19/24/7, appeal notice inside back cover and note inside cover. 12 OL/19/27/1, notice inside back cover. 13 OL/19/14/8, notice inside back cover. 14 OL/19/14/5, pp 10, 12–13, no appearance; p. 19, appeal withdrawn; OL/19/14/9, p. 6, two appeals withdrawn; OL/19/24/2, p. 28, 'Mr Rodes withdraws his objections to this.' 15 OL/19/24/6, p. 8 (field book); OL/19/24/7, note inside back cover: reference to the sheets stored in 'the long box' during hearings in barony of Maryborough West, Queen's County and to the absence of maps for some townlands. 16 Ibid., p. 28.

It appears that some decisions were made immediately and some deferred. Sub-commissioner John Kelly wrote: 'Marked my decisions where there is evidence, pencilled where not, or left blank when no change.'[16] Where changes were made, it was necessary to review and, in many cases, to alter neighbouring tenements in order to maintain the relativity of the valuation. Yet Griffith claimed in a letter to the chief secretary, Somerville, in May 1850 that the relativity of the valuation was destroyed by the appeals.[17]

Further field work was in some cases ordered before a final decision was made, and this was recorded in the revising surveyors' books. In the office, the results were recalculated and the books were examined closely by staff.[18] The notes show that the two sub-commissioners conferred together,[19] the minor differences between the two books were reconciled by clerks, the bigger differences were discussed,[20] and senior staff were consulted.[21] Several books contain tables where the different prices were compared.[22] In the office work, reference was made back to the original field documents, for example, in order to check names,[23] or to copy data into the revising surveyor's book.[24]

The appeal books (and the revising surveyor's books) were also used to carry out important corrections to the *Primary valuation* in matters that did not concern appeals, thereby creating a final copy of the text, ready for its transcription as the first cancelled book. This included updating the information on tenements, boundaries and houses that were said to have been knocked 'down'. With a time lag of at least two years between the field work and the *Primary valuation*, it was inevitable that some of the information was out of date by the time the book was printed. In addition large-scale changes in occupation took place at this period in many parts of the country. Mistakes and typographical errors were also corrected. For example in Aghacrew, Co. Tipperary, the name of a lessor, given in the *Primary valuation* as Edward Bagwell, is corrected to Edward Bagwell Purefoy.[25]

When all the work was completed, including appeals made to quarter sessions, a list of alterations was compiled and signed by the sub-commissioners, usually several months later.[26] No copies of the manuscript lists are now known, but some alterations were printed and are listed with the other appeal books.[27] The settled valuation was copied into the new lists, now known as cancelled books (held in the Valuation Office), which became the

---

17 OL/2/12, p. 411. **18** OL/19/14/7, pp 9, 12. **19** OL/19/24/6, note inside front cover. **20** OL/19/14/8, note by J. Kelly, 25 June 1851, inside front cover. **21** OL/19/14/4, front endpapers. **22** OL/19/24/5, page added before title page; OL/19/24/7, page added before title page; OL/19/14/6/6. **23** OL/19/17/2, p. 85. **24** OL/19/6/1. **25** OL/19/27/5, pp 1–3. A search in the *Primary valuation* books online finds Bagwell (incorrect) but not Purefoy. **26** OL/19/17/18, signed Mar. 1851, hearings held on 5 Dec. 1850. See also OL/19/32/1, alterations signed 19 May 1852 following hearings on 13 Apr. 1852. **27** See list OL/19.

official record of the valuation of each tenement. Copies were issued to the poor law guardians for poor rates and the grand juries for county cess.[28] The data in the cancelled books is the baseline on which all revisions and alterations were made since that time.

The books refer to notices of alterations sent to applicants,[29] but only one example is known: on 20 March 1850 a pre-printed notice, signed by the two sub-commissioners, was sent to John Mulhall in Knocknew, Kilmademoge, Co. Kilkenny regarding an increase in his valuation to £18 10s. and stating a date and place where he could make objections.[30] There is no further correspondence, but the increased valuation appears in the book.[31] In another case, the sequence of events is illustrated by a rare letter from occupiers in Moher, Upperchurch, Co. Tipperary: the hearings were held in early November 1851 and the sub-commissioner signed the book as settled on 4 March 1852. On 6 May 1852 a 'letter' was sent to the occupiers giving the decision, and on 11 May they wrote objecting, but the outcome of the matter is not known.[32] The appeal books also contain a small number of references to further appeals to the court of quarter sessions. In the barony of Eliogarty, Co. Tipperary, the property of a T.F. Carlisle in Clonisnullen was 'appealed to barrister',[33] and a house in Fisher Street, Kinsale, Co. Cork, originally valued at £13 10s., was reduced to £9 10s.[34] At the 1869 select committee, evidence was given that there were at first large numbers of appeals to the court, but that the rate declined once the official side engaged a specialized solicitor.[35]

The 1846 act appeal documents comprise the sub-commissioners' appeal books, appeal application books, revising surveyors' books, printed post-appeal books and a small number of other documents.

The sub-commissioners' appeal books
The sub-commissioners' appeal books were retained as the record of evidence and are the most important documents in this series. These books show how the appeals worked and record the changes made, but their main interest lies in the contemporary notes of oral proceedings. Despite the cramped and difficult handwriting, abbreviations, erratic punctuation and wanderings, they add up to a remarkable record of the concerns, grievances

---

28 *Report from select committee on valuation, 1869*, questions 921–2. **29** OL/19/27/18, note on front endpaper, notice sent on 4 May 1851 following hearings on 11 Feb. **30** OL/19/14/6/5, this is likely to mean a hearing by the sub-commissioners. Quarter sessions were not held in Castlecomer. *Returns of the number of cases prosecuted at each quarter sessions in Ireland, 1849–54*, HC 1854 (515). **31** *PV, Co. Kilkenny, barony of Fassadinin* (1850), p. 97. **32** OL/19/27/7, letter pasted into back of book, and p. 86. **33** OL/19/27/4, inside front cover. **34** OL/19/6/10, p. 21. **35** *Report from select committee on valuation, 1869*, question 5321, evidence of Richard Griffith; see also evidence of J.B. Greene, question 1195.

and interests of the ordinary occupier. The wording of the notes, in the syntax and vocabulary of the vernacular, indicate that they were made as the appellant was speaking. Persons from every situation in society, including those who did not speak English, were prepared to state their complaints in public. The verbatim accounts reveal the human aspect of the process of valuation and how the outcome affected occupiers, in addition to providing insights into rural communities through the incidental information and comments. Several appeals from one townland provide different perspectives, although the dim view of the valuation held by many occupiers needs to be kept in mind. In fifteen baronies, the books of both sub-commissioners are extant.

The multiplicity of circumstances that were taken into account in arriving at a valuation resulted in substantial notes. There are the falling rents, the poor economic climate that caused difficulties for both tenants and landowners, the evictions, emigration and poverty, the deals made between one tenant and another, the arrangements made with landlords and middlemen on taking up tenancies, family, social and community relationships, and tenants' views of landlords (and vice versa). There is also information on farming, buildings and living conditions. From time to time the sub-commissioner recorded his personal opinion. No other series of documents in the valuation archives has this immediacy and connection to the preoccupations of the occupiers and owners of Ireland.

The appeal books were made by interleaving the *Primary valuation* book for the barony with two blank pages. One page was used for reference information transcribed by office clerks and the other was for the sub-commissioners' notes made during the hearings. The clerk's notes vary. At their most complete, they record the lot number, rent, rate per acre, tenure and date of lease for every tenement in the printed book, even those against which there was no appeal.[36] Some record the grounds of the appeal, and many give background details.[37] The manuscript house books, field books and tenure books and the appeal forms were among the sources of this information. A printed questionnaire for appellants was also developed around this time, and although no completed copies are now known, the information requested corresponds to that in the clerks' notes.[38] The average value of land per acre in each tenement was usually written in the margin of the printed pages and frequent reference was made to the Townland Valuation and the Poor Law Valuation.[39] The clerk's notes may be useful for places

36 For example, OL/19/14/7 or OL/19/29/9. 37 OL/19/9/5, p. 39, and examples throughout; OL/19/9/8, throughout. 38 OL/5/4019. One complete page of the questionnaire was used as stationery to provide a cover for this book. Torn fragments were also used for similar purposes in other books. 39 OL/19/24/8 (Townland Valuation) and OL/19/24/5 (Poor Law Valuation).

where the manuscript books are incomplete. At least three copies of each appeal book were made: one for each of the two sub-commissioners, and one for the revising surveyor or for use in the office; the National Archives also holds some blank, unused copies.[40] Most of the appeal books were bound in hard covers, suggesting that they were meant to be preserved. One book bears a note from a later date: 'Appeal book (valuable)'.[41] Care is required in reading the notes to ensure that the information is viewed across the columns on the correct line. The sub-commissioner's notes are in some cases on the page opposite the printed text and in other cases on the inner page, but the lot numbers are usually given.[42] The page numbers given in the footnotes are those of the *Primary valuation* pages to which the notes refer.

The data in the appeal books consists of different elements: the pre-written clerk's notes, the notes taken during the hearings, notes of the follow-up work and the manuscript corrections to the printed *Primary valuation*. The books vary in their markings and in the personal style of the sub-commissioners, some of whom wrote copious notes while others were more concise. Plate 13 shows parts of two pages from the appeal book of sub-commissioner Gaffney for the barony of Ballyadams, Queen's County. In the book the pages are side by side, but they are presented here one above the other. The annotated page from the *Primary valuation* is at the top, with the properties appealing marked and corrections made to names and prices, and the average price per acre noted in the right-hand margin. The lower part of the image shows Gaffney's notes, including the date, the tenement number and the information recited by the appellant. The centre pages (not shown) contain the clerk's notes of background information. In theory, the final settled valuation was written on the printed pages, but detailed comparison with the first cancelled books would be required to establish completeness.

Most appeals were made because of a high valuation price, and these cases appear throughout the books. In Tipperary, 67 per cent of appeals were for excessive valuation.[43] In Newcastle Farm, Newcastle, Co. Dublin, 'Mr Moore says it is the worst land in Ireland, knows no land so bad. Would make a present of it 70 acres to anyone who would pay the county cess.'[44] In Artaine, Co. Dublin, the owner claimed 'the valuation for lot B is preposterous'.[45] In Co. Tipperary, the agent of Lord Ashtown objected to the valuation in Lismaline, Uskane, 'considers this much too high'.[46]

The content or square area of holdings was also a matter of dispute. This included both matters of fact concerning measurement, and changes made to the boundaries of tenements by consolidation or subdivision. Some of the

40 OL/19/14/12, OL/19/20/1, OL/19/24/3 and OL/19/24/13. 41 OL/19/6/7 in 3 parts, note in pencil on front page. 42 See example in OL/19/9/1 and OL/19/24/1, throughout book. 43 *Return of completions and revisions in Co. Tipperary*, HC 1851 (403), p. 3. 44 OL/19/9/8, p. 21 and notes on p. 23. 45 OL/19/9/5, p. 5. 46 OL/19/27/12, p. 173.

confusion arose from the fact that the *Primary valuation* used statute measure and the figures frequently did not tally with what the occupiers themselves believed. Statute measure was used previously in the Townland Valuation and, while some appeals on grounds of content were made then, they did not concern individual tenements, and the outcome for occupiers was not as obvious. Both occupiers and sub-commissioners cited Irish or plantation measure, and Irish currency was commonly used.[47] On the official side, there was a general resignation to the common use of Irish acres and conversion calculations appear in several of the books.[48] In Castlewarden, Lucan, Co. Dublin, the sub-commissioner noted that an occupier 'complains of area, which was made out by Hodges and Smith at 48 [Irish acres] or the equivalent of 79 [statute acres]'.[49] In Howth, Co. Dublin, the clerk noted 'Andrew McKenna complains of the extent of these numbers he says he holds only 33–0–20 (query Irish) if so it comes within 1–1–8 of what's in this book. If statute there is a difference of 22–2–5.'[50] The frustration of the sub-commissioners can be seen in the note by John Kelly in Kilkenny: 'A vast deal of our time occupied in hearing appeals for wrong areas, about one fourth of our time.'[51] Another sub-commissioner seems to have asked all witnesses if they agreed with the area.[52] Occupiers also claimed not to know the acreage of their land: John Harris in Capakeel, Coolbanagher, Queen's County 'thinks he holds 16 acres at will'.[53] In Killeigh, Castleventry, Co. Cork, an occupier 'has no idea of acres'.[54]

However, changes caused by subdivision and consolidation had serious consequences for the work. This led to exasperation in the office in Dublin, and was described by Griffith as 'compound confusion'.[55] In Co. Tipperary the work in some baronies was done several times 'because the changes of tenements were so numerous that we had to go over them again. It was not only that new tenants came in, but the boundaries were altered and new fences were made. We were weary going over it.'[56] The labyrinthine complications of subdivision are illustrated by a case in Brockra, Clonenagh and Clonagheen, Queen's County, where Tom Mulhall held eight acres at £4 3s. rent and gave three and a half acres to Cooke (not listed in the *Primary valuation*), who was to pay £1 15s. rent; Cooke then gave 'the prime acre of the land' to Delaney, who gave him £4 in order to pay for Mulhall's interest, and agreed to pay 10s. a year.[57]

47 The Irish currency was amalgamated with the British in Jan. 1826. For other forms of measure, see for example OL/19/6/3, p. 10, where an occupier describes the area of his holding as 'all 12 gneeves'. 48 OL/19/9/11, p. 151. From 1852 a column for Irish acres was included in the tenure books. 49 OL/19/9/8, p. 21 and notes on p. 23. 50 OL/19/9/5, p. 49. 51 OL/19/14/8, p. 61. 52 OL/19/14/4, p. 45. 53 OL/19/24/8, p. 21. 54 OL/19/6/3, p. 18. 55 OL/2/13, p. 55. 56 *Report from select committee on valuation, 1869*, question 1494. See also *Return of completions and revisions in Co. Tipperary*, HC 1851 (403). This return lists revisions in baronies of Co. Tipperary before the issue of the *Primary valuation*. 57 OL/19/

Where holdings were consolidated, it was frequently the case that one of the existing occupiers took over other tenements. In the parish of Kilmore (barony of Kilnamanagh Lower), Co. Tipperary, there were several instances of this. Patrick Keeffe in the townland of Kilmore Upper became the occupier of seven additional tenements comprising twenty-five acres of land and six houses, now noted as 'down'. In the four years between the field work in 1847 and the appeals in 1851, his tenement grew from eighteen to forty-three acres and where there were previously eight holdings and seven houses, there was now one holding with one house.[58] In Cummer (Mulloghney), Upperchurch all fourteen lots, held by four occupiers in the *Primary valuation*, are crossed through and are now held by one person, and five of the six houses have been demolished.[59] The population of Kilmore parish was almost exactly halved between 1841 and 1851.[60] The 1841 census recorded 168 houses.[61] The field work took place in 1847–8 and based on that work the *Primary valuation* listed 156 houses in November 1850. By the time of the appeals in 1851, seventy-six houses were 'down'. This left eighty houses standing, which is close to the figure of eighty-seven recorded in the census that took place a few months later in October 1851.[62]

The third most frequent reason for appeals was that the houses valued in the first instance had been demolished between the field work and the appeals. This was noted as house 'down' and was related to the depopulation and consolidation of tenements outlined above. The results can be seen on a small scale in the case of one occupier in Gortaderry, Toem, Co. Tipperary, who expanded his holding from twenty to twenty-seven acres in this period: 'Pat Hammersley has taken nos. 5 and 7 and threw down the houses.'[63] In the parish of Upperchurch, Co. Tipperary, all eight tenements in Gortnada were taken over by Edward Buckley, who already held land in another parish. In addition he took over two small farms in Knocknameena Commons, giving him a total of fifty-seven acres in this parish. He demolished five of the six houses in the two townlands.[64]

At the appeal hearings, information was offered by appellants on the wide range of related matters, including rent and landholding arrangements and practices. Rent was expressed as a price per acre, a weekly or a yearly amount, and was gone into in great detail. Robert Metcalf, Acragar, Ardea, Queen's County, 'holds on old lease at £65, lease has fallen out and retook on chancery

---

24/7, p. 8. The total rent of £4 3s. was now paid by three people and Mulhall benefitted by £4. 58 OL/19/27/6, p. 56. 59 OL/19/27/7, p. 77. 60 *Census of Ireland, 1851, part I, volume II, Co. Tipperary* (Dublin, 1852), p. 322. The population was 572 in 1841 and 291 in 1851. 61 *Addenda to the census of Ireland 1841, Co. Tipperary* (S.R.), p. 12. 62 OL/19/27/7, pp 53–6, and *Census of Ireland, 1851, part I, volume II, Co. Tipperary* (1852), p. 322. 63 OL/19/27/7, pp 66–7. 64 OL/19/27/7, pp 81, 85 and *PV, Co. Tipperary, barony of Ikerrin* (1851), p. 47.

lease at £42'.⁶⁵ In some cases the rent was not known or not agreed, such as 'Michael Morris holds 8 acres no lease, taken 2 years, rent not settled' in Knockuragh, Drangan, Co. Tipperary,⁶⁶ or simply not paid, as in Blakefield, Aghnameadle, Co. Tipperary: 'Rent was £20 and is now zero, landlord dead, land in dispute, no rent paid these three years.'⁶⁷ In Reanascreena North, Ross, Co. Cork, the sub-commissioner's note states that half of the tenants do not pay half the rent.⁶⁸ Arrangements for payment of rent other than by cash were recorded in Garranes, Templemartin, Co. Cork ('Let this to Kelleher for about 13s. an acre, paid for by 2 labouring men at 4s. per day each'⁶⁹). In Foulkscourt, Fertagh, Co. Kilkenny, payment was made in kind: 'Rent 20s. an acre but being a butcher paid it by meat accounts to Mr Healy. Allowed last year a quarter's rent.'⁷⁰

The notes show the fall in rents and many mention abatements or reductions. Appellants may have volunteered this information to show that the valuation was too high, but its routine inclusion may indicate that the question was asked. In Ballynoe, Kilshannig, Co. Cork, 'Denis Connell senior has 78 acres Irish, rent £66 of old, abated in 1848 to half. No rent at all fixed upon, they give the landlord what they can and he takes it but gives no receipt.'⁷¹ The same book notes a landlord who was satisfied with half the old rent.⁷² Flexibility in adapting to conditions can be seen in the agent who demanded 'no more than half the rent while the times are bad and if they improve he will change'.⁷³ In better circumstances, the rules were enforced: in Bishopswood, Kilmore, Co. Tipperary, the railway passed through the land and 'as people had some money they were kept to their rent'.⁷⁴ Reference is made in several baronies to high rents during the period of the Napoleonic wars. In Co. Kilkenny 'the whole townland was at 16s. 6d. in 1810, reduced when the war was over' or 'was 25 in Bonaparte's time'⁷⁵ and in Queen's County 'all was let very high in the war and reduced one fifth since'.⁷⁶ Other factors affecting rent received oblique reference: in Donnybrook, Co. Dublin, 'The ground was worth a pound an acre when the potatoes grew more than it is now.'⁷⁷

The role of middlemen is mentioned incidentally but frequently. In Ballydavis, Straboe, Queen's County, John McDonnell 'paid an enormous rent the last 14 years, his landlord raised on a middleman'.⁷⁸ In the same county, the rent of a holding in Cromoge, Clonenagh and Clonagheen 'was

65 OL/19/24/8, p. 2.   66 OL/19/27/10, p. 51.   67 OL/19/27/16, p. 3.   68 OL/19/6/3, p. 51.   69 OL/19/6/8, p. 57. Four shillings a day was the pay of a draftsman, see *Report from select committee on valuation, 1869*, appendix 2, *Return of persons dismissed (or discontinued) the service of the general valuation of Ireland from 1st January 1850 to 1st January 1869*, pp 229–30. In 1838 labourers or spadesmen working with the valuators were paid between 6s. and 9s. a week; see OL/2/4, p. 69.   70 OL/19/14/4, p. 28.   71 OL/19/6/7, part 1, p. 8.   72 Ibid., part 1, p. 7.   73 Ibid., part 2, p. 13.   74 OL/19/27/6, p. 55.   75 OL/19/14/8, pp 65, 101.   76 OL/19/24/7, p. 27.   77 OL/19/9/5, p. 35.   78 OL/19/24/6, p. 39.

formerly set by a middleman. When Lord Milltown came in for the place he reduced the rent,'[79] and in Derrykearn in the same parish the lessor is described: 'Sir Ed. Burrowes, a regular screw. Burrowes worse than any middleman, rent must be paid to the day. Thinks this is a rack rent.'[80]

The overall difficulty of paying rent can be seen throughout the books. In Boherlody, Dolla, Co. Tipperary, 'Edward Purcell holds 13 Irish acres equal to 21 statute acres. Rent was 25s. abated to 21s. last May but he is not able to pay so much. Promised 21s. when evicted last May merely to get in again.'[81] In Clonadacasey, Clonenagh and Clonagheen, Queen's County, the occupiers had disputed the rent without success: 'Mr Kemmis valued this all himself and they went to the Courts and had to give the penny Mr Kemmis valued it to.'[82] Tenants were cautious about taking on rents they thought too high. In Derreens, Fanlobbus, Co. Cork, a tenant said he 'would take a lease at £9 but not at £10, if there was potatoes growing he would not dread £10, but since there is not.'[83] Lessors also had problems with rents. A lessor in Celbridge, Co. Kildare complained that he never received more than two-thirds of the promised rent.[84] The plight of some members of the landed classes can be seen in the case of the Revd Wm Waller, who 'got the place bequeathed to him. It is loaded with debt, has not been able to pay, it is in chancery. There can be no abatement because he has not it in his power. The bequest was a misfortune instead of a benefit.'[85]

In the book for the barony of Maryborough East, Queen's County, sub-commissioner John Kelly listed the main landlords and middlemen with his personal observations on their letting practice. These vary from Viscount de Vesci ('good man, abates'), to representatives of Dr Boys Smith ('Paupers, rack renter') or Mrs E. Broomfield ('High, bad land let at 3 times value').[86] In the book for Maryborough West, de Vesci again receives approval as 'low letter' and owners in other townlands are compared unfavourably with him: 'very high 24 to Lord de Vesci 15.'[87] An occupier in Colt, Clonenagh and Clonagheen, confirmed this view and 'would much rather live under Lord de Vesci than Sir C. Coote'.[88] Occupiers' views of their landlords are not all negative and a certain shared sympathy can be seen in comments such as 'Mr Seale was as good to him as possible, but the £7 was double rent,'[89] or 'He let very high but would forgive a quarter's rent.'[90]

Both the clerk's notes and the sub-commissioners' notes record the tenure, which was broadly by lease or at will. In Kilmore Big, Coolock, Co. Dublin, the holding of Luke Reilly:

---

79 OL/19/24/7, p. 27. 80 Ibid., Kelly, p. 28. Burrowes is listed as Rev Sir E.D. Burrowes and described as 'the highest letter in the barony' in the list of landlords on the page added before the title page. 81 OL/19/27/17, p. 32. 82 OL/19/24/7, p. 13. 83 OL/19/6/3, p. 79. 84 OL/19/13/2, p. 10. 85 OL/19/24/7, p. 22. 86 OL/19/24/5, page added before title page. 87 OL/19/24/7, p. 25. 88 Ibid., p. 24. 89 Ibid., p. 10. 90 Ibid., p. 29.

taken in 1830 about 60 acres plantation £241 of late Irish currency. Pays £21 at the expiration of each life. Built the house and shed, his father in law built the stable. Lease for 3 lives renewable for ever. First taken in 1812 or 1815.'[91]

In Goldenbridge, Co. Dublin, details are given of weekly lettings: lot 78 is corrected to 'in tenements' and the rent is given as '7s. weekly. 7 rooms let at 1s. each at times. Would take £12 yearly.' Similar details were given in relation to Murphy's Court, Dunleary, Co. Dublin.[92] The notes also refer to leases that went back to the eighteenth century. In Balscadden, Co. Dublin 'his mother had a lease made in 1799',[93] or in Derrigra, Kinneigh, Co. Cork, a lease dated from 1775.[94]

The various payments or 'fines' paid on coming into a tenancy are noted, including payments between occupiers for their 'interest' in the holding or for a crop planted but not harvested, and payments made to the lessor. In Inchinattin, Castelventry, Co. Cork, the occupier William Woods 'has this since 1840 and gave Collins the former tenant £20 fine'.[95] In Rahora, Listerlin, Co. Kilkenny, the tenant listed in the *Primary valuation*, John Morrissey, 'went away and Andrew Knox paid £20 or more to Morrissy as a fine for his interest.'[96] Cases where no payment was made on transfer were worthy of mention: 'paid no fine or arrears',[97] or 'gave nothing for the interest'.[98] Many references are made to bidding for a tenement by proposal. In Smithfield, Kilshannig, Co. Cork the occupier 'proposed for it and got it for something less than his proposal'.[99] Witnesses also described unsuccessful proposals, as in Killabban, Queen's County: 'Fishbourne offered £440 for no. 1 Rathtillig, but was outbid by Byrne.'[1]

Many of those appealing argued that their high valuation was not relative to comparable holdings.[2] During the appeal hearings and the follow-up work, everything was compared: land with land, house with house, townlands within parishes, the *Primary valuation* price with the Townland Valuation and the Poor Law Valuation, the evidence taken at hearings was examined in relation to the field documents and the notes of the sub-commissioners. In Ballymount Great, Clondalkin, Co. Dublin: 'Joseph Farran held Fairbrother's no. 3 and considers it better than his own by 15d. an acre. All agree that it is much better and Mr Cummins [occupier of lots 4 and 5] says Fairbrother's is as good as any in that country. Mr Cummins says Michael Smith's [occupier of lot 7] is as good as Farren's.'[3] In Curramarkey, Doon, Co. Tipperary, John Ryan 'would rather have Kilcommon at £30 than this at

[91] OL/19/9/5, p. 37. [92] OL/19/9/10, p. 76. [93] OL/19/9/1, p. 31. [94] OL/19/6/3, p. 2. [95] Ibid., p. 17. [96] OL/19/14/8, p. 65. [97] OL/19/27/15, p. 23. [98] OL/19/24/7, p. 27. [99] OL/19/6/7, part 1, p. 39. [1] OL/19/24/9, p. 23. [2] OL19/17/2, p. 76. [3] OL/19/9/13, p. 8.

£10'.[4] Houses were subject to similar examination. An occupier in Balbriggan, Co. Dublin, William Joynson, pointed out that a better house than his own was valued at a lower price, and the neighbours agreed.[5] In Maryborough town, the house of Mr Harper in Main Street was described, with further information about other parties:

> 7 bedrooms, parlour, drawing room, 4 horse stable, small barn. Mr Harper thinks his house is about equal to Mr Turpin's but not so good, nor so much room as Mr Jacob's. Mr Jacob has a very large accommodation, and he wants it for he has 13 or 14 children.[6]

Grievance also existed, as in: 'Peter Whelan complains of the high valuation would be satisfied if £1 7s. be taken off and added to Pat Doorly who has the best of land.'[7] Not every occupier was prepared to engage in comparison and in Ballyduff, Moyanna, Queen's County, Mary Duigan said she 'knows nothing of any man's land'.[8] Comparison was used to reconcile occupiers to the fairness of the valuation or to encourage them to withdraw the appeal. In Cork, in Aghern East, Aghern, Conor Donovan 'admits that his is relatively fair compared to no. 1, has no more to say.'[9] In Clonshanbo, parish of Clonshanbo, Co. Kildare, sub-commissioner Stawell commented: 'Several of the appellants from this townland withdrew on statements and explanations being made to them.'[10]

Many books refer to evictions of tenants, in some cases with the tenant later retaking the same holding. In Dangans, Ardea in Queen's County, Thomas Delaney held twenty-one acres on a lease of 1798, but 'was ejected and retook land in 1848. Tenant built offices, expects an abatement'.[11] In Lisnamoe, Ballymackey, Co. Tipperary, Cornelius Kennedy held eleven acres taken seventy years earlier by his father on a lease. He was 'evicted in 1847 or 8 for non payment then took it again at the same rent but only paid £6 and is now distrained for the balance. Not worth more than 14s., built all, house in very bad condition.'[12] Occupiers of large holdings were also subject to ejectment: John Dwyer held 205 acres in Ballyconnor, Aghanameadle, Co. Tipperary since 1845, but he fell into arrears and was 'turned out'. He retook the same holding two years before the appeals at a reduced rent of £120.[13] Problems for the owner of un-let property can be seen in Kilmacreddock Upper, Kilmacreddock, Co. Kildare, where the tenants were ejected and the

---

4 OL/19/27/7, p. 5. John Ryan also occupied 128 acres in Kilcommon, p. 55.   5 OL/19/9/1, p. 7: 'William Joynson says that Henry Joynson no. 17 is a better one than his.' William's house was valued at £21 and Henry's at £19.   6 OL/19/24/5, p. 12. John Jacob was listed as occupier of two large houses on Turnpike Road and a further house on Ridge Road.   7 OL/19/24/2, p. 2.   8 OL/19/24/10, p. 23.   9 OL/19/6/9, p. 6.   10 OL/19/13/1, p. 10.   11 OL/19/24/8, p. 11.   12 OL/19/27/15, p. 25.   13 Ibid., p. 3.

lessor was left with the land in an exhausted state.[14] In Monarche Commons, Callan, Co. Kilkenny the fact that the occupier had to give up his land in order to qualify for outdoor relief is noted.[15]

Reference is also made to emigration to America. In Ballybeg, Glanworth, Co. Cork, Thomas Casey explained that '3 or 4 years ago his brother had half the land, went to America, he got all'.[16] In Ballyadams, Ballyadams, Queen's County the name of the occupier was corrected from Daniel Keefe to 'Thomas Burns in his stead. Bought Keefe's crop when going to America. Paid Keefe £5, was clear of arrears.'[17] Similarly, a tenant emigrating was compensated by the lessor: 'Mr Cassan gave Donnel the crop going to America,'[18] or was assisted by the family: 'Thomas Shirley (John gone to America) gave his brother £7 to emigrate.'[19] A note relating to Dunmoon North, Kilwatermoy, Co. Waterford explains that Miss Beauchamp went to New Orleans in America.[20]

Agricultural land was the overwhelming concern of the valuation, and in some cases, great detail was recorded by the sub-commissioners.[21] A number of the valuators had been 'agriculturalists',[22] and Griffith described sub-commissioner John Kelly as 'a farmer and surveyor and an excellent judge of land'.[23] There are references to bad practice and appellants commonly claimed that the land was in poor condition because it was badly farmed by previous occupants. Objections because of flooding,[24] and difficulties arising from the land itself were described, such as 'yellow marigold grows here and smothers everything. Never threshes more than 14 barrels oats to the acre',[25] or 'the land gives the cattle boglame'.[26]

The productivity of farms was frequently noted. In Co. Waterford, an estimate states: '3 firkins of butter to each cow beside many calves on this farm. This has water carriage to bring sea sand up to the door.'[27] An occupier in the parish of Artaine, Co. Dublin, commented: '10 barrels of wheat per acre is a very high average for the County of Dublin.[28] In Brandon Hill, The Rower, Co. Kilkenny the occupier 'gets a firkin a cow'.[29] Further incidental information features costs and wages. The book for the barony of Kilnamanagh Upper, Co. Tipperary, in addition to extensive notes on dairy

14 OL/19/13/2, p. 17.   15 OL/19/14/1, p. 25. From 1847 applicants for relief under the poor law system were not eligible if they held more than a quarter of an acre. This was known as the 'Gregory clause'.   16 OL/19/6/5, p. 75.   17 OL/19/24/1, p. 3; the name is given as Byrne in the printed page.   18 OL/19/24/5, p. 36.   19 OL/19/14/9, p. 16.   20 OL/19/29/1, p. 12.   21 OL/19/24/5, p. 24.   22 *Report from select committee on valuation, 1869*, appendix 3, *Return of the persons who have from time to time been employed on the General Valuation of Ireland, showing the counties or places from whence they came, their professional qualifications*, p. 233.   23 *Report from select committee on valuation, 1869*, question 1339. Kelly had worked with Griffith in various capacities since 1812. He was the superintendent of the office for a period and served as a sub-commissioner for appeals.   24 OL/19/24/8, p. 17.   25 OL/19/24/7, p. 5.   26 Ibid., p. 50.   27 OL/19/29/1, p. 67.   28 OL/19/9/5, p. 7.   29 OL/19/14/8, p. 92.

farming, calculates the expenses of the farmer, including the purchase of firkins for butter, the cost of employing three men 'at drawing and improving' and three women: 'The usual pay of a dairy woman is £10 a year and food. She will take charge of 30 cows but the usual assistants are one girl to 10 cows at say from 10s. to 15s. per quarter.'[30] Other information includes the price of hay in Smithfield market in Dublin[31] and the outlay on drainage works in Co. Cork.[32]

The references to family and social relationships may clarify entries in the *Primary valuation*, where it can be difficult to know if persons of the same family name are related. In Caher (Retrenched), Offerlane, Queen's County, John Bergin was 'brother and successor to Michael deceased'[33] and 'Thomas Moore appears for his uncle Michael'.[34] In Ballinclogh, Ross, Co. Cork, 'the two Hayeses are first cousins',[35] and in Ballyroe, Kilmacabea, also in Cork, William Clarke is noted as 'married to Mr Morris's sister' (Morris was an occupier and lessor in the townland).[36] In Ballysedan, Shanbogh, Co. Kilkenny, 'Mr Joy had three daughters, Jos. Mackessy married one of them'; Mackessy is listed in the *Primary valuation* as occupier and lessor.[37] In Glentane, Ballynoe, Co. Cork, Richard Barry 'came into the land about 26 years ago by marriage, paid about £70 towards the fortune of other sisters'.[38] Where the same name is listed several times in the *Primary valuation* it is unclear if one or several persons are referred to. The book for Mountrath, Queen's County notes 'Finton Phelan of 27 and Finton Phelan of 59b are two different men' and a further person with the same name is described as 'another'.[39]

Some references provide names that do not appear in the *Primary valuation*. In Raheny, Dublin, Thomas Trotter King appealed the valuation of his farm but the occupier listed in the *Primary valuation* was his mother Eliza King, since deceased.[40] In Woodtown, Croagh, Co. Dublin, the father-in-law of Thomas H. Wilkins was named as William Collins, and he is not listed in the printed book.[41] In Blackrock, 'Edward Long is son-in-law and agent to Michael Connor, who is in America and who built 2 cottages in Verschoyle Ave about 3 years since.'[42] The *Primary valuation* lists Connor as lessor of two houses valued at £32 each, but Long is not listed. A complicated situation is described in Ballyspellan, Fertagh, Co. Kilkenny. The occupier, Joseph Moore, 'complains that 3 roods of this holding belongs to Catherine Ready. He is still the occupier until she claims it, which she may never do.' A further note on the endpapers of the book recorded that this holding should be divided between the two: 'Note, this piece was left her by the will of her

30 OL/19/27/7, p. 6. 31 OL/19/9/10, note inside cover. 32 OL/19/6/3, p. 9. 33 OL/19/24/12, p. 6. 34 OL/19/24/1, p. 26. 35 OL/19/6/3, p. 29. 36 Ibid., p. 156. 37 OL/19/14/8, p. 85. 38 OL/19/6/3, p. 14. 39 OL/19/24/7, p. 41. 40 OL/19/9/5, p. 11. 41 OL/19/9/3, p. 21. 42 OL/19/9/10, p. 6.

brother. Moore is still the occupier and tills it, and she may never claim it as she is at service with a family at a distance.'[43] Catherine Ready is not listed in the *Primary valuation*. Many women pleaded their own case in front of the sub-commissioners, but every book contains cases where they were represented by their menfolk, such as 'Eliza Moiles by her son George'.[44] Occupiers also appeared for each other: 'Andrew McLoughlin on behalf of Wm Brennan who is ill,'[45] or 'Mr G. Blackmore appears for the children of the late John Power, in trustee for the children.'[46]

Detailed information on houses and other buildings is found throughout the appeal books. In the suburbs of Dublin many of the appeals concerned houses of high valuation. Griffith described the barony of Rathdown as covering 'Kingstown and bathing villages in villa tenements and rental very high. There has been an outcry made by 10,000 occupiers of tenements who apprehending that other assessments may be levied under my valuation, have one and all objected to it.' He explained that the newspaper editors nearly all live there, that there were public meetings, remonstrances and 'editorial articles written in a very unfair and hostile spirit'.[47] The appeal books of the two sub-commissioners for Rathdown survive and show the high valuations. A house in Dalkey Commons, Cliff Castle, was valued at £70 and said to be in a 'fine situation', but the owner 'refused £100 without a fine. Was £126 furnished.'[48] The development of new grand housing can be seen in the case of surgeon James Parkinson, who took a holding in Dalkey on a 999-year lease: 'The house is built so as to be added to and is unfinished, built 2 large rooms and divided them into four as a temporary residence. The block is that of a large house of the Elizabethan order, but the portion built is only a wing.'[49] The unfinished state of a house on Rathgar Road, Dublin is described: 'Wants chimney pieces in 2 bedrooms and grates, painting and papering.'[50] The Rathdown books contain many accounts of land purchased for speculative building purposes, and of the houses built there. The building materials, ages and conditions of some houses are noted. There may be an element of exaggeration in the descriptions: 'the oldest houses in Maryboro, 500 years old or 400'[51] or 'four houses, his father built them, they are falling every day in the week'.[52]

There are many examples of the poor living conditions of occupiers. In the townland of Killeshin, Queen's County, the family of John Dooge are said to 'think the land well enough but the house too high at 30s. Mud and rotten sticks. The farm small and the family large, they thought to go and never repaired it.'[53] Other examples include 'his house down and living in

43 OL/19/14/3, p. 25 and front endpapers. 44 OL/19/24/8, p. 22. 45 OL/19/24/1, p. 17. 46 OL/19/14/3, p. 60. 47 OL/2/12, p. 197. 48 OL/19/9/11, p. 22. 49 OL/19/9/10, p. 19. 50 Ibid., p. 121. 51 OL/19/24/5, p. 14. 52 OL/19/24/7, p. 43. 53 OL/19/24/9, p. 43.

barn',[54] or 'house has holes in the roof and lets the water in. She is afraid it will fall on her.'[55] In contrast, a house in Co. Tipperary is described as 'thatched, comfortable enough farm house'.[56] One of the circumstances taken into account was if the occupier built the house himself, and this is noted throughout, in some cases with details. In Ballynurney, The Rower, Co. Kilkenny, Matthew Grace was 'allowed £50 for his house, got timber, slates and masons. [Paid] himself for labour, lime and sand. Built 1841.'[57] In Weatherstown, Kilcoan, Co. Kilkenny, Thomas Deniffe recounts how 'his house was burned. Mr Pope promised him to assist in rebuilding but he died, and he got no help.'[58]

Appeals were also made by occupiers of mills, who gave detailed information in support of their cases, including a long explanation by Arthur Izod of Annamult, Danesford, Co. Kilkenny.[59] In Dodsborough, Co. Dublin, Mrs Davis 'got the mill out of order. The water wheel is not hers, a new one would cost about £20, it is an elm wheel. It works a quarter time for 5 months, a barrel of wheat would dry the pond.'[60] The source of grain for the mill in Coolrain, Offerlane, Queen's County was outlined: 'Also purchased Indian corn in Dublin and Liverpool. Egyptian wheat comes from the Nile; about 10,000 barrels of flour ground last year. Bringing wheat from Dublin spoils the miller's profit.'[61]

Many of the notes contain information that is not included in other valuation documents. Descriptions are given of the taxes in Kingstown, Co. Dublin,[62] the possibility of establishing a distillery in Mountrath town,[63] the tolls on the turnpike road in Knocksedan, Co. Dublin,[64] the damage done to the oyster beds by the building of the railway at Malahide, Co. Dublin,[65] the operation of a limekiln in Queen's County,[66] the decline in the value of osieries because 'kishes gone out, carts come in' in Coole, The Rower, Co. Kilkenny[67] and the types of weir and their yields on the river Blackwater in Co. Waterford.[68] An entry regarding Portnacrusha, Stradbally, Co. Limerick contains details of the economics of cutting turf, including the wages of day and night watchmen, the yield of the bog and the price of turf.[69] Several entries in Ross, Co. Cork refer to a local dispute about the sale of sand.[70] In Maryborough town, Queen's County, the location of a national school was perceived as reducing the value of adjacent property. Sub-commissioner John Kelly reported: 'The national school children are a great annoyance,

---

54 OL 19/6/5, p. 131. 55 OL/19/14/8, p. 90. 56 OL/19/27/3, p. 8. 57 OL/19/14/8, p. 92. 58 Ibid., p. 41. 59 OL/19/14/14, p. 9. 60 OL/19/9/8, p. 15. 61 OL/19/24/12, p. 15. 62 OL/19/9/10, note on end papers at back of book. 63 OL/19/24/7, p. 44. 64 OL/19/9/5, p. 9. 65 Ibid., p. 66. 66 OL/19/24/10, p. 34. 67 OL/19/14/8, p. 94; Kish: 'a wicker container or pannier', T.P. Dolan, *A dictionary of Hiberno-English* (Dublin, 2006). 68 OL/19/29/1, p. 133. 69 OL/19/17/2, p. 132: 'Limk' kishes and 'stat' kishes. 70 OL/19/6/3, p. 61.

noisy, dirty.'[71] His fellow sub-commissioner Jonas Stawell merely noted, 'House too high because proximity to school much depreciates its value.'[72] Some instances of the use of spoken Irish are noted in the books for the baronies of Kinnatalloon and Carbery East (West Division), Co. Cork, for example 'John Nagle sworn Irish', and it is likely that detailed examination would find more.[73]

Occupiers and some lessors put up spirited defences at the hearings, and many produced documentary evidence in the form of surveys, valuations and maps.[74] Returns from the map publishers Hodges & Smith were quoted,[75] and in Glebe, Rathmichael, Co. Dublin, Revd John Hunt produced 'a map made by Michael Currin in 1810', which showed the content to be one acre less than in the *Primary valuation*.[76] In other cases the documents were described in vague terms as surveys or maps.[77] Some documents were made by the appellants themselves. In Ballintogher, Graystown, Co. Tipperary, 'Denis Keeffe and Thomas Dwyer, sworn, hand in an applotment which they swear they have made to the best of their belief fairly and relative.'[78]

Some occupiers were uncooperative, such as one who 'refuses to be sworn or to offer any evidence of its value',[79] or openly hostile, like the occupier who stated 'the man that valued [his] land, he never saw it at all. Nor did they come to his neighbour's land either.'[80] Some of the notes of sub-commissioner Jonas Stawell questioned the credibility of the witnesses before him. He described one in Ballynahow, Ballycahill, Co. Tipperary as 'a most mendicating witness'.[81] In Queen's County, he added comments in red ink or diagonally across the page, such as 'a great talker and tricksy',[82] or 'a shuffler wants to hide something',[83] and described witnesses as a 'blackguard'[84] or 'a great blackguard'.[85] He also showed empathy for the situation of occupiers in his comments, for example: 'a decent old man'[86] and 'a very decent fellow, intelligent too'.[87] Sub-commissioner John Kelly recorded that an occupier was 'drunk, not sworn', but took the evidence nevertheless.[88]

Interference in the valuation for political purposes was alleged in a case in Shanahoe, Clonenagh and Clonagheen, Queen's County, where it was

---

71 OL/19/24/5, p. 16.   72 OL/19/24/6, p. 16.   73 OL/19/6/3, p. 42.   74 Some of the appeal books contain notes of names, acreages or valuations that were probably handed in at the appeals, for example OL/19/6/7/1/1 or OL/19/27/21/1. See valuation recited by steward of Hon. Bowes Daly of each part of 500 acres in Killough, Gaile, Co. Tipperary, OL/19/27/10, p. 77.   75 OL/19/6/9, p. 1; OL/19/9/8, p. 18.   76 OL/19/9/10, p. 131. Michael Currin was an established surveyor who made several maps of parishes in this area of Co. Dublin around 1810. Some of these maps are now in the National Library of Ireland, but not this particular map. 77 OL/19/6/10, pp 2, 3 (survey) and OL/19/9/11, p. 19 (map).   78 OL/19/27/21, p. 60. 79 OL/19/6/8, p. 3.   80 OL/19/24/7, p. 12.   81 OL/19/27/4, p. 2.   82 OL/19/24/8, p. 13.   83 Ibid., p. 29.   84 OL/19/24/10, p. 23.   85 OL/19/24/8, p. 24.   86 Ibid., p. 11. 87 OL/19/24/10, p. 19.   88 OL/19/6/3, p. 2.

believed that an excessive price was put on a tenement because of the behaviour of the occupier at an election: 'They valued him at 25s. an acre in 1832 because they told a lie on him that he was shouting and spitting at the election, when they only put 16s. on all the neighbours round him. They reduced him after to 20s. which is too high yet.'[89] At the 1869 select committee, several allegations were made of the valuation being deliberately kept below the qualification for voting of £12 in rural areas and £8 in towns. This included a case where the valuation of a troublesome member of a board of guardians was reduced in order to disqualify him from voting,[90] and a separate situation where a low valuation was made in parts of Dublin for a similar purpose.[91]

The appeal documents show the level of care taken to ensure that the valuation was correct. Tables of comparison were drawn up to provide data for the sub-commissioners and evidence was taken from expert witnesses. Several books contain tables of data abstracted from the field books, the re-valuation by experienced members of staff like John Boyan[92] and the Townland Valuation. General comparisons were also carried out, as can be seen in the notes of sub-commissioner Stawell.[93] One such table set out the rents, the data presented at the hearings, the *Primary valuation* and the sub-commissioner's proposal.[94] Some books contain details of rent, for instance in Mountrath, Queen's County.[95] The Poor Law Valuation was frequently used as a reference by both sides.[96] Public opinion was also used as a measure of fairness and relativity, and was actively sought: 'The popular opinions Mr Jones got in the barony of Maryborough East are about half or two-thirds of the rents, very difficult to get a popular scale from them. It was so also in Upperwoods.'[97]

The qualifications and experience of the experts consulted were noted, giving authority to their evidence. William Fitzpatrick, the poor law valuator in parts of Queen's County, was an important witness in several baronies there and weight was given to his opinion by the sub-commissioners.[98] Other poor law valuators included Mr G. Wilson, who had valued Carlow union.[99]

89 OL/19/24/7, p. 57. The valuation of 1832 is likely to refer to a local or a landlord's valuation. The Townland Valuation of Queen's County began in 1842, the tithe valuation in this parish was made in 1829 and the Poor Law Valuation did not begin before 1838. The holding of James Fitzpatrick, lot 15, consisted of 7 acres, valued in the *Primary valuation* at £3 10s. or 10s. per acre. 90 *Report from select committee on valuation, 1869*, question 2940–3.   91 Ibid., questions 3096–8 and 4927.   92 OL/19/9/11, p. 131.   93 OL/19/24/8, p. 30: '101 too little, 99 too great'. 94 OL/19/27/16/2.   95 OL/19/24/7, p. 30.   96 See example in OL/19/6/7, part 1, p. 8; OL/19/14/8, p. 87 and throughout.   97 OL/19/24/5, note on page added before title page. 98 OL/19/24/5, p. 39 and throughout; see barony of Slievemargy OL/19/24/9, p. 7 where Fitzpatrick was a sworn witness; this book contains pages of notes on his opinions: pp 8, 17. See also references to his valuations in baronies of Ballyadams (OL/19/24/1), Stradbally (OL/19/24/10) and Upperwooods (OL/19/24/12), where a note on the back endpapers gives the rates he charges for valuations.   99 OL/19/24/9, p. 37.

In Mountrath town, a comparison of houses was made by the priest.[1] In the barony of Middlethird, Co. Waterford, Mr Gamble had valued the barony for county cess about 10 years previously.[2] In the barony of Ida in Kilkenny, Thomas Jekyll valued land for landowners wishing to rent, and his opinion was quoted at various points,[3] as was that of Mr Carmichael, who had carried out valuations for the Encumbered Estates Court in Co. Cork.[4]

The checking done after the appeals also demonstrated concern for accuracy. In the barony of Clanwilliam, Co. Limerick, sub-commissioner Henry Buck noted matters where he was not satisfied, and these were later ticked off to show they had been dealt with. In Clooncunna North, Abington, he did not accept measurements submitted by an appellant but arranged to check the house book and ensured that the proper deductions were made.[5] In Ballybrood village, the entire townland had been purchased under the Encumbered Estates Court by Matthew Gabbett, who claimed the houses were all 'down'. Buck had this looked at by the surveyor, who found only twelve houses 'down' out of thirty-five.[6]

Appeal application books
Manuscript appeal application books for fourteen baronies in counties Clare, Cork, Limerick and Tipperary are held by the National Archives. The books were compiled in the office from the appeal applications and their format varies slightly.[7] The books note the reasons for appealing, which varied from one place to another. In Askeaton, Co. Limerick, approximately 20 per cent of tenements made appeals, and of those, 66 per cent stated that the reason was that the valuation was too high, with the next most frequent reason, 'house down', at more than 10 per cent.[8] In Kilbolane, Co. Cork, almost 30 per cent of tenements were appealed, with 33 per cent of these citing 'over value' and more than half citing 'house down'.[9] In contrast, the parish of Killeenagarriff, Co. Limerick lists only two cases of 'house down' in thirty-eight appeals from 309 tenements.[10]

In a number of cases both the appeal application book and the sub-commissioners' appeal books survive for the same barony, and comparison shows a surprising lack of correlation. It appears that the sub-commissioner made notes in the appeal books only in non-routine cases, and that conclusions cannot be drawn about the number of appeals in any townland or parish based on the cases written up in the sub-commissioners' books alone. For example, in the parish of Kilbolane, Co. Cork, the appeals for houses down

1 OL/19/24/7, p. 31. 2 OL/19/29/7, note on front endpaper and Mr Gamble's evidence, p. 51. 3 OL/19/14/18, p. 4 and throughout. 4 OL/19/6/7, part 1, pp 2–5. 5 OL/19/17/2, p. 2. 6 Ibid., p. 9. 7 See list OL/19. In Co. Limerick, copies of the *Primary valuation* have paper pasted to the edge of the pages, on which the reason for the appeal is written. 8 OL/19/17/4, pp 1–15. 9 OL/19/6/11, pp 53–66. 10 OL/19/17/1, pp 71–9.

were noted in the list of applications to appeal, but although many of these appear to have been successful as the houses are crossed through in the sub-commissioner's book, no notes concerning them were made there.[11]

Revising surveyors' books and other documents
These books record the work on queries arising at the appeal hearings and contain important information on the last changes made. They mostly concerned matters of fact that required checking in the field, such as the boundaries of tenements or names of the occupiers. Ten books are held by the National Archives and a microfilm of another book,[12] for baronies in counties Cork, Limerick, Tipperary and Waterford, but it is likely that there was originally a book for every barony. The surveyor used an interleaved copy of the *Primary valuation* book, and also noted changes in names and holdings in cases that did not involve appeals. In the barony of Middlethird, Co. Waterford, both an appeal book and a revising surveyor's book are extant. Sub-commissioner Edward Gaffney marked 'S' in the margin, stating the work required. This was attended to by the surveyor, Francis Roberts, who wrote his findings in his own interleaved book, opposite the entry on the printed page.[13]

An example of further changes identified in the post-appeal survey work, but not necessarily connected with the appeals, can be seen in Curraghbridge, Adare, Co. Limerick, where almost every piece of data in the townland printed in the *Primary valuation* in December 1850 was altered. The original field work was carried out in 1849–50 and the appeals were heard in March 1851. The post-appeal survey work took place in September 1851 and reduced the number of tenements from the original forty-five to thirty-three and the number of houses from thirty-three to twenty-two. Of the remaining tenements, ten had changes of name noted.[14]

Other documents now exist only in fragments. Some appeal notices were fortuitously kept with the appeal books, a few appeal forms are extant and a small number of notebooks and field books related to the checking work have survived.

The printed post-appeal books
Some books arising from the 1846 act appeals were printed: lists of alterations, statements of alterations and refusals, and the valuation as revised and amended. A total of thirty-six of these books have been identified, twenty-four of which are held in the National Archives, and some others are

11 OL/19/6/11, pp 53–66 and OL/19/6/12, pp 53–66.   12 MFA/16.   13 OL/19/29/10, p. 4, lot 12: 'boundary & content correct'; and p. 24, lot 19AB: 'boundary correctly marked. Calculations also correct.'   14 OL/19/17/15, p. 3.

included in the Askaboutireland.ie database of the *Primary valuation*. Most of the books relate to parts of Dublin and Kilkenny and others cover some baronies in counties Cork, Kildare, Limerick, Tipperary and Waterford. The printed books appeared in 1849–51 under the 1846 act, before being discontinued on grounds of expense; thereafter the lists were produced only in manuscript, although one book is known to have been printed under the 1852 act.[15] The books were published in the sequence *List of alterations* or *List of alterations and refusals, Valuation as revised and amended* or *Valuation as finally revised and amended*. In some baronies in Dublin, up to three books were printed. The 1846 act was vague about the outcome of the appeals, and section 22 stated that it was to be made public in the same manner as the *Primary valuation*. It is not known how many copies of each of these post-appeal books were printed, but few have survived.

The lists of alterations and refusals give the number, townland, occupier, primary valuation of land and buildings, valuation as altered by sub-commissioners and observations that in some cases explain the changes. They cover only properties that were appealed. The 1846 act required that lists of alterations be sent to the local board of guardians and only these printed lists are now known.[16]

The valuation as revised and amended relists all tenements and contains the same information as the *Primary valuation* books, but amended.

Conclusion

The documents relating to the 1846 act appeals are among the most informative and wide-ranging of the valuation archives. They are the intermediary documents between the *Primary valuation* and the cancelled books and subsequent amendments to the valuation. The appeal books show changes to the names listed in the *Primary valuation* that are significant because they were made within a few short years and can be dated. The few surveyor's books that have survived show alterations that are later again and can also be dated. However, the most important aspect of these books is the direct testimony of the occupiers, and the alterations made to the valuation, which on a wider scale of townlands, parishes and baronies provide rich and deep detailed background that is not available in any of the other series. The appeals were important in gaining public confidence in the valuation, and demonstrated attention paid to detail and accuracy and a willingness to correct mistakes, all in the interest of obtaining the best outcome.

The appeals took place in the aftermath of the Great Famine, at a moment of profound change in rural and urban Ireland, and provide insight into

---

15 *Report from select committee on valuation, 1869*, question 922 and see notices printed in *Primary valuation* from 1854.   16 9 & 10 Vict., c. 110, sec. 18.

society at that moment. Against the background of rural depopulation, the books outline how some small occupiers created more viable farms, long in advance of the radical changes in ownership that took place from the latter part of the century. The combination of first-hand testimony by the citizens of the country with the professional judgment of the sub-commissioners is unique. These documents contain a wide range of information not only on how the valuation operated, but on a host of extraneous matters. The work carried out after the appeals was the last field work of the initial valuation.

B. APPEALS UNDER THE 1852 ACT

A new system of appeals was brought in when the second Tenement Valuation Act became law on 30 June 1852. The right of appeal by all occupiers and lessors was retained, but the appeals became an administrative matter, dispensing with the troublesome and expensive hearings by sub-commissioners. The 1852 act applied to places where the Tenement Valuation had not been completed under the 1846 act, that is, in some parts of eleven counties and all of the seventeen remaining counties.[17] Appeal documents under the 1852 act survive for parts of Cos. Antrim, Cavan, Cork, Donegal, Dublin city, Galway, Kildare, Kilkenny (appeal letters only), Leitrim, Mayo, Meath, Monaghan, Sligo, Tipperary, Tyrone and Westmeath.

The *Primary valuation* books included a sample appeal form and an explanation of how to appeal. Forms were submitted to the clerk of the local poor law union and forwarded to the office in Dublin. The grounds of the appeal were investigated in the field before the decision of the commissioner was issued. Appellants who were still dissatisfied could make further appeal to the court of quarter sessions. Changes could also be made to properties that were not appealed. The final valuation was written into the cancelled books that are still held in the Valuation Office and copies were sent to the boards of guardians and the grand juries, giving them authoritative lists for the collection of poor rates and county cess. This series consists of appeal books and a small quantity of other documents. Only one post-appeal book is known to have been printed under the 1852 act.[18]

The appeals were investigated by revising valuators, who visited the

17 Counties valued partially under the 1846 act and partially under the 1852 act: Clare, Cork, Dublin, Kerry, Kildare, King's, Limerick, Louth, Meath, Tipperary and Wicklow. Counties valued entirely under the 1852 act: Antrim, Armagh, Cavan, Donegal, Down, Fermanagh, Galway, Leitrim, Londonderry, Longford, Mayo, Monaghan, Roscommon, Sligo, Tyrone, Westmeath and Wexford. 18 OL/20/9/1, *List of alterations, union of Dublin South* (Dublin, 1854).

locality, spoke to the appellants and their neighbours, and made themselves available. The revising valuators were senior members of staff, some of whom had previously been sub-commissioners of appeal under the 1846 act.[19] The valuators were assisted by surveyors. Their recommendations were subject to approval in the office and difficult cases were referred to the commissioner.[20] Where changes were made, recalculations and corrections were carried out in the office.[21] Many of the appeal documents are undated, but the work seems to have been carried out with dispatch. In most cases under the 1852 act, the period between the printing of the *Primary valuation* and the new valuation coming into force was reduced to a matter of months.[22] Under the 1846 act, it took a year or two for the final valuation to be issued.

The appeal books contain the notes of the revising valuators. Copies of the *Primary valuation* were used, most of which were interleaved with blank pages for notes. Some books have the notes written in the margins. They were prepared in the office by recording the appeals received, and some background notes but fewer than the 1846 appeal books. The books consist of the same elements as the 1846 books, that is, clerks' notes, revising valuators' notes, a record of the follow-up work, and alterations made to update and correct the printed *Primary valuation*. Some have the averaged figures of the valuation per acre written in the margin on both tenements appealed and neighbouring holdings.[23] The appeal books are a significant source of names that do not appear in the printed *Primary valuation*. The page for the parish of Moyrus, Co. Galway (plate 14) shows the arrangement of the appeal book. The printed page is marked and the revising valuator noted his comments on the blank page and made alterations, including corrections to names, on the printed page.

The revising valuator's notes cover circumstances relating to the cases appealed, including rent and tenure, farming, family and social conditions, economic activity and development, descriptions of property, comments on individuals and some rare insights into the lives of the valuators. These books

---

19 The former sub-commissioners Edward Gaffney, William Jones and Abraham Woffington worked as revising valuators on the 1852 appeals. Thomas Cox and Robert Bell were senior valuators since the early years and also worked as revising valuators. **20** OL/20/7/8, p. 57: uncertainty about how to value a ferry in Killydonnell, Aughnish, Co. Donegal, saw the matter referred to the commissioner, and his decision is noted in the book. **21** See OL/20/16/1, p. 9, for example. **22** *Returns showing the counties in Ireland in which the Tenement Valuation has been completed ... 1. Returns showing the counties in Ireland in which the Tenement Valuation has been completed ... the cost of the valuation by the acre, the cost by the £100 of the valuation, the whole cost to each county, and the date when it first came into force in each county*, HC 1856 (180), p. 2 (hereinafter cited as *Return showing counties in which Tenement Valuation is completed, 1856*, HC 1856 (180)); *Report from select committee on valuation, 1869*, appendix 1. **23** See OL/20/22/2, p. 87 and other books in Co. Meath.

lack the spontaneous testimony of occupiers at the hearings under the 1846 system and are less discursive, but they are nevertheless an excellent source. The revising valuators followed up the investigations as they thought best, expressed their opinions freely, and in general were less constrained than under the earlier formal procedure. The overall impression is that there were fewer appeals than in the earlier period, but detailed study of each book would be needed to establish the facts. The commissioner J.B. Greene claimed that the numbers of appeals declined because of improved public understanding of the valuation.[24]

As in earlier appeals, the main reason for appealing was excessive or irrelative valuation. A house in Bailieborough, Co. Cavan was appealed because of 'value excessive, not being in the marketable part of the town', and similar cases are found throughout the books.[25] In Ballyshannon town, it was accepted that buildings were dilapidated and the valuation was reduced from £85 to £50.[26] In Cloontyprughlish, Rossinver, Co. Leitrim, the revising valuator William Jones wrote: 'this valuation is very high. The mountain is very remote and horned cattle can scarcely be got to it and it is altogether land for sheep.' The valuation was reduced.[27] While many appeals appear to have been successful, there were also refusals.[28] An appeal claiming the valuation is 'too high and irrelative' receives the response: 'Valuation is not too high, on the contrary rather low. House should not be under 15s.' The valuation of the house was raised from 10s. to 15s.[29] Valuations considered too low could also be appealed. The board of guardians of the union of Galway, whose revenues were based on the valuation, objected to the low valuation of the village of Salt Hill, but their appeal was refused.[30] In Dunmuckrum, Inishmacsaint, Co. Donegal, neighbours objected to a low valuation. This was investigated by revising valuator Edward Gaffney, who redid the field work and calculations, and noted: 'I have valued this farm carefully and it is here quite plain to my judgment that this valuation so much cried out against is not too low.'[31]

Appeals based on incorrect content or square area were also frequent, arising from changes in tenements, mistakes by the original valuators or misunderstandings. Where tenements were subdivided, the content of each part needed to be stated separately and the valuator sought recalculation 'by altered boundaries'. In the townland of Gortnasillagh, Rossinver, Co. Leitrim, Robert Johnston and William Johnston appealed, the acreage of each holding was corrected and the latter's name was added in manuscript to the printed page.[32] The books for Mayo contain many references to the alter-

24 *Report from select committee on valuation, 1869*, questions 374–6. 25 OL/20/4/1, p. 51. 26 OL/20/7/3/1, p. 67. 27 OL/20/16/1, p. 14. 28 For example, OL/20/7/1, p. 50 and throughout. 29 Ibid., p. 49. 30 OL/20/11/4, p. 51. 31 OL/20/7/1, p. 64. 32 OL/20/16/1, p. 26.

ations in the boundaries, and the changes in the liability of occupiers, consequent on striping the land,[33] including a note on the difficulties caused.[34] Claims concerning small areas were examined with the same care, and an occupier in Cornalara, Shercock, Co. Cavan, 'says she holds but 8 Irish acres'; the recorded content was reduced by just over 3 roods.[35]

Many appeals for content were turned down, for example with the comment 'content right enough'.[36] In Co. Monaghan, the revising valuator wrote: 'I have examined the bounds of this townland carefully and cannot find anything to alter. They appear to have been carefully marked on maps and of course the calculations are also carefully made.'[37] A long-standing disputed boundary through a mountain was noted: 'It was latterly decided by the agent to the property that it should be made accordingly with the dotted line on the map made by me.'[38]

Changes made without appeal, and other matters examined
Changes, known as 'alterations', were made in cases where there was no appeal. These were made on the initiative of the revising valuator and concerned matters that arose in the course of the work, from changes of occupiers or tenements, to cases of houses that had been demolished. The number of changes varies greatly from place to place, but can outnumber the appeals. The book for the union of Ballyshannon, Co. Donegal contains many examples. In the townland of Rossnowlagh Upper or Crockahane, Drumhome there was one appeal, which was accepted, and two further alterations were made in neighbouring tenements, the valuations of which had not been appealed. One concerned a house that had been extended since the original valuation, and an increase was made. In the second case, the original valuation of the house was considered a mistake and was reduced from £10 to £5.[39] In Omey, Co. Galway, on a sample page where three appeals were noted, corrections were made to twenty-one tenements, but most books contain fewer.[40] Some of the changes arose because of new occupiers, and names were altered throughout the books. For example, in Ballyshannon town, Co. Donegal, Honoria Gorman was changed to Pat Hughes.[41] An occupier in Cattan, Cloone, Co. Leitrim 'says Rose Higgins has a garden and house in his farm which is charged to him'. The two holdings were separated and Higgins' name was added in manuscript.[42] There are many examples of names being added to the printed lists,[43] including the Revd Henry Newman, noted as the occupant of University College at 86 St Stephen's Green, Dublin, and the new building at 86a for University Church.[44] Some books

33 Examples in OL/20/21/15, p. 129. 34 OL/20/21/38/1. 35 OL/20/4/2, p. 91. 36 OL/20/4/4, p. 9. 37 OL/20/23/5, p. 25. 38 OL/20/7/1, p. 50. 39 OL/20/7/3, p. 10. 40 OL/20/11/3, p. 96. 41 OL/20/7/1, p. 68. 42 OL/20/16/4, p. 73. 43 OL/20/7/1, p. 3, and OL/20/4/1, p. 49. 44 OL/20/9/1, p. 156, and throughout for examples of name

give additional lists of occupiers, as in Ardmore, Moyrus, Co. Galway, where the two names given in the printed book as holders of common land were expanded to show twenty-five occupiers.[45]

Corrections to errors in the printed *Primary valuation* include misspelled names: for example, Faucett was corrected to Fawcett,[46] Le Monte to Lamont,[47] McCauley to McCawley.[48] Agnomens or nicknames are also altered.[49] A note in Kilfian, Co. Mayo states: 'The name spelled Roughan [in the printed book] should be properly Rowan, but most commonly Ruane.'[50] In Ballyshannon, Co. Donegal, a title is corrected: 'Should be Right Revd Daniel McGettigan. He is coadjutor bishop of Raphoe.'[51] The notes also name persons involved but who do not otherwise appear as either tenants or lessors, for example, land agents with whom the valuation was discussed.[52]

The many alterations in Dublin city between the publication of the printed book in February 1854 and the revision that was carried out a few years later are listed. A house in Pleasants Street was built in November 1856, first reduced in November 1857 and then further reduced in November 1860.[53] The demolition of old houses, the building of new, and the division of existing houses are recorded, as well as new developments such as the terminus of the Dublin and Wicklow Railway at Harcourt Street, valued at £500,[54] or the new occupier of a house in Lower Baggot Street given as 'Irish Institution, Picture Gallery', with a note that it was exempt by order of Mr Greene.[55]

References to rent and tenure are present in many of the notes. The book covering part of Cork city gives information on rent and tenure,[56] and the one for Rathmolyon, Co. Meath, gives the rent, the type of tenure with the year and precise information about leases.[57] A house on Leeson Street, Dublin was noted as 'taken 20 years ago for £63 and £450 fine'.[58] A property in Galway is described as 'shop only, rent £18 and taxes',[59] and in another part of the county a list of rent paid is given on an additional page.[60] The book for the union of Clifden, Co. Galway contains several lists of rent paid by occupiers of common land.[61]

Notes of matters taken into account include descriptions of farming practices. In Bridge End, Tullyfern, Co. Donegal, a holding is 'let as grazing to the townspeople this year, 12 cows at £3 5s. each and would make as much almost every year either in meadow or pasture. It was formerly a bleach

---

changes. **45** OL/20/11/3, p. 80. Similar on p. 93 and throughout. **46** OL/20/7/1, p. 46. **47** OL/20/1/1, p. 280. **48** OL/20/7/1, p. 49. **49** OL/20/21/44, p. 26. **50** OL/20/21/38, p. 42. **51** OL/20/7/1, p. 32. **52** OL/20/11/3, p. 445, 'C. Sherrard is agent'; OL/20/21/10, p. 82, 'Mr Keavney, the agent to Lord Kilmaine.' **53** OL/20/9/1, p. 153. **54** Ibid., p. 146. **55** Ibid., p. 134. **56** OL/20/6/1, pp 202, 204. **57** OL/20/22/29, pp 58, 63. **58** OL/20/9/1, p. 150. **59** OL/20/11/4, p. 34. **60** OL/20/11/5, p. 193. **61** OL/20/11/4, pp 98, 101.

green.'[62] In Rossnowlagh Lower, Co. Donegal, the importance of seaweed in agriculture can be seen: 'A great portion has been brought under potato tillage which the facility of procuring sea weed encourages, as by its means a poor crop of potatoes can be grown, the only crop they dare risk.'[63] In Achill, Co. Mayo, the valuator commented that a farm 'is only fit for three or four summer months not fit at all for winter, there being no black sedge on it', and there are notes concerning the new charges introduced by the lessor for grazing livestock on mountain land.[64]

The appeal books may assist in elucidating family matters or dates. The comment that the valuation of John Healy in Firmount West, Clane, Co. Kildare is 'rather high compared to his brother Phil' establishes a relationship that is not known from the printed text.[65] The family connections of the lessor in Drummond's Court, Belfast can be seen in the correction 'Mary Magill of 82 Little Donegall St or 1 Birch St with her son in law McManus'.[66] The note stating that a tenement is 'held by the widow of James Mitchell' may help in dating a death.[67] The comment in Foyagh, Drumhome, Co. Donegal, 'Francis Walsh, died recently, his widow retains the land', is a similar case. The name in the printed book was corrected to Susan.[68]

In Killinangel Beg, Drumhome, Co. Donegal, the background to names listed in the printed book was given, where an appeal claimed the wrong occupier had been listed. The occupier's name was not on the rental, although he occupied the holding, and his father wished him left out of the valuation also. Here no alteration was made in the printed book.[69] In another case of the wrong occupier being listed, the explanation was made: 'Francis [Donagher] *is the proper occupier* but his father James who put him into possession wishes to have his own name returned for it. It is supposed to give him a qualification for a poor law guardian which he has hitherto managed.' James Donagher is listed elsewhere in the townland with the letters 'PLG' (poor law guardian) after his name.[70] In the neighbouring townland of Killinangel More, the name of an occupier was changed: 'John Watson occupier. Elizabeth his sister took care of this place during his absence in America.'[71]

Useful incidental information on occupations was sometimes included. The exemption from taxes of the house of the scripture reader of the Irish Church Mission Society in Ballinaboy, Ballindoon, Co. Galway was related to his professional activity.[72] The status of the occupant of stables and a yard

---

62 OL/20/7/8, p. 50.   63 OL/7/1/, p. 9.   64 OL/20/21/44, pp 14, 22.   65 OL/20/13/15, p. 111.   66 OL/20/1/3, p. 463. James McManus is listed in Birch Street, p. 450, but Mary Magill is not listed. The entry for 82 Little Donegall Street, p. 449, cross-refers to Birch Street. 67 OL/20/13/15, p. 104.   68 OL/20/7/3, p. 10.   69 OL/20/7/1, p. 2.   70 Ibid., p. 49. 71 Ibid., p. 3.   72 OL/20/11/3, p. 13.

in Belfast determined which name was listed: 'John Garland is only the hostler of the yard at weekly wages from Miss Anderson,' and the name was corrected to Jane Anderson.[73] Further mention of occupations included a clergyman in Knappagh More, Aghagower, Co. Mayo who was employed by the Additional Curates Fund Society,[74] and an appellant in Co. Mayo who was a relieving officer.[75]

Additional information was sometimes recorded on the use of buildings, such as notes on shops in Belfast.[76] A Belfast property with many functions comprised:

> a shop, Masonic lodge room, 3 bedrooms, kitchen, 4 rooms over and WC. The lessor is member of the lodge and the dining room floor is used as a lodge room monthly. Tenant has use of it at other times. Hence the low rent.[77]

In Monaghan town, a building purchased by private subscription as a reformatory for female offenders was described. The government paid for the maintenance of the children, but 'no salaries paid to the staff and it is wholly a charitable institution. As yet there are only 21 children as the place is not quite fitted up to receive more.'[78] The background to an exemption given to the house attached to a female orphan nursery and school in Clifden, Co. Galway was explained: 'Employed to give a home to young persons embracing the Protestant faith and there is a glebe house being built on the grounds with a view of giving them spiritual consolation.'[79] The revising valuator examined houses in Ballymacrorty, Co. Donegal, where the late Colonel Conolly had encouraged the building of good houses and given slates for roofing, but the houses were over-valued: 'Those houses are usually well glazed and the outside whitened, but within they are all in the rough, seldom plastered or rendered and not in comfort or value what they appear on the outside.'[80] Some of the expanded descriptions indicate dates for buildings or alterations. In Belfast, a note dated the extension to a school as having been added in 1861,[81] and six houses in Carr's Row were 'to be taken down and rebuilt, in bad repair'.[82] Reference was made in June 1861 to the recent demolition of the market house in Carrickmacross.[83]

Many occupiers defended their appeals strongly. A document given by an occupier in support of his case in Drumharriff, Donaghmoyne, Co. Monaghan is entitled 'Owen Hall's probable valuation', and was annotated by the valuator with the words 'or as he would wish to have it'.[84] In

73 OL/20/1/1, p. 217.   74 OL/20/21/54, p. 56.   75 OL/20/21/39, p. 38.   76 OL/20/1/1, p. 227 and examples throughout.   77 OL/20/1/5, p. 177.   78 OL/20/23/7, p. 214.   79 OL/20/11/3, p. 82.   80 OL/20/7/1, p. 6.   81 OL/20/1/1, p. 299.   82 Ibid., p. 265.   83 OL/20/23/1/2.   84 OL/20/23/1/1.

Fohanagh, Co. Galway, a list of occupiers and stock was submitted, probably in support of an appeal.[85] A tenant in Ray, Aghamullen, Co. Monaghan complained 'very bitterly' about too much square area being ascribed to his tenement, and produced an applotment of the county with the areas copied from the landlord's maps.[86] Another occupier claimed not to have known about the appeal and 'thinks himself much wronged by the valuation'.[87]

Appeals were also withdrawn, in some cases without a reason stated,[88] and in other cases with an explanation, as in Galway, where Charles Lynch, an appellant, wrote: 'In consequence of the explanations given me by the revising valuator Mr Cox which are very satisfactory, I hereby beg to withdraw my appeal made against the valuation of my property both in unions of Oughterard and Ballinrobe.'[89] Not everyone was satisfied though, and a memorial from an occupier in Clones, Co. Monaghan described how he had lodged a preliminary notice of appeal, which had resulted in a reduction of £3. He was aggrieved to find it was not further reduced, but 'not wishing to be litigious, did not proceed to have the final notice of appeal'.[90]

Many of the alterations indicate economic activity and development. In Belfast, a new machine shop where the occupier invested £100 had its valuation reduced,[91] and there are notes about 'building ground used for temporary timber yard for rough timber only, it is not enclosed'.[92] The taxes of the town of Monaghan were the property of Lord Rossmore, who gave them to the town commissioners, who then let them to the highest bidder and used the benefit for public purposes of 'cleaning, watching and lighting'.[93] The dividend paid by the gas company in Carrickmacross is noted, and the fact that the distillery had ceased working was deplored as 'a great loss to the trade of the town generally'.[94] The accounts of the ferry at Pollranny, Achill, Co. Mayo were produced by the owner in support of his appeal, claiming 'he does not make a shilling of it', and it was reduced from £5 to £3.[95] A loss of business due to new developments could result in a reduction of valuation, as in the livery stables in Coburg Street, Cork, now 'much depreciated in value since railway commenced'.[96]

In Wardhouse, Rossinver, Co. Leitrim, the appeal of a 'bag net salmon fishery' resulted in a £2 valuation being placed on each of the three persons concerned, despite the advice of the revising valuator Jones that only two of them should be charged:

> Only one bag net now. Roger Dowdican and Michael Cassidy are the fishermen and get half the fish caught for their trouble. These

85 OL/20/11/9/2. 86 OL/20/23/4, p. 18. 87 OL/20/21/24, p. 10. 88 OL/20/22/19, p. 124. 89 OL/20/11/2/1. 90 OL/20/23/3/2. 91 OL/20/1/4, p. 351. 92 OL/20/1/1, p. 219. 93 OL/20/23/7, p. 213. 94 OL/20/23/1, p. 88. 95 OL/20/21/44, p. 10. 96 OL/20/6/1, p. 225.

parties make all that is made by the fishery as Mr Ellis pays all the expenses which from his returns amount to more than the sale of his half of the fish. I would be inclined if anything is to be charged to have the £2 10s. each on the tenants and 0 on Mr Ellis as valuation.[97]

The accounts of a tile works and kiln in Aghadunvane, Rossinver, Co. Leitrim showed a loss in 1856, but as tiles were given to the tenants free of charge for drainage works, Jones wrote in justification of reducing the £25 valuation to £2:

I do not think the tilery is properly chargeable in this case. The spirit of our act is to give encouragement to improvements whereas rating such a useful speculation is a direct discouragement. If it was worked for the purpose of making money by it there could be some reason given for taxing it but as it is a losing matter to the proprietor as will appear by the annexed account it is ever hard to charge for the tilery house and kiln the £2 which I have entered in the building column against them.[98]

There are also the usual random pieces of information. For example, a temporary circus was noted in the printed book for Belfast ('circus taken down April 1861'[99]), and the valuation of a house in Hatch Street, Dublin was appealed on the grounds: 'valuation excessive, house being askew'.[1] In Rareagh, Conwal, Co. Donegal an appeal was turned down but the occupier claimed to have been misled: 'He says the porter at the workhouse told him his valuation was £6 10s. and the porter had an interest in causing appeals inasmuch as he charged a shilling for filling them.'[2] In Camden Street, Dublin, the date of a fire that damaged two houses is given as November 1856.[3] A note referring to Knockduff, Templeshanbo, Co. Wexford describes how land was acquired by Dr Morrison. His father-in-law was the law agent to the former owner, who won the estate 'with the wife of his opponent, at play'.[4]

A small number of notebooks are also part of this series, and loose documents are attached to some of the books. These comprise mostly correspondence and some lists of alterations made as a result of the appeals. The correspondence contains some letters of appeal, including letters from occupiers in County Kilkenny where the valuation was carried out under the 1846 act but they appealed under the 1852 act.

---

97 OL/20/16/1, p. 44. 98 OL/20/16/1/1 and OL/20/16/1, p. 2. 99 OL/20/1/1, p. 212.
1 OL/20/9/1, p. 148. 2 OL/20/7/6, p. 73. 3 OL/20/9/1, p. 136. 4 OL/20/31/1, p. 37.

The role of the valuator

The presence of the valuator in the locality was important, and may have improved public satisfaction with the valuation, as many showed themselves to be willing to listen. Edward Gaffney described two separate chance encounters with occupiers in Co. Monaghan. In Aghanamullen, tenants 'whom I met on the road, returning home from work, complain to me of the valuation of this portion of the townland'.[5] In Doohat, Aghabog, a tenant approached him about the valuation of his farm because 'he was deterred from appealing by the police who told him it would be attended by great expense. He states the valuation is £2 above the rent although he holds as tenant at will.' Gaffney investigated and found that roads were mistakenly included in the acreage.[6] The valuator also had contact with local officials and landowners, and in some cases was happy to accept external advice. The agent of Lord Kilmaine in Islandeady, Co. Mayo, gave a valuation to Gaffney 'which he assures me has got done with great care. As this does not materially alter the valuation of any of the tenements and is calculated to give more satisfaction to all, I think it right to adopt it.' Changes were made to most holdings in the townland.[7]

The investigations of the valuator required the co-operation of the community, but he was in an ambiguous position, as the valuation could be seen as not in the interests of the occupiers. He needed to demonstrate impartiality and tact. Examining cases during the appeal process also meant judging the work done by his predecessors in making the *Primary valuation*. Thomas Cox revised parts of Co. Mayo and remarked on the carelessness of the earlier work.[8] In Keel East, Achill, he found that the valuator had overvalued one house, while failing to value the house where he had lodged.[9] Edward Gaffney investigated the union of Ballyshannon, Co. Donegal and found criticism to make on nearly every page of the *Primary valuation* for that area. He accepted many of the appeals and made many other reductions in this book, for example: 'There must be some mistake in the valuation of this house. It is an ordinary farm house thatched and hardly fit for the reception of lodgers,' or 'This is greatly too high.'[10]

The appeal books again demonstrate the thoroughness of the work. The cases varied from simply checking facts, as in an appeal for 'house down', which was annotated, 'House is not down, he lives in it,'[11] to the more complex matter of the motivation of occupiers in Ratheskin, Kilfian, Co. Mayo: 'That they are too high is believed by every person except the agent. But I believe they will to sell, and therefore are anxious to have the rents much lower than the valuation, for purposes of their own.'[12] The valuator

5 OL/20/23/4, p. 2. 6 OL/20/23/5, p. 27. 7 OL/20/21/10, p. 82. 8 OL/20/21/38, p. 45. Several of the Mayo books contain remarks of this kind. 9 OL/20/21/44, pp 36–7. 10 OL/20/7/1, pp 27, 40. 11 OL/20/4/9, p. 30. 12 OL/20/21/38, p. 34.

Philip Ryan recorded finding everything 'quite correct' after examining a whole townland.[13] A note on the book for the union of Ballyshannon, Co. Donegal, explained that many items were marked because they were examined by the revising valuator, Edward Gaffney 'for his own satisfaction in getting through the appeals of the union'.[14]

There was a general acceptance that some occupiers would appeal without serious cause. William Jones commented on an appeal in Rossollus, Clontibret, Co. Monaghan: 'Mrs McGuire is satisfied her valuation is low enough and does not wish it disturbed, but a younger son of hers, she says, when he saw others putting in appeals, thought he would try his hand at it also.'[15] In Sligo town the revising valuator wrote a long note warning about a large number of appeals seeking increases in valuations, or substitutions of names, in an apparently organised attempt to obtain voting qualifications.[16] There was also acceptance that some taxpayers would dispute the valuation to the end. In Cuiltycreaghan, Bekan, Co. Mayo: 'The appellant Mr John Treston is quite prepared to follow up his appeals at quarter sessions. He is fond of litigation and generally so successful that he won't hesitate to go into court even against difficulties.'[17]

The staff were often sceptical about the evidence produced. An appeal by Patrick Curry in Cloondace, Knock, Co. Mayo was contested by the valuator: 'This is not a correct statement. Some of the persons named above cut turf only on the bog but he has the exclusive grazing. Valuation fair.' A possible increase in the valuation of a turbary in Legland, Kilgarvan, Co. Donegal was treated with caution and the revising valuator Robert Bell wrote that the owner, Mr Montgomery 'should be put down at £25 a year instead of £10 as published. He makes upwards of £50 a year by this turbary free of expenses, but I did not wish to change it until I could get reliable information from the bog bailiff and others.'[18]

The frustration of the rules being overturned by further appeals can be seen in a case in Knockgeeragh, Burrishoole, Co. Mayo that Cox investigated. It was appealed to the quarter sessions on the grounds that the valuation was too high in relation to the low rent, but Cox anticipated that the court would fail to take account of the good price obtained for the seaweed from the property:

> It is quite wrong they should be reduced below what they are, no matter what rent they pay. The occupiers called on me and were *furious* because they would get no reduction, they will lose £50 or get it reduced they say – and I have no doubt from the rule the barrister made for himself but they will get it reduced.[19]

13 OL/20/21/21, p. 87. 14 OL/20/7/1, p. 1. 15 OL/20/23/2, p. 96. 16 OL/20/26/2, p. 119. 17 OL/20/21/32, p. 135. 18 OL/20/7/8/1. 19 OL/20/21/45, p. 40.

Occupiers were not always helpful. For example, one valuator noted the difficulty he had in obtaining cooperation in Emlagharan, Ballindoon, Co. Galway, where a Mr Hart invited the valuator to call, and 'I called at his place three times and he gave me no list, nor do I think he would give me an explanation, except with a view of leading me astray.'[20] Edward Gaffney expressed his irritation at confusion in Kinnewry, Ballintober, Co. Mayo: 'The person who lodged the objection here appears to have no interest in the place and his objection is such as could not be noticed to any effect. I shall await the owner's objection.'[21]

In general, the revising valuators showed sympathy for the situation of occupiers, and the books contain many negative comments on the living conditions of tenants. In Eskermorilly, Knock, Co. Mayo, it was noted that 'John Forde's is a hovel not worth any valuation'.[22] In Aughrusbeg, Omey, Co. Galway, Abraham Woffington described dwellings as 'mere rubbish scarcely deserve the name of houses' and the occupiers as 'pauper tenantry, paying rack rents, a good deal of which has to be allowed in labour and some produce supplied at the highest penny'.[23] In Rooaunmore, Claregalway, Co. Galway the notes describe a difficulty:

> They hold from Michael Burke but their houses are going to ruin, they want thatch and other repairs and he won't repair them and therefore they will pay him no rent, nor have they paid him any for some time. If he does repair the houses they will pay him rent, but I believe he wishes to send them off without having recourse to harsher means, but they are living on his lands and are his tenants.[24]

Thomas Cox recited the background to a case in Killerduff, Doonfeeny, Co. Mayo. Here, a bequest under the will of Mr Kirkwood gave a house, garden and the grass of a cow, in the farm occupied by Revd Mr McNamara, to the occupier, Michael O'Malley. The property was later sold subject to these provisions and the new lessor, Colonel Knox Gore, 'was inclined not to allow Mally to have the grass but he asserted his right to it and has it'. O'Malley sent to Dublin for a copy of Kirkwood's will and Cox transcribed extracts from it in the appeal book.[25]

A small number of appeal forms survive for Co. Mayo. In 1857, two occupiers in Garrymore, Kilcommon, in the union of Claremorris submitted late appeals, claiming to have been out of the country at the time of the appeals, that their land was poor and the valuation too high. The forms are

---

20 OL/20/11/3, p. 2. 21 OL/20/21/5, p. 39. 22 OL/20/21/27, p. 61. 23 OL/20/11/3, p. 97. 24 OL/20/11/5, p. 228. 25 OL/20/21/35, p. 7.

written in the same hand and use similar wording but they may have been completed by the clerk of the union. Gaffney was instructed to investigate when in the townland. In the first holding, he increased both the content and value. In the second case, he reduced the valuation, but did not believe the excuse of the occupier: 'He strains his facts to make a case. It is not true that he was out of the country during the appealing time.'[26] In a third and similar case in Ballyglass, Crossboyne, also in Claremorris union, an appeal form giving a similar excuse was completed on the same date in the same hand and signed with a mark. On this occasion, Gaffney accepted neither the case nor the excuse: 'This statement is untrue as all his neighbours assert he never left home during the whole season and it is equally untrue to state that the valuation is higher than the remainder of the townland.'[27] A note in another book shows how the clerk of a poor law union assisted, or failed to assist, in these matters: 'Notice given to the clerk to appeal against these two and he forgot it. The notice was not written out and given to him to forward but he was asked to write out the appeal himself and he forgot it.'[28]

An incomplete letter regarding a farm in Feighcullen, Co. Kildare, by an unknown person, sent to valuator William Jones at the post office in Edenderry, King's County, indicates trust on behalf of the public, although it is not clear if Daniel Dunne had appealed his valuation (and, despite a note in the appeal book stating that it was too high, the price was not changed):

> Mr Jones, Sir, I was wrong on Thursday last the day you had your car at my house at Feighcullen, when I told you many things about Mr Dunne's farm that were untrue, that is the farm you were looking at behind my house. I was hard upon the man and I am now sorry for it. The truth is the land was so bad when he took it this time two years that it was dear at the rent of £45 per year. I am now sorry for many things I said, and I was wrong. I write these few lines hoping you will not expose my weakness. I am, sir, sorry for all I said.[29]

Conclusion

In addition to the data on the appeals, these documents are full of interesting and surprising information gathered at first hand by staff who travelled the country, verifying the truth or otherwise of every claim. The investigations exposed and recorded a multitude of details and connections that provide background and context to the facts of the valuation. The complaints raised against the valuation under the 1852 act were consistent with those in the

---

26 OL/20/21/34, pp 2–3, OL/20/21/34/1–2. 27 OL/20/21/24, p. 21 and OL/20/21/24/1. 28 OL/20/21/55, p. 70. 29 OL/20/13/45/1 and OL/20/13/45, p. 3.

Townland Valuation and the 1846 Tenement Valuation in showing that public concern was centred on the price being too high or unfair and on general confusion about the correct square area of holdings. The 1852 appeal documents were made up to the very last stages of the initial valuation, and their late date makes them particularly valuable in recording changes. The careful work is again clearly visible, and the non-adversarial contact with occupiers and owners may have created better understanding of the process.

7

Keeping the archives safe

The valuation archives now exist in large numbers because they were well looked-after from the time of their creation, with the result that they are now a major resource. Apart from the large quantity now in the National Archives, some documents are held in other repositories. Facilities for public inspection of the documents are available at these locations, but researchers should check any specific conditions, requirements and opening hours before visiting.

A. MANAGEMENT AND PRESERVATION OF ARCHIVES IN THE VALUATION OFFICE

The valuation work was based on a complex system of linked information recorded in the very large collection of documents. Order and method were essential to managing both the physical records and the data. The records were an integral part of the standardized methodology and were retained for reference and as proof. Rules about the creation, format and retention of the records were outlined in the first act in 1826, and the later acts and instructions all make reference to record-keeping. Provision was made in the 1834 act to deposit the documents in the Chief Secretary's Office in Dublin Castle, and although this does not seem to have been done, other arrangements ensured their safety and preservation.[1] The inclusion of these provisions in the legislation shows recognition of the importance of this aspect of the work. The result of the good arrangements made at the time can be seen today in the high rate of survival of valuation archives. Despite the criticism of the Valuation Office's management by the select committee of 1869,[2] much of the success of the valuation can be attributed to high standards of records-management, which maintained and made available the evidence on which the valuation was based. The archives of the initial valuation now comprise almost 30,000 items, and while this is a very large quantity, not all of the original documents have survived.

The order and method behind the work can also be seen in the arrange-

---

[1] See 4 & 5 Will. IV, c. 55. See also OL/2/5, p. 63, Griffith's letter to the undersecretary for Ireland, Sir William Gossett, resisting compliance with this requirement. [2] *Report from select committee on valuation, 1869.*

ments made for the physical preservation of the records. In the 1860s, the office moved from Griffith's private house in Fitzwilliam Place in Dublin to two very grand eighteenth-century houses in Ely Place.[3] Nothing is known about the physical storage in Fitzwilliam Place, and in the early 1880s, specific provision was made for preservation when an extension was built in Ely Place. This was designed as a purpose-built repository that gave protection to the documents, allowed order to be maintained and permitted convenient consultation. The rooms were fitted with wooden shelves around the walls, in sizes appropriate to the books, and with banks of wooden drawers in the centre and on some sides for the full-sized valuation maps. The books were arranged in order on the shelves by county, and the maps were kept in order by county and sheet number. This arrangement allowed the storage in proximity of related books and maps, and the upper surface of the map cabinets facilitated the laying out of documents for side-by-side consultation. This system continued until the Valuation Office moved out of this building in 1998. A full-time custodian was in charge of maps in 1835,[4] and a small number of office books confirm that removal and use of the documents was controlled.[5] This situation has continued to the present day. The record keeper was one of the witnesses examined by the 1869 select committee, and the commissioner described how the books were in use every day, and how they were taken out and returned.[6]

In addition to the good storage, several other factors contributed to the preservation of this collection, including a culture of respect and appreciation throughout the organization. The longevity of the valuation system, which continued to use the documents for reference until recent times, and the occupation of the same premises for over a hundred years were also important. Additional storage space was created several times in the twentieth century through the removal of some documents. Those relating to Northern Ireland were removed to Belfast in the early 1920s, and are now in the Public Record Office of Northern Ireland,[7] and several transfers were made to the National Archives from the 1940s onwards.[8] One exception to the good survival rate is the appeal books of the Tenement Valuation. Only approximately half of the number of these books that once existed was transferred to the National Archives, and some were later acquired from private sources. The valuation archives were not affected by the destructions that

3 Griffith was paid £100 a year rent for the offices in his house and over the adjoining stables between 1828 and 1868. See *Report from select committee on valuation, 1869*, questions 1429 and 5096. The houses in Ely Place were formerly the home of John Fitzgibbon, earl of Clare, lord chancellor of Ireland (1708–1802).   4 OL/2/5, pp 58–60.   5 OL/1/3/1–26.   6 *Report from select committee on valuation, 1869*, questions 5298–327 and 848–50.   7 See Parkhill, 'Valuation records in the Public Record Office of Northern Ireland', p. 46.   8 Transfers were made to the Public Record Office of Ireland (now the National Archives) in 1947 and 1949, and to the National Archives in 1977, 1979 and 1998.

have plagued other Irish archives. The work continued routinely through the period of the Great Famine and the later disturbances of the nineteenth century. Situated, as the office was, in a quiet street off St Stephen's Green, its records appear to have been untouched by the events of both 1916 and 1921–2, although its staff was disrupted by both the First World War and the establishment of a separate Valuation Office in Northern Ireland. The proactive role of the Valuation Office in Dublin in the management and preservation of the records should not be underestimated.

The 1869 select committee heard evidence from the storekeeper, who described how the cold and humidity were kept under control in the stores:

> when you go down stairs in the under basement there are two stores, and every day in the year a fire is lit in each of them; then there is a rear building, you go through a long passage and there is a building that was occupied as a kitchen in the days of Lord Clare, there is a kitchen fire-grate, and above stairs there are three other stores. It is my business to see that the papers are all preserved from damp and every day there are large fires lighted.[9]

B. ARCHIVES NOW HELD IN THE VALUATION OFFICE, DUBLIN

The Valuation Office (located at Irish Life Centre, Abbey Street Lower, Dublin 1) holds the records of the valuation from the mid-1850s to 1990, and to the present day for commercial property. These documents are the continuation of the archives held in the National Archives. They consist of cancelled books where the results of the initial valuation were recorded and were revised since that time, and the corresponding maps. The revisions were made arising out of changes in property such as new occupiers or boundaries. Revisions were made at the request of the local rating authorities and went through a statutory procedure, including appeals. The results of the revisions were marked up in the cancelled books, using different-coloured inks for each year, allowing identification of the year when an alteration was made. The results were issued in revised lists to the local authorities who then used them for levying rates on occupiers.

There is an overlap in dates between documents held in the National Archives and the Valuation Office because of the varying dates when the initial work in each county was completed and the revision work was commenced. In some cases the latest maps and town plans in the National Archives relate to books held in the Valuation Office. The cancelled books for

---

9 *Report from select committee on valuation, 1869*, question 5311.

some counties have been digitized and are available for consultation in the reading area. Facilities for research and copying are available at the Valuation Office premises. The conditions and opening times should be checked on the website before visiting. It is useful for the researcher to record the revisions in the cancelled books in a manner that distinguishes the year.

C. VALUATION ARCHIVES IN THE PUBLIC RECORD OFFICE OF NORTHERN IRELAND

Following the partition of Ireland into two states, a separate Valuation Office was established in Belfast, and records relating to Northern Ireland were transferred there. The documents of the initial valuation are now held in the Public Record Office of Northern Ireland, where they can be inspected. Northern Ireland was re-valued several times in the twentieth century, and the archives of those valuations are also available. All of the Valuation Office archives held in the Public Record Office of Northern Ireland relate to the six counties of Northern Ireland. The archives consist of the books and maps of the valuation from its beginnings in 1830 until 1993.

The documents now divided between Belfast and Dublin arose from the same legislation and were created by the same body, but some differences can be perceived. The content of all the documents varied with the date at which they were created. The northern counties were both the first counties to be valued under the Townland Valuation and the last counties to be valued under the Tenement Valuation. For example, the valuation first carried out in Co. Londonderry from 1830 was experimental; in the second valuation of these counties, a fully formed and perfected system was used. The Townland Valuation of northern counties was complete, published and in force before the first steps towards a tenement valuation were made in 1844. These counties escaped the complications of the transitional stages seen in counties such as Tipperary or Kilkenny. This fact created two distinct sets of documents made at two well-separated periods of valuation.

The arrangement of the documents and the catalogue descriptions vary between the two institutions. In PRONI all the manuscript books are described as 'field books'. This encompasses books described by the National Archives as field books, house books, quarto books for the Townland Valuation and house books and tenure books for the Tenement Valuation. Similarly, the terms used to describe the maps may vary. The catalogue of valuation documents under the reference code 'VAL' is available online at nidirect.gov.uk/proni, and introductory explanations can be accessed there. The annual revision lists (or cancelled books) relating to Northern Ireland, 1864–1930, are digitized and can be searched on the website above. The National Archives holds some books relating to parts of Northern Ireland.

D. LOCAL ARCHIVES AND LOCAL-STUDIES LIBRARIES

Local archives and the local-studies sections of public libraries are likely to hold copies of the *Primary valuation* and manuscript valuation archives relating to the annual revision in the county or city. The annual revision took place from the mid-1850s. These documents are the copies of revised valuations sent by the Valuation Office to local authorities, which levied rates. This work was initiated by the local authorities requesting that the commissioner revise the valuation of property where the occupiers, boundaries or value had changed. A time-bound statutory procedure was followed, and the revised valuations could be appealed through a process similar to that used in the Tenement Valuation.

8

Conclusion

The archives of the valuation are a rich source of information on nineteenth-century Ireland. This is a large archive of nearly 30,000 individual items, books and maps, which fit together to show a picture of the entire country at points between 1830 and 1865. Over a period of thirty-five years the baseline valuation was created by establishing the facts about individual properties and their occupiers. This was revised and updated for all property until the late twentieth century, and is still in operation for commercial premises. Valuations of various kinds had been carried out before this one, and the concept was understood, but there were particular difficulties associated with this work, including the large scale and long duration, the technical content and the need for a uniform result. The achievement of the valuation cannot be exaggerated, and neither can that of Commissioner Richard Griffith, who dominated the work for forty years. The records contain an enormous mass of data, which was subjected to a rigorous process. It was collected manually by staff who were dispersed across the country at a period when travel and communication were not easy, and was then collated and transformed into a valuation that withstood public scrutiny and appeal, and endured for more than 150 years. Despite the criticism to which it was subjected, which has been described as 'savage', its longevity is an indication of its high quality and status in the public mind. Although this longevity could be attributed to inertia, it was also a recognition of the inherent difficulties of this complex work.[1]

The experimental nature of the work can be seen in the large number of changes that were made, from the acts of parliament to the instructions and minor changes, and also in the alternative methodologies that were considered, as seen in the correspondence. The work always depended on the same method, of painstaking collection of minute pieces of data, of extraordinary numbers of calculations done in duplicate, checked and re-checked before being opened to examination by the public. This was done for the highest public purpose of establishing an impartial, fair and justifiable valuation based on facts that were preserved as evidence, even if it was not always perceived as such.

---

1 Vaughan, 'Richard Griffith and the Tenement Valuation' in Herries Davies & Mollan (eds), *Richard Griffith, 1784–1878*, pp 104–8.

The period in which the valuation was made saw major changes resulting from the Great Famine and, although the tragedy of the period is scarcely referenced in the documents, the effects were recorded in great detail. The valuation also needs to be put in the context of other state activities. In the early years it was linked directly to the Boundary Survey and Ordnance Survey as part of the basic recording of the country's vital statistics that also included activities such as the census and the making of agricultural statistics. Gradually, over the second half of the century, the valuation became a reference point for state services and benefits in a context of expanding infrastructural activity, such as the installation of town water and sanitation systems and the building of labourers' cottages.

The valuation was a record-based activity and the documents were created with the intention that they should be preserved. Fortunately for present-day researchers, the preservation extended to a wider range of documents than the main series. While there have been losses that may affect research in individual cases, this is a whole archive in the sense that the majority of the documents and the series in which they were created have survived. It is also universal in applying to every part of the country, and is uniform throughout – with minor variations. The archives cover a period for which census returns do not survive, and they contain lists of names in every townland, village and city. The incidental information recorded includes fascinating insights into the human aspects of the entire operation.

Making the valuation was a complex undertaking and the archives can be challenging, although they are accessible at many different levels. Many of the documents are technical and the researcher's experience will be enhanced by understanding the meaning of the information in front of them. The documents can be used for simple searches for names, or wider investigations of families and communities, or analytic socio-economic studies. Many of these archives were available to researchers in the past (in the National Archives and the Valuation Office), but they are now all held in the National Archives. This has allowed the previously fragmented information to be arranged in coherent archival series and the relationships between the series to be elucidated. The possibilities of these important archives as a research resource remain to be explored.

Appendix A

Procedures for appeals under valuation acts of 1826–52

TOWNLAND VALUATION ACT 1826

Under this act, separate hearings were held for each barony and a further hearing was held for the county as a whole. The grand jury appointed a committee of appeal for each barony and a committee of revision for the county. The composition of the committees was prescribed.

Barony-level appeals (sections 10–20)
When the work on each barony was completed, a draft valuation list was made in the prescribed form, showing the parishes and townlands, with the number of acres and the total value of land and houses and stating the day and place of the meeting of the committee of appeal, six weeks hence. This was sent to the high constable of the barony, who fixed copies in places used for posting grand-jury notices and forwarded copies to the churchwardens of parishes in the barony concerned for posting on the doors of places of worship, where they remained for two successive Sundays. The churchwardens called a select vestry (membership of which has a property qualification) that could decide to appeal. The appeals stated the grounds in writing and were sent to the commissioner. The latter notified the clerk of the peace, who organized the committee of appeal meeting in the sessions house of the barony and advertised in a local newspaper fourteen days before the meeting. The commissioner presided over the appeal hearings. Evidence was taken under oath, with a penalty for perjury specified. The field books were produced at the appeals as necessary. The decision of the committee was conclusive, unless the commissioner disagreed. In such case, it was referred to the county-level committee of revision. If there was no appeal, the valuation stood.

County-level appeals (sections 21–5)
When appeals in all of the baronies in a county were heard, the commissioner made a list in the form prescribed and sent it to the clerk of the peace, stating the day for the meeting of the county-level committee of revision in the county court house, six weeks hence. The clerk notified the members of the

committee and advertised in a local newspaper fourteen days before the hearings. The committee of revision considered if baronies were equally and properly valued, and could make corrections, provided that the proportional valuations of parishes and townlands within the barony were not affected. Records were produced at the hearings. Once the valuation was agreed, the documents were signed by the chairman and at least three members of the committee and were published in the *Dublin Gazette* and a local newspaper. This valuation was used for the county as a whole from the assizes following the date of publication.

ALTERATIONS TO APPEALS PROCEDURE MADE UNDER THE 1836 ACT

The 1836 act required (section 19) that the draft valuation list for a barony be printed before it was sent to the high constable to be posted in public.[1] Section 33 brought the new valuation into force for each barony once agreed by the committee of appeal. The draft valuation list was published in a local newspaper and used for taxes until the valuation for the entire county was issued by the preliminary committee of revision and also published in a local newspaper. A new and final meeting of the committee of revision within three years of the first was added (section 41). The signed valuation was sent to the lord lieutenant, who published it in the *Dublin Gazette* within thirty-one days. This valuation was used in the county for local taxes from the next assizes.

TENEMENT VALUATION: APPEALS UNDER THE 1846 ACT

The 1846 act authorized two appeal systems. The existing system was retained for the valuation in townlands made for county cess, and a new one was introduced that applied to the valuation in tenements made for poor-law purposes.

Appeals under the Poor Law Valuation provisions (sections 16–25)
The valuation for poor law could be appealed by individual occupiers. The appeals were heard by two sub-commissioners, who were professional valuators appointed by the lord lieutenant (section 6). As work in each barony or city was completed, the commissioner set out the valuation in a prescribed format (that is, the printed *Primary valuation*), specifying the place and date

[1] All of the documents in the National Archives date from after 1836, and the format of the lists before this date is not known.

of the appeal hearings, and sent printed copies to the board of guardians. The printed books contained model appeal forms and explained how to make the appeal. The clerk of the union posted a notice on church doors stating when and where (the workhouse, constabulary station or other place) the valuation list could be inspected by occupiers for the following twenty-eight days. Copies could be made. Persons aggrieved had forty days from the posting of the notices to submit a signed appeal, stating the grounds, to the clerk of the union. These were forwarded to the commissioner, who prepared a statement of the notices of appeal, which was laid before the board of guardians. The commissioner could cause the re-valuation of the tenements appealing, and notified appellants of the appeals (section 19). The appeal hearings were held by the sub-commissioners, who summoned witnesses and examined them on oath. The field documents were made available at the hearings. The sub-commissioners could alter the valuation and gave the amended list to the clerk of the union for dissemination as previously. Further appeal could be made to the court of quarter sessions.

Appeals under the county-cess provisions (sections 45–62)
The procedure for appeals against the county-cess valuation was the same as for those under the Townland Valuation Act of 1836, described above, with the new requirement that the commissioner transmit alterations made by the sub-commissioners at appeal to the barony committee of appeal.

Final valuation (section 64)
When completed, the commissioner made a copy of the valuation lists of each parish, attested by his signature, and delivered the lists to the county treasurer, who kept them in his office.

APPEALS UNDER THE 1852 ACT (SECTIONS 17–23)

A new system of administrative appeals was created under the 1852 act. On completion of the valuation of any county, barony or poor law union, the commissioner made a list of the tenements in each townland and their valuations (that is, the printed *Primary valuation*) and sent it to the county treasurer, town council and the clerk of the union concerned. Within three days of receiving the list, the clerk of the union placed notices on the doors of the places of worship, stating the time and place for inspection of the lists at the workhouse or constabulary station. The lists were available for inspection for twenty-one days and extracts could be taken. The printed books contained model appeal forms and explained how to make the appeal. Any person aggrieved could notify the clerk of the union in writing stating the cause of grievance. The notices were forwarded immediately to the office in Dublin. Changes could also be made to the valuation or the area of properties that had not appealed (section 20). The commissioner made enquiry into the complaints, sent a valuator or surveyor to report and could make alterations. The commissioner made out a list of alterations or refusals and sent it to the clerk of the union, who publicized it in the same manner as the preliminary lists. Persons still aggrieved could appeal within twenty-one days to the court of quarter sessions, informing the clerk of the union, who notified the commissioner as respondent. The clerk of the union made out a list of all such notices, that were open to inspection at the workhouse. The decision of the court of quarter sessions was final.

Final valuation (section 25)
Following the completion of appeals, the commissioner had the final list made in the format prescribed (same as *Primary valuation*, with new heading), setting out all the tenements. Copies (in manuscript) were sent to the clerk of the union, town council and the county treasurer. The latter struck out houses under £5 and the valuation after these deductions was deemed to be the valuation for county cess.

Appendix B

Chronology of principal measures and amendments, 1826–64

1826　Townland Valuation Act (7 Geo. IV, c. 62)
- Valuation in townlands, parishes and baronies to be carried out by commissioner and valuators
- The work to take place by parish and to be recorded in books and on maps
- Land to be valued according to a scale of prices and houses by letting value, less one-third
- A system of appeals was established, and the procedure and duties of the grand jury set out

1830　Field work started in Co. Londonderry
- *Instructions 1830* circulated
  - Valuators to work in parties of three under supervision of baronial valuator
  - Local circumstances to be taken into account
  - Rules on maps set out

1831　1 & 2 Will. IV, c. 51
- Threshold of £3 set, under which houses are not to be valued
- Buildings other than dwelling houses to be valued

1832　2 & 3 Will. IV, c. 63
- Exempt buildings defined

1833　*Instructions 1833* published
- Standardized descriptions of land
- Houses to be measured and classified according to tables showing materials and condition
- Houses worth over £3 to be valued and houses worth over £2 10s. to be noted
- Rent of houses in towns to be recorded and system for additional value of house in towns defined (see quarto books)
- Influence of proximity of towns on value of agricultural land defined
- Valuator to enter his estimate of rent

Appendix B: Chronology

1834   4 & 5 Will. IV, c. 55
- Number of valuators expanded
- Copies of books and maps to be deposited with county treasurer for public inspection

1835–6   *Instructions 1835–6* issued
- Name of occupier of every house measured to be entered in field book and numbered to correspond to field map
- Quality lots to be limited to 30–50 acres
- Check valuation introduced
- Lines of percentage around towns to be shown
- Information to be noted on tenure, dates of tenancy and lessors in towns
- Information to be noted on grazing lands and mills

1836   6 & 7 Will. IV, c. 84
- Threshold for valuation of houses raised to £5
- Requirement for valuators to work in parties of three dropped
- Final meeting of county committee of revision introduced
- Draft lists of valuation to be printed
- Mills to be valued
- Commissioner to give progress report and statement of costs to grand juries at assizes

1838   Poor law introduced in Ireland under 1 & 2 Vict., c. 56.

1839   *Instructions 1839* issued
- Quality lots to correspond to farms
- Detailed instructions about valuing mills
- Houses worth over £4 to be noted in field work

1844   Valuation in tenements authorized by order of lord lieutenant
- *Instructions to valuators 1844* and *Instructions to surveyors 1844* issued
  - All tenements to be recorded and names of occupiers noted
  - All tenements over 1 acre to be shown on map
  - Tenements under 5 acres to be measured
- Tenement Valuation field work started in Cos. Dublin and Tipperary

1846   Tenement Valuation Act (9 & 10 Vict., c. 110)
- Valuation to be made in tenements for poor law in specified counties where Townland Valuation was not made and restated in townlands for county cess

	- Valuation of land and houses to be based on rent and to be revised
- New system of appeals established
1848–50	- Cos. Carlow and Kilkenny, Queen's County and town of Drogheda request valuation in tenements
- Request for valuation in tenements of poor law unions in parts of Cos. Clare, Kildare, Meath, Wexford, Wicklow and King's County
1852	Tenement Valuation Act (15 & 16 Vict., c. 63)
- Valuation in tenements to apply to whole country for poor rates and county cess
- Valuation of land to be based on scale of prices, and valuation of houses to be based on rent
- Half of rent of exempt buildings to be valued
- Additional property valued (for example, railways, mines)
- Revisions to be carried out
- New valuation to be made every fourteen years
- New system of administrative appeals introduced
1853	*Instructions 1853* issued
- Comprehensive statement of all requirements for valuing land, houses and water power
- Include tables and ready reckoners

16 & 17 Vict., c. 7
- Amended procedure for annual revision |
| 1854 | 17 Vict., c. 8
- Houses under £5 valuation to be included in assessment for county cess
- Provisions regarding revision and exempt properties amended |
| 1856 | Grand Jury Act (19 & 20 Vict., c. 63), section 13
- Errors in valuation not to affect rates |
| 1860 | 23 Vict., c. 4
- Half of the cost of annual revision to be paid from consolidated fund
- Valuation brought under control of Treasury |
| 1864 | 27 & 28 Vict., c. 52
- Power given to boards of guardians to appeal against revisions of valuation |

Appendix C

Field work in Townland Valuation and Tenement Valuation

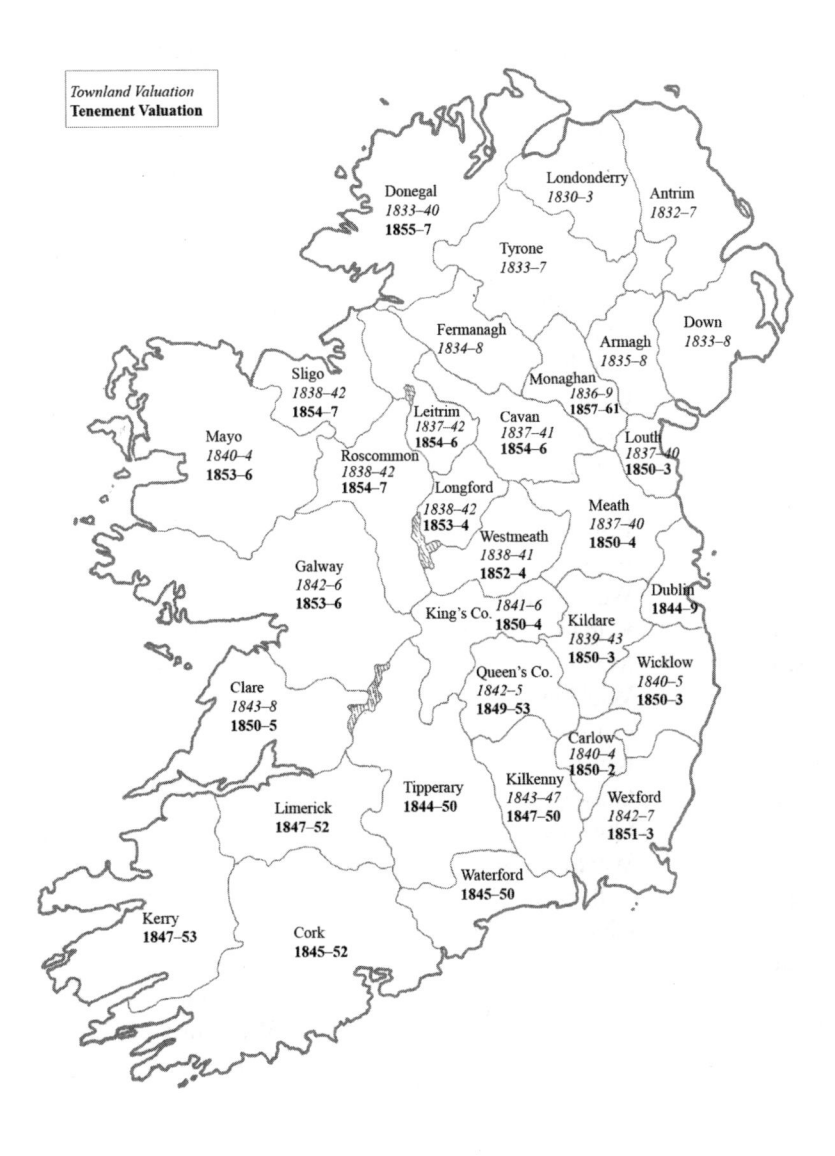

Townland Valuation
Tenement Valuation

Donegal
1833–40
1855–7

Londonderry
1830–3

Antrim
1832–7

Tyrone
1833–7

Fermanagh
1834–8

Armagh
1835–8

Down
1833–8

Sligo
1838–42
1854–7

Leitrim
1837–42
1854–6

Monaghan
1836–9
1857–61

Mayo
1840–4
1853–6

Roscommon
1838–42
1854–7

Cavan
1837–41
1854–6

Louth
1837–40
1850–3

Longford
1838–42
1853–4

Westmeath
1838–41
1852–4

Meath
1837–40
1850–4

Galway
1842–6
1853–6

King's Co. *1841–6*
1850–4

Kildare
1839–43
1850–3

Dublin
1844–9

Queen's Co.
1842–5
1849–53

Wicklow
1840–5
1850–3

Clare
1843–8
1850–5

Carlow
1840–4
1850–2

Tipperary
1844–50

Kilkenny
1843–47
1847–50

Wexford
1842–7
1851–3

Limerick
1847–52

Waterford
1845–50

Kerry
1847–53

Cork
1845–52

207

Appendix D

Start dates of field work, by county, 1830–57[1]

	Townland Valuation	Tenement Valuation
1830	Londonderry	
1832	Antrim	
1833	Donegal	
	Down	
	Tyrone	
1834	Fermanagh	
1835	Armagh	
1836	Monaghan	
1837	Louth	
	Cavan	
	Meath	
	Leitrim	
1838	Roscommon	
	Longford	
	Sligo	
	Westmeath	
1839	Kildare	
1840	Mayo	
	Wicklow	
	Carlow	
1841	King's	
1842	Galway	
	Queen's	
	Wexford	
1843	Kilkenny	
	Clare	
1844		Dublin
		Tipperary
1845		Waterford
		Cork

1 Based on books held in the National Archives. No Tenement Valuation field documents are held for counties in Northern Ireland.

	Townland Valuation	**Tenement Valuation**
1846		Limerick
1847		Kerry
		Kilkenny
1849		Queen's
1850		Kildare
		King's
		Meath
		Clare
		Louth
		Carlow
		Wicklow
1851		Wexford
1852		Westmeath
1853		Longford
		Galway
		Mayo
1854		Sligo
		Leitrim
		Cavan
		Roscommon
1855		Donegal
1856		
1857		Monaghan

Appendix E

Main book types extant, by county

County	Field book OL/4 Original	Field book OL/4 Inc. house book	Field book OL/4 Check	Field book OL/4 Calculation	Field book OL/4 Fair copy	House book OL/5 Original	House book OL/5 Check	House book OL/5 Copy	Quarto book OL/7	Mill book OL/9	List book OL/10	Appeal book OL/13	Printed book OL/14
Antrim	✓		✓		✓				✓			✓	✓
Armagh					✓					✓		✓	
Carlow	✓	✓	✓	✓	✓	✓	✓		✓		✓	✓	✓
Cavan	✓	✓	✓	✓	✓	✓	✓		✓	✓		✓	✓
Clare	✓	✓	✓	✓	✓	✓			✓	✓	✓	✓	✓
Cork													
Donegal	✓	✓	✓	✓	✓	✓	✓		✓			✓	
Down	✓				✓				✓	✓		✓	
Dublin													
Fermanagh	✓		✓	✓	✓							✓	✓
Galway	✓	✓	✓	✓	✓	✓	✓		✓	✓	✓	✓	✓
Kerry													
Kildare	✓	✓	✓	✓	✓	✓	✓		✓		✓	✓	✓
Kilkenny	✓	✓	✓	✓	✓	✓			✓	✓		✓	✓
King's Co.	✓	✓	✓	✓	✓	✓	✓	✓	✓	✓		✓	✓
Leitrim	✓	✓	✓	✓	✓		✓			✓		✓	✓
Limerick													
Londonderry	✓												✓
Longford	✓		✓	✓	✓	✓	✓		✓	✓		✓	✓
Louth	✓	✓	✓	✓	✓	✓	✓	✓	✓	✓	✓	✓	
Mayo	✓	✓	✓	✓	✓	✓	✓		✓	✓	✓	✓	✓
Meath	✓	✓	✓	✓	✓	✓	✓		✓			✓	
Monaghan	✓	✓	✓	✓	✓	✓		✓	✓			✓	
Queen's Co.	✓	✓	✓	✓	✓	✓	✓		✓	✓		✓	✓
Roscommon	✓				✓	✓	✓		✓			✓	✓
Sligo	✓	✓	✓	✓	✓					✓		✓	✓
Tipperary	✓	✓											
Tyrone	✓		✓		✓								✓
Waterford													
Westmeath	✓	✓		✓	✓	✓	✓		✓	✓			✓
Wexford	✓	✓	✓	✓	✓	✓	✓		✓	✓		✓	✓
Wicklow	✓	✓	✓	✓	✓	✓			✓	✓			✓

Appendix E: Main book types extant, by county 211

Tenement Valuation													
Tenement field book OL/4					Tenement house book OL/5				Tenure book OL/6	Quarto book OL/7	Mill book OL/9	List book OL/10	Rent book OL/16	1846 appeal book OL/19	1852 appeal book OL/20
Original	Inc. house book	Check	Copy	Calculation	Original	2nd original	Check	Copy							
										✓					✓
		✓			✓		✓		✓				✓	✓	
					✓				✓						✓
					✓			✓	✓					✓	
✓	✓	✓	✓	✓	✓	✓			✓	✓	✓	✓		✓	✓	✓
					✓					✓	✓					✓
✓	✓	✓		✓	✓	✓			✓	✓	✓	✓		✓	✓	✓
		✓		✓	✓		✓		✓						✓
✓		✓	✓	✓	✓	✓			✓	✓	✓	✓	✓	✓	✓	
		✓	✓		✓		✓	✓	✓				✓	✓	✓	✓
		✓			✓			✓	✓					✓	✓	✓
		✓			✓				✓					✓		
					✓		✓		✓							✓
✓	✓	✓	✓	✓	✓	✓			✓	✓	✓	✓		✓	✓	
					✓					✓						
		✓			✓			✓	✓	✓					✓	
								✓	✓	✓						✓
		✓			✓					✓						✓
					✓			✓	✓							✓
		✓			✓									✓	✓	
					✓					✓						
		✓			✓					✓						✓
✓	✓	✓	✓	✓	✓	✓			✓	✓	✓	✓		✓	✓	✓
✓	✓	✓	✓	✓	✓	✓	✓	✓	✓	✓	✓	✓	✓	✓	✓	
					✓					✓						✓
		✓			✓					✓					✓	✓
					✓					✓					✓	✓

Appendix F

Main map types extant, by county

	Townland Valuation			Tenement Valuation		
County	Townland Valuation original field map	Townland Valuation office map	Townland Valuation fair-copy map	Original field maps (counties valued for the first time)		
				(Surveyor)	(Valuator)	(Field map)
Antrim	✓					
Carlow	✓					
Cavan	✓		✓			
Clare	✓	✓				
Cork				✓	✓	✓
Donegal	✓		✓			
Down	✓					
Dublin						✓
Galway	✓	✓	✓			
Kerry				✓	✓	✓
Kildare	✓	✓	✓			
Kilkenny	✓		✓			
King's Co.	✓		✓			
Leitrim	✓	✓	✓			
Limerick				✓	✓	✓
Longford			✓			
Louth	✓	✓	✓			
Mayo	✓	✓	✓			
Meath	✓	✓	✓			
Monaghan	✓		✓			
Queen's Co.	✓		✓			
Roscommon	✓	✓				
Sligo	✓	✓				
Tipperary				✓	✓	✓
Waterford				✓	✓	✓
Westmeath	✓	✓				
Wexford	✓		✓			
Wicklow	✓	✓				

Appendix F: Main map types extant, by county

Original field maps (counties also valued in Townland Valuation)			Office maps (counties also valued in Townland Valuation)		Other	Fair copy map
Drawn on Townland Valuation original field map	Drawn on Townland Valuation copy field map	Drawn on printed Ordnance Survey map	Drawn on Townland Valuation office map ruled	Drawn on Townland Valuation copy map ruled		Fair map and revised fair copy
		✓				✓
✓	✓		✓		✓	✓
✓	✓		✓	✓		✓
					✓	✓
		✓			✓	✓
		✓				✓
✓	✓		✓	✓		✓
						✓
✓	✓	✓	✓		✓	✓
		✓				✓
✓		✓	✓		✓	✓
	✓		✓	✓		✓
						✓
✓	✓		✓		✓	✓
✓	✓		✓	✓		✓
✓	✓	✓	✓		✓	✓
	✓	✓	✓			✓
		✓				✓
		✓	✓			✓
✓	✓				✓	✓
✓	✓		✓		✓	✓
					✓	✓
						✓
✓	✓		✓	✓	✓	✓
✓	✓	✓	✓			✓
✓	✓	✓	✓			✓

Appendix G

Classification of buildings

The term 'house' applied to dwelling houses and public buildings. The term 'office' applied to farm buildings, outbuildings and other non-dwellings.

1. CLASSIFICATION OF BUILDINGS IN *INSTRUCTIONS 1839*

Classification of houses and offices

New or nearly new
- A⁺ Built or ornamented with cut stone, and of superior solidity and finish
- A Very substantial building, and finished without cut-stone ornament
- A⁻ Ordinary building and finish, or either of the above when built 20 or 25 years previously

Medium
- B⁺ Not new, but in sound order and good repair
- B Slightly decayed, but in good repair
- B⁻ Deteriorated by age and not in perfect repair

Old
- C⁺ In repair
- C Out of repair
- C⁻ Dilapidated, scarcely habitable

Descriptions of houses
1. Slated dwelling house built with stone or brick and lime mortar
2. Thatched house built with stone or brick and lime mortar
3. Thatched house, having stone walls with mud or puddle mortar, dry stone walls pointed, or mud walls of the best kind
4. Basement stories of slated houses, used as dwellings

Descriptions of offices
1. Includes all slated offices, built with stone or brick walls, with good lime mortar
2. Thatched offices built with stone or brick walls and lime mortar

Appendix G: Classification of buildings

3   Thatched office, having stone walls, with mud or puddle mortar, dry stone walls pointed, or good mud walls
4   Thatched offices built with dry stone walls
5   Basement stories or cellars used as stores

2. CLASSIFICATION OF BUILDINGS IN *INSTRUCTIONS* 1853

Classification of Buildings with Reference to Their Solidity
1   Slated house or office built with stone or brick and lime mortar
2   Thatched house or office built with stone or brick and lime mortar
3   Thatched house or office with dry stone walls with mud mortar, with dry stone walls pointed or with good mud walls
4   Basement of 1
5   Office with dry stone walls

Classification of Buildings with Reference to Age and Repair
New or nearly new
A^+ Built or ornamented with cut stone, and of superior solidity and finish
A   Very substantial building and finished without cut stone ornament
A^- Ordinary building and finish, or either of the above when built 20 years previously

Medium
B^+ Not new, but in sound order and good repair
B   Slightly decayed, but in good repair
B^- Deteriorated by age and not in perfect repair

Old
C^+ In repair
C   Out of repair
C^- Dilapidated, scarcely habitable

Appendix H

Statutes, 1826–64

1. 7 Geo. IV, c. 62 (26 May 1826)
   An act to make provision for the uniform valuation of lands and tenements in the several baronies, parishes and other divisions of counties in Ireland, for the purpose of the more equally levying of the rates and charges upon such baronies, parishes, and divisions respectively

2. 1 & 2 Will. IV, c. 51 (20 Oct. 1831)
   An act to amend an act of the seventh year of the reign of his late majesty King George the Fourth, for making provision for the uniform valuation of lands and tenements in the several baronies, parishes, and other divisions of counties in Ireland, for the purpose of the more equally levying of the rates and charges upon the same

3. 2 & 3 Will. IV, c. 73 (1 Aug. 1832)
   An act to amend two acts, of the seventh year of the reign of his late majesty King George the Fourth, and in the first and second years of the reign of his present majesty, for the uniform valuation of lands and tenements in the several baronies, parishes, and other divisions of counties in Ireland

4. 4 & 5 Will. IV, c. 55 (13 Aug. 1834)
   An act to amend three acts, made respectively in the seventh year of the reign of his late majesty King George the Fourth, and in the first and second years and in the second and third years of the reign of his present majesty, for the uniform valuation of lands and tenements in the several baronies, parishes and other divisions of the counties in Ireland; and to provide for the more effectual levy of grand jury cess

5. 6 & 7 Will. IV, c. 84 (17 Aug. 1836)
   An act to consolidate and amend the several acts for the uniform valuation of lands and tenements in Ireland, and to incorporate certain detached portions of counties and baronies respectively whereto the same may adjoin, or wherein the same are locally situate

6. 9 & 10 Vict., c. 110 (28 Aug. 1846)
   An act to amend the law relating to the valuation of rateable property in Ireland

7   15 & 16 Vict., c. 63 (30 June 1852)
    An act to amend the laws relating to the valuation of rateable property in Ireland

8   16 & 17 Vict., c. 7 (21 Feb. 1853)
    An act to amend an act relating to the valuation of rateable property in Ireland

9   17 Vict., c. 8 (12 May 1854)
    An act further to amend an act relating to the valuation of rateable property in Ireland

10 19 & 20 Vict., c. 63 (21 July 1856)
    An act to amend acts relating to grand juries in Ireland

11 23 Vict., c. 4 (23 Mar. 1860)
    An act to enable the commissioners of her Majesty's treasury to defray one moiety of the expense of the annual revision of the valuation of rateable property in Ireland out of the consolidated fund

12 27 & 28 Vict., c. 52 (25 July 1864)
    An act to amend the law relating to the valuation of rateable property in Ireland

Appendix I

Research in the valuation archives

The original documents described in this guide are all held by National Archives, Bishop Street, Dublin 8 (see nationalarchives.ie). All the documents are listed, and the lists are available in the reading room of the National Archives. The notes on each county and series should help the researcher to understand the documents that are extant for that county.

Researchers wishing to use the reading room of the National Archives will need to obtain a reader's ticket. See the website of the National Archives for requirements, conditions and opening hours. Documents are viewed in the reading room and copies of some documents can be obtained.

PLACES

All of the documents made in the valuation are based on place, and researchers wishing to inspect documents in the reading room of the National Archives will need to know the name of the place in order to identify the relevant documents. The hierarchy of places comprises townlands in parishes, parishes in baronies and baronies in counties. It is also helpful to know the name of the poor law union in which the place is situated. This information can be found in the *Townland index* published with the censuses in 1851, 1871 and 1901, available in the reading room and in some local-studies libraries. Some of this information can be searched online on logaimn.ie/en. Images of the *Townland index* for 1851 and 1871 are available on dippam.ac.uk/eppi. Some parishes are in more than one barony, and the valuation treated each part as a separate parish. In this case the information should be noted on all parts.

Some documents are searchable online free of charge, including some of the manuscript documents, see census.nationalarchives.ie/search/vob/home.jsp, and for the *Primary valuation* or *Griffith's valuation*, see askaboutireland.ie/griffith-valuation. The *Primary valuation* is a convenient entry point and the results can be printed. Searches can be carried out by name or by place. Searching for a name without a place is likely to produce a very large number of results. A name with a place, or a place alone, will narrow down the number of possibilities. If a name is identified in a townland in the *Primary valuation*, it is advisable to note other information printed on the page, or the next page, including the name of the parish and the Ordnance Survey map reference number. The name of the barony and poor law union can be found by scrolling back to the title page and table of contents of the volume. The Ordnance Survey sheet numbers are not printed on books published before mid-1850. This information can also be found in the *Townland index*.

While the initial valuation established the situation once, during that process information may have been noted more than once because of the long period that elapsed between the beginning of the work and the completion of the appeals. Cos. Cork, Dublin, Kerry, Limerick, Tipperary and Waterford were valued once, but some revisions and amendments were made. In other counties valuation work was carried out twice – in the Townland Valuation and the Tenement Valuation. This work took place at an interval of years that varied from one county to another. A large number of documents are extant, but some documents did not survive, and there are gaps. Revisions were carried out in all counties. This means that between the start date of townland work in a particular county, and the end of the tenement appeals in that county, information was noted on at least two different dates, and possibly more.

USING THE BOOKS

The manuscript books were made in parishes, and in the lists the parishes are in alphabetical order by county. If the place concerned is in more than one townland or more than one parish, the researcher needs to check the names of the related parishes, baronies or poor law unions of all parts. If the place researched is a town, it may have a different name from the parish and the name of the parish or parishes needs to be established using the *Townland index* or websites.

USING THE MAPS

The valuation maps are listed in counties and in order of six-inch Ordnance Survey sheet number. The sheet number of the townland or parish can be found using the *Townland index*. A townland is a manageable area on a map, but a search for a parish will involve looking at several different sheet numbers.

Time and careful examination are necessary to identify the data required on the valuation maps (scale 1:10,560 or six inches to the mile). Researchers will usually need to see specific townlands, and it is useful to have prepared in advance a diagram showing the position and boundaries of the townland, or a tracing on transparent material at the scale of the six-inch map for rural areas. The data on the town plans is easier to read as they are at the larger scale of 1:1,056 or sixty inches to the mile.

LISTS IN THE NATIONAL ARCHIVES

The lists in the National Archives are outlined below. These are broad series and some contain several different types of book.

Townland Valuation	OL/4	House books
	OL/5	Field books
	OL/7	Quarto books (towns)
	OL/11	Valuation maps
	OL/12	Valuation town plans
Tenement Valuation	OL/4	House books
	OL/5	Field books
	OL/6	Tenure books
	OL/7	Quarto books (towns)
	OL/11	Valuation maps
	OL/12	Valuation town plans
	OL/18	*Primary valuation*
	OL/19	
	and	
	OL/20	*Primary valuation* appeals

A more advanced search might also look at

OL/1	Acts, instructions and administration
OL/2	Valuation letter books
OL/9	Mill books
OL/13	Townland Valuation appeal books
OL/14	*Townland Valuation* printed books
OL/15	Other valuations (including re-valuation of Co. Dublin, 1865)
OL/17	Query sheets (Dublin and Belfast cities only)

Researchers interested in the process of valuation might also look at

Appendix I: Research in the valuation archives 221

OL/8   Registry books
OL/10 List books
OL/16 Rent books

TAKING NOTES

The documents are numerous and can appear confusing. The researcher should take care to note the reference and date of each book and map. Putting the data from the various books into a table may also be helpful in understanding how each piece relates to the others.

RELATED SOURCES IN THE NATIONAL ARCHIVES

These include the Chief Secretary's Office Registered Papers (detailed catalogue available online, currently 1818–30), the Ordnance Survey and the Boundary Survey.

VALUATION ARCHIVES IN OTHER REPOSITORIES

See pp 195–7 for valuation archives held in other repositories.

MOST IMPORTANT

These archives are complex and made more difficult for the user by the manner in which different books were combined. There are unexpected combinations of books, cases where books from separate series are combined and cases where the combinations were not used consistently. The researcher needs to look closely at the lists in the National Archives, including the introductory notes, in order to know what documents are extant for each county and whether books have been combined. The rule for the researcher should be to look at all the entries for the place of interest in the lists for all series of documents.

HOW THE DOCUMENTS GO TOGETHER: ILLUSTRATIONS

Plates 1–5 are examples of the field map, field book, house books and tenure book for the townland of Crannagh, Kilmacduagh, Co. Galway, and they show how the documents connect to each other. The Townland Valuation work was carried out in late 1842 and the original field book (plate 2) describes lots 9, 10, 11, 12 and 13. The quality lots are numbered and described, with the acreage, the field price and the price reduced to allow for local circumstances. The figures in the 'amount of land' column are calculated by multiplying the acreage by the field price, and the figures in the house column are the acreage multiplied by the reduced price. The corresponding map is sheet 122 of Co. Galway (plate 1). The townland is outlined on the map, which shows the Tenement Valuation original field map overlaid (in red lines and numbers), on the Townland Valuation original field map, where the quality lots are marked out in black lines and numbers. A house is marked in lot 11 but crossed out. The Townland Valuation lots 9–13, in the lower right-hand corner, are described in the field book. The Townland Valuation house book page (plate 3) shows the details of this house, occupied by James Ryan but marked exempt as it was under the £5 threshold, with the prices given by the two valuators written in. The Tenement Valuation work was done in late 1853. The Tenement Valuation house book (plate 4) values the house and offices at £2 and this figure is entered in the tenure book. No measurements are given for this house. It was common for houses measured in the Townland Valuation not to be re-measured in the tenement work, and also from 1852 measurement was no longer a requirement. The tenure book (plate 5) draws the new and old information together: under James Ryan's name, the column for original numbers lists 9, 10, 11 and 12 and the new revised number as 16A. This tenement consists of a house, offices and ninety acres of land. He also holds land at 16B (old lot 13) and 16C (old lot 5) that is also visible on the map. The book also gives information on his rent and tenure and the total valuation.

Plates 6–9 provide a further example of how the documents can be linked. The Townland Valuation work in Ballina, Co. Mayo took place in late 1841. The manuscript valuation town plan of Ballina (plate 6) was made at this time and was in use until September 1877. This illustration shows part of the town centre. The houses are numbered using one series of numbers for the town and not by numbering each street separately. The gasworks and sawmills at the river were added at a later date, as were the rows of houses in Pawn Office Lane at the top, and they were sketched in black. The railway was added in the bottom left corner (not shown) on Rahans Road. The Townland Valuation house book (plate 7) includes the additional columns used in town books for the valuator's estimate, the yearly rent, garden and observations. The page for part of Bridge Street describes three premises: a printer (no. 11), an iron monger (no. 12) and a public house (no. 13.). The buildings are measured, including all their parts, the price is calculated and the names of occupiers are given. The valuator's estimate appears to be taken from the quarto book, see below. The notes describe the advantages or inconveniences of the buildings and give some information on the rent and tenure. On the plan, the numbers are highlighted, but the houses concerned are at either side of the corner of Hill Street. The alterations to some numbers can be seen. The quarto book (plate 8) was made in 1842 by Robert McMicken and the same building numbers are used. The multiplier of additional value for towns by which the figures in the house book were augmented is shown in the column 'relative value, multiplied by' and is as high as seven in the case of some houses in this street. This book shows the range of data taken into consideration before the final price. The Tenement Valuation house book (plate 9) was made in 1854. Here the new format town house book is used. The numbering is new and does not relate directly to the town plan. The premises now numbered 12, occupied by Sidney Dixon, can be identified as the same building as number 13 in the earlier book by the measurements and the description.

Plates 10–12 are examples of how the information was disseminated in the two valuations, using the barony of Castlerahan, Co. Cavan and the parish of Munterconnaught. It illustrates how the information became more detailed. The November 1840 list of the draft valuation (plate 10) was folded into the appeal book. It shows the townlands in parishes in the barony and gives the acreage, the value of the land and houses and the total. The exemptions are given at the end of each parish and the information on the meeting of the barony-level committee of appeal is printed at the foot of the document. A copy of this list was posted in the prescribed places in advance of the meeting. The manuscript corrections made to this document record alterations made at the meeting. The Townland Valuation printed book (plate 11) shows the result of the meeting for this barony. The parish is printed on one small page and the opposite page includes the abstract for the barony and the declaration of the committee. The extract from the *Primary valuation* (plate 12) shows one townland from the parish. Where there was previously one line for the townland, there are now more than twenty separate and detailed entries, including names.

Plates 13 and 14 show examples from the Tenement Valuation appeal books. Queen's County was valued and appealed under the 1846 act at hearings by sub-commissioners. The page (plate 13) from two pages of the interleaved *Primary Valuation* book, is here presented with part of the printed page above the related notes, with the properties appealing marked on the printed page, and corrections to names and prices. The figures in the right margin give the average price per acre. The left-hand page contains sub-commissioner Edward Gaffney's notes made at the hearings. The tenement number is noted, the date of the hearing and the information recited by the appellant. The centre pages (not shown) contain the clerk's notes of background information. The new system of appeals under the 1852 act is seen on the page for the parish of Moyrus, Co. Galway (plate 14). The revising valuator noted his comments on the blank page and made alterations, including corrections to names, on the printed page.

Bibliography

PRINTED SOURCES

Aalen, F.H.A., Kevin Whelan & Matthew Stout (eds), *Atlas of the Irish rural landscape* (Cork, 1997)
Andrews, J.H., *A paper landscape: the Ordnance Survey in nineteenth-century Ireland* (Oxford, 1975)
——, *History in the ordnance map: an introduction for Irish readers* (2nd ed., Kerry, Wales, 1993)
——, *Plantation acres: an historical study of the Irish land surveyor and his maps* (Belfast, 1995)
——, *Maps in those days: cartographic methods before 1850* (Dublin, 2009).
——, *Atlas of Ireland* (Dublin, 1979)
Connolly, S.J. (ed.), *The Oxford companion to Irish history* (Oxford, 1998)
Crossman, Virginia, *Local government in nineteenth-century Ireland* (Belfast, 1994)
Crowley, John, William J. Smyth & Mike Murphy (eds), *Atlas of the Great Irish Famine* (Cork, 2012)
Donnelly, James S., Jr., *The land and the people of nineteenth-century Cork* (London, 1975)
Dooley, Terence, *The big houses and landed estates of Ireland* (Dublin, 2007)
Hamilton, Gertrude (ed.), *A catalogue of large scale town plans prepared by the Ordnance Survey and deposited in PRONI* (2nd ed., Belfast, 1981).
Helferty, Seamus & Raymond Refaussé (eds), *Directory of Irish archives* (5th ed., Dublin, 2011)
Herity, Michael (ed.), *Ordnance Survey letters: letters relating to the antiquities of County Galway* (Dublin, 2009)
Herries Davies, Gordon L. & Charles L. Mollan (eds), *Richard Griffith, 1784–1878* (Dublin, 1980)
Hogg, W.E., *The millers and the mills of Ireland of about 1850* (Dublin, 2000)
——, *The old mills of Ireland*, 4 vols (Dublin, 2015)
Lyne, Gerard J., *The Lansdowne estate in Kerry under W.S. Trench, 1849–72* (Dublin, 2001)
Maguire, James & James Quinn (eds), *Dictionary of Irish biography*, 9 vols (Cambridge, 2009)
Nolan, William & Anngret Simms (eds), *Irish towns: a guide to sources* (Dublin, 1998)
Prunty, Jacinta, *Maps and map-making in local history* (Dublin, 2004)
Scott, Thomas Colville, *Connemara after the Famine: journal of a survey of the Martin estate, 1853*, ed. Tim Robinson (Dublin, 1995)
Simms, Anngret & J.H. Andrews (eds), *Irish country towns* (Cork, 1994)

——, *More Irish country towns* (Cork, 1995)
Stout, Geraldine, *Newgrange and the bend in the Boyne* (Cork, 2002)
Townland index, 1851
Townland index, 1871
Townland index, 1901
Vaughan, W.E., *Landlords and tenants in mid-Victorian Ireland* (Oxford, 1994)

WEBSITES

Dictionary of Irish architects: dia.ie, accessed 15 Sept. 2017
National Archives: nationalarchives.ie, accessed 15 Sept. 2017
National Inventory of Architectural Heritage: buildingsofireland.ie
Ordnance Survey Ireland: www.osi.ie/products/professional-mapping/historical-mapping, accessed 15 Sept. 2017
Parliamentary papers relating to Ireland: dippam.ac.uk/eppi, accessed 15 Sept. 2017
Place-names in Ireland: logainm.ie/en, accessed 15 Sept. 2017
Primary valuation and associated documents: askaboutireland.ie/griffith-valuation, accessed 15 Sept. 2017
Public Record Office of Northern Ireland: apps.proni.gov.uk, accessed 15 Sept. 2017
Valuation documents in National Archives: census.nationalarchives.ie/search/vob/home.jsp, accessed 15 Sept. 2017
Valuation Office: valoff.ie/en/Archives_Genealogy_Public_Office, accessed 15 Sept. 2017

Index

administrative documents 114–16
  valuation letter books 115–16
agricultural land 61
  abolition of rates 19, 61
  appeals 170
  scale of prices 25, 27
  see also farms; land
alterations (changes) 182–3
Andrews, J.H. 132, 156
appeal application books 176–7
appeal books (Tenement Valuation) 43, 45, 61, 94–9
  additional information 170–2, 184–5, 187
  agricultural land 170
  appellants' defences 174, 185–6
  emigration 170
  evictions 167, 169
  farms, productivity of 170
  houses down 176–7
  houses/buildings, information on 172
  information offered by appellants 165–6
  low valuations 181
  mills 173
  names, source of 180, 184
  printed post-appeal books 177–8
  reasons for appeal 163–4, 165, 168, 169, 172, 176, 181–2
  rents 165–6
  revising surveyors' books 177
  revising valuators' notes 180–1, 182, 188–9, 190
  sub-commissioners' 161–76
  voting, valuations and 175
  withdrawal of appeals 159n14, 186
appeal books (Townland Valuation) 40
  additional information 98–9
  baronial appeals 95, 96
  county appeals 29, 95, 100
  draft valuation list 96
  late appeals 98
  printed *Townland Valuation* 100–2
  reasons for appeal 97
  Townland Valuation 94–9
appeal forms 190–1
  submission of 179
appeals (against Tenement Valuation/*Primary Valuation*)
  (1846 Act) 34, 36, 38, 43, 45, 157–79
  (1852 Act) 179–92

arrangements 159–61
  sub-commissioners 43, 49
  venues 159
appeals (against Townland Valuation) 26, 40, 97
  arrangements 40
  committee of appeal 94, 95, 100
  committee of revision 94, 96, 101
  draft valuation list for 40
  grand juries and 94–5
  venues 95
applotment 30
applotters 30
Aran Islands 59, 69
Armagh union 153
Armstrong, William 99, 99n19

Ballinasloe union 145–6
Ballyshannon union 138, 182
baronies 22
  maps 119–21
  Ordnance Survey sheets and 24–5
  Primary valuation and 25
  Tenement Valuation and 25
Belfast 185
  query sheets 112, 113
Bell, Robert (valuator) 58, 180n19, 189
Bianconi, Charles 146
Board of Ordnance 23
Board of Works 15, 136
Bog Survey 15, 57
boundaries
  of lots 29
  of poor law unions 24
  tenement 44, 125–6
Boundary Survey 15, 16, 23, 47, 97, 199
  Griffith and 23–4, 57
Boyan, John (valuator) 30, 49–50, 51, 52, 55–6, 175
Boyan, Michael (engineer) 56
Boyle union 138
Buck, Henry (valuator) 57, 157n1, 176
buildings
  exempt properties 26, 29, 30, 36, 37, 72, 87, 88, 97, 101, 183, 184
  net annual value (rent) 36
  public buildings 26, 36
  valuation of 26, 36
  see also houses
built environment (1833–61) 78–80

227

cadastral surveys 23, 117, 131
Caherconlish, County Limerick 107, 149–50, 151
calculation books (field) see field books
cancelled books 25, 46, 160–1, 179, 195–6
Carlow union 175
chain surveys 33, 104
check field books see field books
check house books see house books
Christ Church Dublin 148
civil parishes 22, 62
clerks 40, 47, 48, 54
clerks' notes 162, 163, 167
Clifden union 148
Coffey, Martin (valuator) 57
Coffey, Stephen (draftsman) 57
Colby, Colonel Thomas F. 23
Colville Scott, Thomas (private surveyor) 59
commissioner of valuation 16
  salary 48
  see also Greene, J.B.; Griffith, Richard
common land 140, 150
comparison books see field books
congested districts 19
Cork County 104, 106, 108, 112
  maps 126
  Primary valuation 154
Cork grand jury 32
counties, divisions of 22
county administration, grand juries and 22
county cess 17, 22–3, 33, 34, 36, 95, 102, 103, 161
  based on acreage 97
  calculation of 26, 97
  Inishmore island 69
  Select Committee (1836) 28
  Select Committee (1844) 31
county treasurers 22, 26–7
court of chancery 69, 107, 139, 167
Cox, Thomas (valuator) 51, 54n54, 55, 69
  appeals and 186, 188, 189, 190
Currin, Michael (private surveyor) 174

death duties 18
distilleries, valuation of 27
Down Survey 22
draftsmen 40, 48, 56, 124, 126
Dublin city
  alterations 183
  Bow Street lodgings 141–2
  department stores 146–7
  query sheets 112
  town plans 132
Dublin County 102
  rents 167–8
  re-valuation (1865) 113–14
Dublin Gazette 96, 101
Duffy, Henry 49n24, 127

electoral franchise 31
emigration 105, 106, 107, 162, 170
Encumbered Estates Court 18, 139, 176
evictions 106, 107, 162, 169
exempted properties 36, 37, 72, 87, 88, 97, 101, 183, 184
  background to 185
  defining 29, 30

fair-copy field books see field books
fair-copy maps see maps
Famine see Great Famine
farms
  alternatives to paying rent 106
  boundaries of quality lots 29, 63
  expenses 171
  farming practices 183–4
  productivity of 170
  rents 104, 105
Ferguson, Sir Robert, MP 98–9
field book (term) 61
field books 20, 61–72
  combinations of books 62, 65, 73
  format 61–2
  staff names 53
field books (Tenement Valuation) 33, 65–8
  calculation books (field) 66
  check field books 66
  comparison books 68
  copy field books 66
  original field books 65–6
  preliminary books 67
  survey books 67
field books (Townland Valuation) 62–5
  calculation books (field) 40, 62, 64, 76
  check field books 62, 63
  copy field books 60–1
  fair-copy field books 62, 64–5
  original field books 62–3
  time bills 58, 70
  Townland Valuation 38–9, 62–3, 68, 71
  types of 62
  worksheets in 40, 53
field maps see maps
field price 39
field work
  1830 instructions 27–8, 123
  1833 instructions 28, 39, 84, 86, 123
  1835–6 instructions 28–9
  1839 instructions 29–30, 86, 104, 134
  1844 instructions 33, 34, 35
  1853 instructions 37, 65–6, 77, 134, 139, 140
  Tenement Valuation 42, 44–5
  Townland Valuation 38–9
  transitional period (1844–52) 33–6
fines 168
fisheries 36, 108, 186–7
Fitzpatrick, William (poor law valuator) 175

Frain, James (private valuator) 70
freeholds 139
Fremantle, Sir Thomas (chief secretary for
    Ireland) 41

G. & J. Grierson (printers) 153
Gaffney, Edward (valuator) 50, 51, 58, 68–9
    appeals and 163, 177, 181, 188, 190, 191
Ganly, Patrick (draftsman) 56, 58
gardens 28, 33, 75, 84
General Valuation of Ireland 16
geological map of Ireland 37, 49n24, 56, 116
Glandore, County Cork 130, 132
Government Stationery Office 137, 153
Government Valuation of Ireland 16, 25–7
grand juries 99
    administration of counties 22
    applotment, responsibility of 30
    committees of appeal and revision appointed
        by 94–5
    county cess and 17, 22, 26, 28, 32, 34, 95, 161
    old book records 22
    progress and expenditure reports to 30
    valuation in tenements 41, 43
Great Famine 20, 58, 81, 109, 136, 178, 195, 199
    relief works 52, 55
Greene, J.B. 49n24, 52, 57, 114, 130–1, 136, 158,
    178, 181, 183
Griffith, Richard 15, 33, 47
    achievement of the valuation 198
    appeals 95, 96–7, 98, 99, 160
    applotment 30
    barony of Rathdown 172
    Board of Works 136
    boundary surveyor 23–4
    commissioner of valuation 24, 30, 136
    correspondence 115–16
    exemptions 30
    geological map of Ireland 37, 49n24, 56, 116
    house books and 72
    Instructions for land surveyors 33
    maps 117
    printing costs 153
    records storage 194, 194n3
    rent/rent books 104, 112
    residence 143, 194
    scale of prices and 36–7
    Select Committee (1824) 23
    Select Committee (1836) 28
    Select Committee (1844) 31–3
    Select Committee (1869) 127
    staff management 47–54
    subdivision changes 164
    Tenement Valuation 32, 41, 124
    townland work, legislation and 36
    travel at night 58
    valuators, training of 26, 47, 56
Gunn & Cameron (printers) 153

half rent 138
Hampton, John (valuator) 70
Hardinge, Sir H. (chief secretary of Ireland) 26
Harton, James (valuator) 86–7, 88
Hitchcock, George (clerk) 54
Hodges & Smith (map publishers) 164, 174
Hogg, William 92, 94
house books (term) 72
house books 20, 39, 61, 72–83
    additional information in 81–2
    built environment (1833–61) 78–80
    combinations of books 62, 65, 73
    commercial enterprises 79–80
    format rural parishes 72, 77–8
    format towns 77–8
    mills 91, 92, 93, 94
    numbering system in towns 75, 87, 134
    occupiers' names 72–3, 75, 78
    quality letter code 74
    rural parishes 61, 72, 73–4
    sketch plans of buildings 79
    town plans and 134–5
    towns 72, 74–5, 77
    value by tables 74
house books (Tenement Valuation) 45, 76–8, 83
    compared with *Primary Valuation* 149–52, **149**,
        152
    in counties previously valued 77–8
    in counties valued for the first time 76–7
    original house books 76–8
    surveyors and 42
    valuators and 42
house books (Townland Valuation) 73–6, 83
    calculation books (field) and 76
    check house books 75–6
    original house books 73–4
houses
    £3 threshold 26, 39, 78
    £4 threshold 87
    £5 threshold 29, 30, 39, 78, 124, 135, 147
    annual rent 27
    built by occupiers 173
    demolition of (house down) 165, 176
    exemptions 26
    instructions regarding 72
    interiors 79
    letting values 25
    lodgings 141–2
    percentage increases 75
        see also quarto books
    quality letters assigned to 28
    query sheets 45
    rules for numbering in towns 75, 87, 134
    rural 39
    in towns 28, 39, 75, 135
    valuation appeals 169, 172–3
    valuation of 25, 26, 27, 28, 36, 147
    see also buildings

Inishmore Island 69
initial valuation 16–17
  books and maps of 20–1
  four stages of 38
  Tenement Valuation and 17
  Townland Valuation and 17
Innes, George (valuator) 55
Innes, Robert (valuator) 55, 58

Jones, Francis P. (valuator) 57
Jones, William (valuator) 57, 59
  appeals and 181, 189, 191
Jones, William E. (valuator) 57

Kelly, John (valuator) 49, 58
  appeals and 157n1, 160, 164, 167, 173–4
Keogh, Thomas (valuator) 51

labourers (chainmen) 38, 47, 48, 54, 54n54–5
land
  basis for valuation 15
  scale of prices 25, 27
  see also agricultural land
Land League 18
landlords 167
landowners
  complaints made by 51
  private valuations and 18, 50–1
Lansdowne estate (Kerry) 55, 143
Law Life Assurance Company 148
lessors 148
  immediate lessors 139, 140, 143
  lodgings 141–2
  poor rates shared with occupier 17–18
  rents and 167
  see also occupiers
letter books 115–16
Leveson Gower, Sir Francis (chief secretary for Ireland) 26
libraries, local-studies sections 197
lines of percentage 28–9, 123
list books 40, 61, 110–11
local archives 197
local taxation 18, 38
  dissatisfaction with system 22, 97
  exemptions 97
  Spring Rice report recommendations 23
  see also county cess
Locke, John (private surveyor) 58
Lynam, James (valuator) 54n59, 56, 57

McMicken, Robert (valuator) 52, 87, 88, 89
manuscript books
  versus *Primary valuation* 149–55, **149, 152**
  see also field books; house books; quarto books; tenure books
maps 23–4, 117–35
  additional information 130–1

  cancelled maps 119, 129
  data interpretation 130
  dates 121–2
  geological map of Ireland 37, 56, 116
  multiple copies of 119–21
  poor law unions 120
  preservation of 194
  printed valuation 119
  reuse of existing maps 120, **121**, 122–31
  territorial divisions and 24–5
  union maps 25, 129
  valuation maps 118–25
maps (Tenement Valuation)
  in counties previously valued 126–9
  in counties valued for the first time 125–6
  fair-copy maps 126, 129
  field maps 125–6, 127–8
  office maps 126, 128–9
  re-use of Townland Valuation documents 43, 44, 45, 119, 120, **121**
maps (Townland Valuation)
  fair-copy maps 64, 124
  field maps 123
  office maps 123
  working conditions 130–1
Martin estate (Galway) 59, 148
Mathew, Revd Theobald 78
Meagher, Thomas, MP 141
measurement systems
  Armstrong's survey 99
  Cunningham acres 99
  Irish acres 97, 99, 103, 164
  Primary valuation and 164
  statute acres 61n5, 97, 99, 103
  Townland Valuation and 97, 164
middlemen 63, 105, 112, 162, 166–7
mill books 40, 61, 90–4
  format 90–1
  location of mills 93
  mill buildings 91, 93
  prices, information on 92–3
  types of mills 91–2
mills 79
  machinery, valuation of 29
  valuation of 27, 90, 91
Montgomery, James (valuator) 52, 56–7
Municipal Corporations Act amendment 31
municipal government 18

names
  agnomens (nicknames) 141, 183
  exclusion of 141–2
  rules for recording 140–1
Napoleonic wars 166
National Archives, archival arrangement and lists 20–1
National Inventory of Architectural Heritage 93
National Library of Ireland 100

Index

Norreys, Sir Denham 19
Northern Ireland 61
  documents relating to 61, 72, 83, 119
  PRONI 17, 46, 194, 196–7
  Valuation Office 195

O'Brien, Thomas (valuator) 50
occupiers 148
  county cess paid by 17
  meaning of term 138–9
  names of 28, 63, 151
  non-cooperation of 190
  poor rates shared with lessors 17–18
  tax liability 30
  see also lessors
O'Donovan, John 59
office maps *see* maps
Ordnance Survey 16, 23, 24, 47, 57, 97, 199
  boundaries of baronies, parishes and townlands 24, 25
  field fences included on 29
  registry books 42, 109
  revision of maps 26
  town plans 131–2, 133
  town plans, publication of 134
  valuation maps 118
original field books *see* field books
outbuildings, valuation of 26

parliamentary franchise 18
parliamentary papers 53
Parnell, John (landowner) 52
perambulation books *see* tenure books
perambulation maps *see* field maps (Tenement Valuation)
Pettigo Estate 70
poor law
  introduction in Ireland 31
  letter books 115
  lists 103, 105
  Tenement Valuation and 17, 102–3
Poor Law Act 31, 32, 34, 138
poor law unions 24–5
  1846 valuation act 35
  boundaries of 24
  maps 120
  union maps 25, 129
  valuation 31, 34, 41, 138
Poor Law Valuation 31, 32, 96, 117, 168, 175
poor rates 17–18, 31, 32, 78, 103
preliminary books *see* field books
Primary valuation (*Griffith's valuation*) 18, 43, 44, 45, 136–56
  appeal forms included 159, 179
  appeals against 43, 157–92
  businesses 146–7
  in chancery 139
  common land 140, 150
  compared with manuscript books 149–52, **149**, **152**
  corrections 160, 183
  descriptions (terminology) 138–9, 143–5
  detached portions of a tenement 139–40
  format of the text 138
  freeholds 139
  italicized letters 140
  lessors/immediate lessors 139, 140, 143, 148, 151
  lodgings 141–2
  monuments/historic buildings 147
  names, exclusion of 141–2
  names, rules for recording 140–2
  occupier, meaning of 138–9
  occupiers, names of 140–3, 151
  poor law unions 138
  printed books 136–8, 153–4
  publication in baronies and poor law unions 137–8
  publication by Government Stationery Office 137, 153–4
  research and 149–52, 218
  statute measure used 164
  subletting 143–4, **144**, **145**, 152
  tenement, definition of 138
  tenement, numbering of 139–40
  waste, meaning of term 139
  workhouses 148
printed post-appeal books *see* appeals
PRONI *see* Public Record Office of Northern Ireland
Public Record Office of Northern Ireland (PRONI) 17, 46, 194, 196–7
Purdon, Augustus (clerk) 56
Purdon, Robert (valuator) 52, 56

quality lots 27, 28, 38, 39, 42, 62, 63, 109
  maps and 123, 124, 127, 128, 129
quarto books 40, 45, 61, 75, 83–90
  classification of streets 86–7
  classification of towns 86
  format 84, **85**, 86
  house numbering system 87
  revised information 87–8
  town plans and 134, 135
  towns, observations on 89
query sheets 45, 83, 112–13

railways, valuation of 36, 37, 113, 138
rates, abolition on agricultural land 19, 61
registry books (registers of calculation) 40, 42, 45, 109–10
rent books 42, 61, 103, 104, 111–12
rents 18, 104, 165–6
  abatements 105–6, 107, 166
  alternatives to paying 106, 166
  factors affecting 166

Napoleonic wars, effects of 166
rack rents 107
revising surveyors' books *see* appeal books
revising valuators *see* appeal books
revision books 25n12, 43
Roberts, Francis (surveyor) 177
Ryan, Philip (valuator) 189

salaries 48
Scarriff union, County Clare 142, 148
schools 101, 146, 151
Scott, William (surveyor) 58, 132
Select Committee on County Cess (1836) 28
Select Committee on general valuation (Ireland) (1869) 57, 127, 193, 194, 195
Select Committee on the survey and valuation of Ireland (1824) 16, 23
  see also Spring Rice Committee
Select Committee on Townland Valuation (1844) 31–3, 44
Smyth estate (County Wicklow) 19
Smyth, William J. 81
Somerville, Sir William (chief secretary for Ireland) 36, 157n1, 160
Spring Rice Committee 23, 24, 25, 31, 117, 131
Spring Rice, Thomas 23
stamp duties 18
Stawell, Jonas (valuator) 169, 174, 175
Stout, Geraldine 147
Strafford Survey 22
subletting 106, 143–4, **144**, **145**, 152
survey books *see* field books
surveyors 42, 44, 48, 52, 180
surveyors' books 177

taxation 173
  see also county cess; local taxation
temperance movement 78
tenement
  definition of 138
  detached portions of 139–40
  numbering of 139
Tenement Valuation 16, 17, 32–3, 35, 41–6
  1846 act 33–6, 42
  1852 act 36–7, 44
  appeals against 43, 158
  based on baronies 25
  books (field/house/quarto/tenure) 61
  cancelled books 46
  chain survey measurement 33
  commencement of 42, 102
  county cess and 36
  documents created 42, 43, 45, 46
  establishment of 33–4
  extension of 43–4
  field books 65–71
  field work 42, 44–5
  final valuation 46

house books 76–8, 82, 83
  maps 119, 120, **121**, 122, 124–31
  mills 90, 91
  models 31
  occupiers named 137
  office work 42–3, 45
  overlap with Townland Valuation 17, 35–6, 41
  poor rates and 36
  query sheets 112–13
  rateable hereditaments 34
  registry books 109, 110
  re-use of Townland Valuation documents 43, 44, 45, 119, 120, **121**
  tenure books 102–9
  town plans 131, 132, 135
  Townland Valuation re-plotted in tenements 44
  transitional period 33–6
  union maps and 25
  work under 41–6, 103
tenure books 42, 44, 61, 77, 102–9
  additional information 107–8, 109
  county cess 103
  court of chancery as lessor 107
  economic conditions 106–7, 108, 109
  emigration 106, 107
  evictions/ejectments 107, 108
  format 103–4
  names of occupiers and lessors 102
  occupations 106
  poor law lists 103
  poor rates 103
  Primary valuation and 105
  purpose of 103
  rents 103, 104, 105–6, 107
  revision 105, 107
  Tenement Valuation 102–9
  towns 102
Thom, Alexander (printer) 153, 154
time bills 58, 70
Tipperary County
  appeals 158, 159, 174
  holdings, consolidation of 164–5
tithe applotment books 99
Tithe Valuation 31
town plans 131–5
  additional information 135
  cancelled plans 133–4
  dates of 133, 134
  house books and 134–5
  improvised plans 132
  Ordnance Survey 131–2, 133
  printed plans 134
  quarto books and 134–5
  reference plans 132
  revisions 132, 133
  rules for numbering houses 134

scale of 131
working plans (base plans) 132, 133, 135
Townland index, 1901 25, 74
Townland Valuation 17, 34–5
  1826 act and amendments 25–7
  appeals against 26, 29, 40, 94–7
  books (field/house/quarto) 61
  commencement 24
  difficulties for 30–1, 35
  documents created 39, 40, 41
  draft valuation for appeal 40
  field books 62–5, 68–70, 71
  field work valuing land and houses 38–9
  house books 73–6, 78, 83
  house books, revision of 45
  list books 110–11
  maps 119, 120, **121**, 122–4
  mills 90, 91
  occupiers' names 28, 63
  overlap with Tenement Valuatioin 17, 35–6, 41
  printed *Townland Valuation* books 100–2
  quality lots *see* quality lots
  registry books 109–10
  Select Committee (1844) 31–3
  statute measure 97
  town plans 131–5
towns
  advantage of proximity to 28–9
  classification of streets 86–7
  classification of towns 86
  percentage increases (houses) *see* quarto books
  value of houses in 28, 75, 84, **85**, 86
triangulation
  of Britain 23
  of Ireland 24
Trinity College Dublin 148

union maps 25, 129
Universal exhibition Paris (1855) 116

valuation
  check valuation 39
  commencement of work 24
  four stages of work 41
  legal basis of 18
  purpose of 17–18
  scale of prices, based on 15
  state services' eligibility and 19
  uses of 18–19
valuation acts 15, 17, 18, 23, 25–7, 29, 33, 36
  1826 act and amendments 25–7, 47, 137
  1831 act 26, 72
  1832 act 26
  1834 act 26
  1836 act 29, 34, 94, 137
  1846 act 33–6, 41, 135, 136, 137
  1852 act 36–7, 41, 45, 77, 138, 158

valuation archives, information contained in 19–20
Valuation bill (1865) 113
valuation commissioner, salary and expenses 27
Valuation Office 16, 17, 23, 61, 157
  archives now held in 195–6
  cancelled books 25
  management of archives 193–5
  research facilities 196
valuation staff 47–59
  clerks 40, 47, 48, 61
  discontinuation of service notices 48–9
  dismissals 50
  draftsmen 40, 48, 124
  Famine relief works and 52, 55
  field staff 50–1
  labourers (chainmen) 38, 47, 48, 54n54–5
  management 50, 51, 52
  number of 47
  pensions 49–50, 55, 56
  professional standing of 51–2
  recruitment 47, 50
  researching individual members 53–9
  salaries 48, 54, 55
  specialization 52
  sub-commissioners of appeal 49
  surveyors 42, 44, 48, 52
  see also valuators
valuation system
  development of 22–46
  field work instructions 27–30, 33, 37
valuators 25–6, 47–59
  backgrounds 47, 52
  check valuators 29, 52
  indoor duties 28
  itinerant life of 58
  labourer assistants and 38
  profession of 47
  recruitment 47, 50
  revising valuators 179–80
  role of 188–91
  town valuators 52
  training of 26, 47
  weather and 58, 70
  work of 57–8
  see also field books; field work
Vaughan, W.E. 19, 37
villages *see* towns
voting, valuations and 175

Wake, William 153
Warwick, Robert (valuator) 54
Wexford grand jury 30
Williamson, David (valuator) 50, 52
Wilson, G. (poor law valuator) 175
Wilson's Hospital 148
Woffington, Abraham (valuator) 180n19, 19